In his new book, *The Dreams of a Child*, Claudio Colace details a seven-year longitudinal study of his son's dreams. This book takes readers on a journey into the developmental course of dreaming and vividly shows how dreams reach a crescendo of dynamic complexity in childhood. *The Dreams of a Child* is a must-read for anyone interested in the contemporary Freudian view of children's dreams.

Calvin Kai-Ching Yu, Professor at Hong Kong Shue Yan University

The Dreams of a Child

This fascinating and highly original book presents a longitudinal systematic study of the earliest form of human dreaming in a child, from ages 4 through 10.

Claudio Colace draws upon his extensive research on children's dreams, his expertise in brain science and an intimate knowledge of a single subject, his son Marco, to demonstrate the validity of an ontogenetic approach to the understanding of dream processes. The availability of 'first-hand' information about the daytime experiences of the author's son in relation to dream contents, as well as the longitudinal approach of the study, prove to be useful for a qualitative in-depth analysis of the nature and function of infantile dreams and of the changes that occur in the dreaming process as the child grows, from the early forms to more complex ones. Affirming the significance of Freud's explorations of infantile dreaming, this book attests to the nature of dreaming as a meaningful psychic act rather than the result of random processes.

Expanding beyond a purely psychotherapeutic context, the book analyzes the development of dreams systematically and in relation to Freud's theories on the human mind, making it an important read for clinicians, scholars and researchers interested in dream functions, child development and psychodynamic theory.

Claudio Colace, M.D., Ph.D., is a psychologist and psychotherapist at the Operational Unit of Psychology of the ASL Viterbo (National Health Service Office, Italy), where he works at the Outpatient Psychology Department and at the Center for Drug Addictions of Civita Castellana (Viterbo). He obtained an M.D. in Psychology at the University of Rome "La Sapienza", a post-graduate Master in Neurophysiology of Consciousness State, Psychopathology and Psychotherapy at the University of Rome "La Sapienza" and a Ph.D. in Psychology at the Department of Psychology of the University of Bologna, Italy. He is the author of scientific contributions published in *The American Journal on Addictions*, *Neuropsychoanalysis*, *Alcohol and Drug Review*, *Sleep and Hypnosis*, *Sleep* and *Sleep Research*. He is the author of *Children's Dreams: From Freud's Observations to Modern Dream Research* (London, 2010, Karnac Books); *Drug Dreams: Clinical and Research Implications of Dreams about Drugs in Drug-addicted Patients* (London, 2014, Karnac Books); and of some *Encyclopedia of Personality and Individual Differences* entries: "Dream", "Latent Dream Content" and "Manifest Dream Contents" (eds. V. Zeigler-Hill and T. Shackelford, Springer International Publisher, 2018).

The Dreams of a Child

A Case Study in Early Forms of Dreaming

Claudio Colace

Routledge
Taylor & Francis Group

LONDON AND NEW YORK

Cover image: Chan2545

First published 2022
by Routledge
4 Park Square, Milton Park, Abingdon, Oxon OX14 4RN

and by Routledge
605 Third Avenue, New York, NY 10158

Routledge is an imprint of the Taylor & Francis Group, an informa business

British Library Cataloguing-in-Publication Data
A catalogue record for this book is available from the British Library

Library of Congress Cataloging-in-Publication Data
Names: Colace, Claudio, 1965– author.
Title: The dreams of a child: a case study on early forms of dreaming / Claudio Colace.
Description: 1 Edition. | New York, NY: Routledge, 2022. | Includes bibliographical references and index.
Identifiers: LCCN 2021060362 (print) | LCCN 2021060363 (ebook) | ISBN 9781032027241 (paperback) | ISBN 9781032027265 (hardback) | ISBN 9781003184874 (ebook)
Subjects: LCSH: Children's dreams. | Children—Sleep.
Classification: LCC BF1099.C55 C646 2022 (print) | LCC BF1099. C55 (ebook) | DDC 154.6/3083—dc23/eng/20211216
LC record available at https://lccn.loc.gov/2021060362
LC ebook record available at https://lccn.loc.gov/2021060363

ISBN: 978-1-032-02726-5 (hbk)
ISBN: 978-1-032-02724-1 (pbk)
ISBN: 978-1-003-18487-4 (ebk)

DOI: 10.4324/9781003184874

Typeset in Times New Roman
by Apex CoVantage, LLC

Contents

Acknowledgements

I would not have been able to carry out this study without the presence of my son Marco, who is now thirteen. All the observations and findings in this study are based on his dream reports. Therefore, my gratitude and the dedication of this volume go to Marco.

I would like to thank Simon Boag, who, with his writings on dream bizarreness and metapsychology, helped me clarify various aspects of the Freudian theory about dreams and the general psychological theories of psychoanalysis.

After the publication of my first book on children's dreams, I had e-mail exchanges with Adolf Grünbaum, who sadly passed away in 2018. He was so kind as to read with interest my chapter about the epistemological debate on psychoanalysis and agreed with me that certain hypotheses of Freud's dream theory could indeed be eligible for empirical testing, at least potentially. This is the first opportunity I have to thank him publicly for his words, which encouraged me in pursuing my research on the Freudian dream theory.

I would also like to thank Brian Johnson for his continuing and sincere consideration of my studies on dreams along these years and for his helpful clarifications in the study on "drug dreams" and of several aspect of psychoanalysis.

Last but not least, I would like to thank Cristiana Pirrongelli for her tangible contribution to the dissemination of my studies on children's dreams and adults' infantile dreams in Italy and Alessandra Maugeri for her accurate and timely supervision in my efforts to write this book in English.

Acknowledgements

Introduction

Freud's intuition about children's dreams

The study of dream processes in children have proved to be an effective and feasible research paradigm to investigate the dream process systematically (in general) through the analysis of its early simple forms of manifestation in the individual (Foulkes, 1982, 1999, 2017; Colace, 2010, 2013, 2021; Sándor, Szakadát, & Bódizs, 2014, 2016; Sándor et al., 2015).

This research perspective rests on Freud's original intuition, according to which a dream can be better understood through the investigation of its ontogenetically early and elementary forms of realization. In Freud's view, the study of children's dreams facilitates the understanding of the formation process of dreams and their nature and meaning, as well as their function. This means that the essential and constitutive elements of dreaming are thought to appear already in its early forms but at the embryonic stage (the most elementary) since the *dreaming function* in a child takes place in a simpler and less complex psychic and cognitive system than that of an adult (Freud, 1900, 1901, 1916–1917).

Such a research strategy is even more promising when we consider that Freud suggested that the study of infantile dreams is not in fact exclusive to psychoanalysis or of its psychotherapeutic setting and interpretation techniques. According to Freud, infantile dreams can be an elective field of investigation for common psychological research. It is no coincidence that such a theoretical and methodological option was later followed, albeit from a different perspective, by two other great (non-psychoanalyst) researchers: J. Piaget and D. Foulkes (e.g., Foulkes, 1982; Piaget, 1962).

In the end, the path indicated by Freud may prove very useful for the knowledge of dreams. But we are still at the beginning. In fact, while the studies on children's dreams have increased in recent years, they still represent a sporadic approach compared to the much wider research on adult dreams.

This volume draws inspiration from the Freudian intuition about the value of infantile dreams as research strategy and tries to expand it by proposing an in-depth investigation on the onset of dreaming, in an attempt to describe also the further developments of this psychic function in middle childhood, those that precede the more complex forms of adult dreaming.

DOI: 10.4324/9781003184874-1

The systematic study of children's dreams in the perspective of Freudian dream theory

This volume comes out just over 12 years after my first book on the dreams of young children (Colace, 2010) and represents its ideal continuation in terms of study and research. In that book, I reported the results of an extensive systematic research programme on children's dreams, from their first appearance up to 7–8 years of age. That study had succeeded in three general purposes: (a) to broaden the empirical basis of Freud's observations on infantile dreams; (b) to identify, on a theoretical and methodological level, guidelines for a systematic research on Infantile dreams from a psychodynamic perspective, where other studies were later carried out (e.g., Colace, 2012, 2013; Mari, Beretta, & Colace, 2018); and (c) to prove that the Freudian observations and assumptions about children's dreams lend themselves to empirical testing unambiguously (see Colace, Violani, & Solano, 1993; Colace, 2010, 2012; Colace & Boag, 2015a, 2015b). Those results also highlighted major implications for an evaluation of the empirical value of the Freudian dream theory in general (e.g., censorship model, day residue, etc.). I believe that the 2010's study demonstrates that it is possible, through the study of children's dreams, to investigate systematically the empirical validity of important parts of the Freudian dream model. This path will take us forward in terms of judging whether this theory may be relevant in the present scenario of sleep and dream research.

Methodological pluralism in the study of children's dreams

During the past three decades, studies on young children's dreams have increased and have contributed to several aspects of dream research and theory, in particular about the nature of dream bizarreness, the role of wishes in dreaming, the nature of day residues in dream reports, the role of cognitive and personality development in the dreaming process, the possible function of dreams and their general meaning and contents and also the possible role of dreams contextualizing the emotional traumatic impact of the coronavirus disease (COVID-19) pandemic (e.g., Colace, 2006, 2010, 2012, 2013, 2015, 2021; Colace, Violani, & Solano, 1993; Mari, Beretta, & Colace, 2018; Colace, Ceccarelli, & Angiletti, 2022; Foulkes, 1982, 1999, 2017; Resnick et al., 1994; Gartner, 2014; Sándor et al., 2015; Sándor, Szakadát, & Bódizs, 2016; Honig & Nealis, 2011; Kráčmarová & Plháková, 2012; Parker, Freer, & Adams, 2013; Eti & Sigirtmac, 2016; Medina Liberty, 2017; Maggiolini et al., 2020; Strauch & Meier, 1996).[1]

In spite of the advantages offered by this type of approach, the researchers noticed that the results of the studies conducted do not always converge on certain characteristics of children's dreams. If, on the one hand, certain conflicting results may be due to different methods of collection (i.e., home interviews, school interviews, parent questionnaires, sleep laboratory interviews), on the other hand, it is exactly that methodological pluralism that allows us to understand the full spectrum and potential of children's dreams (Sándor, Szakadát, & Bódizs, 2014).

An important issue that emerged from the research on children's dreams is that many of their important aspects (e.g., their possible meaning and motivational significance) can be highlighted by collecting dream reports within a family setting and having "first-hand" information about the children's daytime life experiences in order to explain dream contents in relation to them (Colace, 2010, 2013; Mari, Beretta, & Colace, 2018; Sándor, Szakadát, & Bódizs, 2014). Actually, the past clinical investigation and qualitative observations on the infantile dream reports of one child or of a very small number of children, well known to the investigator (e.g., the researcher's own children) who has full details about the young dreamers' personal experiences, provided valuable and enlightening indications about the nature of their dreams that are comparable to the results of systematic studies (e.g., Freud, 1901; Piaget, 1962; De Sanctis, 1899; Von Hug-Helmuth, 1919; Grotjahn, 1938).

The aim of this book

This book reports a systematic longitudinal study of the earliest form of human dreaming in a child, from the age of 4 to the age of 10. The child whose dreams have been studied is my son Marco. From a methodological point of view, this has ensured the maximum availability of information about the child's daytime experiences, with the possibility of having a clearer picture of the relationships between those experiences and the dream contents as well as on the child's psychological and behavioural development. I have extensive previous experience with children's dreams based on several studies that reached 900 children aged between 3 and 8 and systematically collected over 650 dream reports, the results of which have been published (Colace, 1997, 2006, 2010, 2013, 2020; Colace, Doricchi et al., 1993; Colace, Tuci, & Ferendeles, 1997; Colace, Tuci, & Ferendeles, 2000; Colace & Violani, 1993; Colace, Violani, & Solano, 1993). However, this was the first opportunity to investigate in full detail the ontogenetic development of dreaming under a longitudinal approach.[2]

The main purpose of this study is an attempt to replicate and possibly extend certain results of the previous studies based on more systematic conventional methods of collecting dream reports, also hoping to provide some qualitative insights into the dreaming process. I am referring here—especially but not exclusively—to my studies conducted from the standpoint of the general Freudian psychodynamic theory of dream and mental apparatus. In the context of the Freudian dream theory, dream development has been related to intrapsychic apparatus development. Although Freud did not have a specifically evolutionary approach to the study of dreams, he often correlated certain changes in dream contents and form with the development of the ego and superego and with the age of the children.[3] From this point of view, this study is also an attempt to describe certain *longitudinal developmental changes* in dreaming in relation to some intrapsychic changes, particularly those that occur between 4 and 7 years of age (ego and superego formation).

Notes

1   For a review on children's dreams, see Ablon and Mack (1980); Colace (2010); Ramsey (1953); DeMartino (1959); Despert (1949); and Sándor, Szakadát and Bódizs (2014). From the psychoanalytic point of view, see Catalano (1990); Lempen and Midgley (2006); and A. Freud (1927, 1965).
2   A very preliminary attempt in this sense was made in 2010 (see Colace (2010, pp. 183–193).
3   While the psychodynamic approach was focused on the changes that occur in the dream process in relation to the development of the intrapsychic structure, other authors, such as Piaget and Foulkes, have analyzed dreams in developmental age in relation to the development of symbolic functions, visuospatial abilities and general cognitive development. I believe that these approaches should be considered complementary and not alternative to the Freudian approach.

References

Ablon, S. L., & Mack, J. E. (1980). Children's dreams reconsidered. *Psychoanalytic Study of the Child, 35,* 170–217.

Catalano, S. (1990). *Children's Dreams in Clinical Practice.* New York: Plenum Press.

Colace, C. (1997). *I sogni dei bambini nella teoria psicodinamica: un contributo teorico e sperimentale [Children's Dreams in Psychodynamic Theory: A Theoretical and Experimental Contribution].* Unpublished Ph.D. dissertation, Department of Psychology, University of Bologna, Italy.

Colace, C. (2006). Children's dreaming: A study based on questionnaire completed by parents. *Sleep and Hypnosis, 8* (1), 19–32.

Colace, C. (2010). *Children's Dreams: From Freud's Observations to Modern Dream Research.* New York: Routledge.

Colace, C. (2012). Dream bizarreness and the controversy between the neurobiological approach and the disguise censorship model: *The Contribution of Children's Dreams. Neuropsychoanalysis, 14* (2), 165–174.

Colace, C. (2013). Are wish-fulfilment dreams of children the royal road for looking at the functions of dreams? *Neuropsychoanalysis, 15* (2), 161–175.

Colace, C. (2015). *Iniziazione ai sogni dei bambini.* Roma: Edizioni Mediterranee.

Colace, C. (2020). Dreams help us to resolve affective states. How young children's dreams could reveal the function of the dream. *Psychoanalysis Today.* www.psychoanalysis.today/en-GB/PT-Psychoanalytic-Reflections/Dreams-Help-Us-to-Resolve-Affective-States.aspx.

Colace, C. (2021). The motivational trigger and the affective function in infantile dream. In: T. Giacolini & C. Pirrongelli (Eds.), *Neuropsychoanalysis of the Inner Mind a Biological Understanding of Human Mental Function.* New York: Routledge.

Colace, C., & Boag, S. (2015a). Persisting myths surrounding Sigmund Freud's dream theory: A reply to Hobson's critique to scientific status of psychoanalysis. *Contemporary Psychoanalysis, 51* (1), 107–125.

Colace, C., & Boag, S. (2015b). The empirical study of infantile wish-fulfillment dreams. A reply to response of Allan J. Hobson. *Contemporary Psychoanalysis, 51* (1), 132–134.

Colace, C., Ceccarelli, V., & Angiletti, M. (2022). An investigation on children's dreams during the social isolation due to Coronavirus disease (COVID-19) pandemic. *In preparation.*

Colace, C., Doricchi, F., Di Loreto, E., & Violani, C. (1993). Developmental qualitative and quantitative aspects of bizarreness in dream reports of children. *Sleep Research, 22,* 57.

Colace, C., Tuci, B., & Ferendeles, R. (1997). Bizarreness in early children's dreams collected in the home setting: Preliminary data. *Sleep Research, 26,* 241. University of California, Los Angeles.

Colace, C., Tuci, B., & Ferendeles, R. (2000). Self representation in young children's dream reports. *Sleep (abstract supplement 2), 23,* A176–A177, 1198.D.

Colace, C., & Violani, C. (1993). La bizzarria del sogno infantile come correlato della capacità di provare sensi di colpa. *Psichiatria dell'infanzia e dell'adolescenza, 60* (4–5), 367–376.

Colace, C., Violani, C., & Solano, L. (1993). La deformazione-bizzarria onirica nella teoria freudiana del sogno: indicazioni teoriche e verifica di due ipotesi di ricerca in un campione di 50 sogni di bambini. *Archivio di Psicologia, Neurologia e Psichiatria, 54* (3), 380–401.

De Martino, M. F. (1959). A review of the literature on children's dreams. In: M. F. De Martino (Ed.), *Dreams and Personality Dynamics* (pp. 87–96). Springfield: Charles C. Thomas Publisher.

De Sanctis, S. (1899). *I sogni. Studi clinici e psicologici di un alienista.* Torino: Bocca.

Despert, J. L. (1949). Dreams in children of preschool age. *The Psychoanalytic Study of the Child, 3–4,* 141–180.

Eti, İ., & Siğirtmaç, A. (2016). The investigation of dream concepts and contents of preschool children. 2nd International Conference on Social Sciences and Educational Research, İstanbul, Turkey, 4–6 November, pp. 131, XX. Bir Okul Öncesi Öğre.

Foulkes, D. (1982). *Children's Dreams, Longitudinal Studies.* New York: Wiley-Interscience Publication.

Foulkes, D. (1999). *Children's Dreaming and the Development of Consciousness.* Cambridge and London: Harvard University Press.

Foulkes, D. (2017). Dreaming, reflective consciousness, and feelings in the preschool child. *Dreaming, 27* (1), 1–13. https://doi.org/10.1037/drm0000040.

Freud, A. (1927). *Four Lectures on Child Analysis.* The Writings of Anna Freud (Vol. 1). New York: International Universities Press.

Freud, A. (1965). *Normality and Pathology in Childhood.* New York: International Universities Press.

Freud, S. (1900). *The Interpretation of Dreams.* S.E., 4–5. London: Hogarth Press.

Freud, S. (1901). *On Dreams.* S.E., 5. London and New York: Norton & Company, Inc.

Freud, S. (1916–1917). *Introductory Lectures on Psycho-Analysis.* S.E., 15/16. London: Hogarth Press.

Gartner, Y. (2014). *Immature Recall Ability in Dream Reporting with Children Aged 3–5.* MA Dissertation, University of Cape Town.

Grotjahn, M. (1938). Dream observation in two-year, four-months-old baby. *Psychoanalytic Quarterly, 7,* 507–513.

Honig, A. S., & Nealis, A. L. (2012) What do young children dream about? *Early Child Development and Care*, *182* (6), 771–795. DOI: 10.1080/03004430.2011.579797.

Hug-Helmuth, H. (1919). *A Study of the Mental Life of the Child*. Washington, DC: Nervous and Mental Diseases Publishing.

Kráčmarová, L., & Plháková, A. (2012). Obsahová analýza dětských snů. *E-psychologie*, *6* (4), 1–13 [cit. vložit datum citování]. Dostupný z www: http://e-psycholog.eu/pdf/kracmarovaplhakova.pdf. ISSN 1802–8853.

Lempen, O., & Midgley, N. (2006). Exploring the role of children's dreams in psychoanalytic practice today: A pilot study. *The Psychoanalytic Study of the Child*, *61*, 228–253.

Maggiolini, A., Di Lorenzo, M., Falotico, E., Gargioni, D., & Morelli, M. (2020). The typical dreams in the life cycle. *International Journal of Dream Research*, *13* (1), 17–28.

Mari, E., Beretta, M., & Colace, C. (2018). L'appagamento di desiderio e il ristabilimento affettivo nel sogno infantile: nuove osservazioni. *Psychofenia*, *XXI* (37–38), 17–28.

Medina-Liberty. (2017). The sociocultural sources of our dreams. *International Journal of Arts & Sciences*, *9* (4), 647–654.

Parker, J., Freer, K., & Adams, K. (2013). Characters, social interactions, emotions and self-representation in 7–8 and 9–11 year olds' dream reports: A mixed methods study. *International Journal of Dream Research*, *6* (1), 13–21.

Piaget, J. (1962). *Play, Dreams and Imitation in Childhood*. New York and London: W.W. Norton & Company.

Ramsey, G. V. (1953). Studies of dreaming. *Psychological Bulletin*, *50* (6), 432–455. https://doi.org/10.1037/h0062305.

Resnick, J., Stickgold, R., Rittenhouse, C., & Hobson, J. A. (1994). Self-representation and bizarreness in children's dream reports collected in the home setting. *Consciousness and Cognition*, *3*, 30–45.

Sándor, P., Szakadát, S., & Bódizs, R. (2014). Ontogeny of dreaming: A review of empirical studies. *Sleep Medicine Reviews*, *18* (5), 435–449.

Sándor, P., Szakadát, S., & Bódizs, R. (2016). The development of cognitive and emotional processing as reflected in children's dreams: Active self in an eventful dream signals better neuropsychological skills. *Dreaming*, *26* (1), 58–78.

Sándor, P., Szakadát, S., Kertész, K., & Bódizs, R. (2015). Content analysis of 4 to 8 year-old children's dream reports. *Frontiers in Psychology*, *6*, 534. DOI: 10.3389/fpsyg.2015.00534.

Strauch, I., & Meier, B. (1996). *In Search of Dreams Results of Experimental Dream Research*. Albany, NY: SUNY Series in Dream Studies.

Part I

Methodological aspects of the study

Chapter 1

The credibility of children's dream reports

The authors who conducted studies on children's dreams pointed out the many methodological difficulties of this research, particularly those concerning the evaluation of *dream report credibility* (Ablon & Mack, 1980; Becker, 1978; Cicogna, 1991; Colace, 1998, 2010; Colace & Violani, 1993; De Martino, 1959; Despert, 1949; Foulkes, 1982, 1993, 1999; Kimmins, 1920; Piaget, 1945; Sándor et al., 2015). (See Table 1.1.)

An important question is the problem about the understanding of the term and the concept of dreams in children. The experimenter should evaluate the extent to which the child is able to understand what it means when he is asked to report a dream (especially a young child). On the one hand, Piaget (1926) claimed that children only achieve a full picture of the psychical, private, inner nature of dreams by the age of 11 years, but on the other hand, post-Piagetian studies on how children understand the phenomenon of dreaming suggest positive results concerning the possibility to collect sufficiently reliable dream reports in young children. Kinoshita (1994), for instance, suggested that children of preschool age are able to distinguish dream entities from real ones. Woolley and Wellman (1992), suggested that 3- to 4-year-old children give proof of understanding the fantastic (unreal), non-physical and mental/private nature of dreams. Accordingly, Woolley and Boerger (2002) found that children up to 5 years have a notion of dreams similar to that of older children and adults. Meyer and Shore (2001) have shown that 5-year-old children, despite their scarce ability to recall dreams,

Table 1.1 Main methodological difficulties in evaluating the credibility of children's dream reports

- problems with understanding the term and the concept of "dream";
- problems with evaluating the accuracy of dream reports and the effects of a possibly distorted recall;
- problems with detecting what is really of dream origin out of the stories reported by the child

Reproduced from: Colace, 2010

DOI: 10.4324/9781003184874-3

begin to understand that dreams are an unreal, private and psychological event. On the other hand, children as early as the age of 4 can use mental categories to define dreams (Cassi, Pinto, & Salzarulo, 1999) and seem to be able to recognize the boundary between imagination and reality better than we would commonly suppose (Sharon & Wolley, 2004; on this topic, see also Goulding & Friedman, 2020). A more recent study showed that children aged five and six can appropriately define the concept of dreams, which they consider something unreal (Eti & Siğirtmaç, 2018).

Children also seem to be able to represent dreaming mental experience, and they seem to be somewhat competent dream reporters. Gartner (2014), in a study on the dream reports of children aged 3 to 5, suggests that children of this age do possess the cognitive ability to both dream and report their dream; in fact, they report rich dream experiences (i.e., active self-representation, emotions, etc.).[1]

Sándor et al. (2015, p. 14) quote Fonagy et al. (2004) who "have shown that children as young as 3 years old are able to understand and engage in pretense play, which requires the simultaneous symbolic representation of the outer and inner reality". Based on previous studies as well as on their own findings, Sándor et al. (2015) assume that even preschoolers are able to represent mental imagery such as vivid and eventful dream scenarios.

Finally, along the same lines, other studies showed that at the age of five, children already begin to show a certain interest in dreaming by asking parents questions about them (Colace, 2006) and a certain competence in evaluating their dreaming experience—for example, in reliably self-assessing their dream recall frequency—that is, compared to their objective percentage rate of dream recall (Colace, 2010, p. 78). During the interviews, in most cases the children also revealed a good degree of cooperation and diligence in the attempt to recall their dreams (Colace, 2010).

Credibility indices

In my previous studies (Colace, 1998, 2010) I found *eight objective characteristics* in children's dream reports that may indicate their credibility. A description of these characteristics is given as follows.

1   *Short interval before the start of the dream report.* The child starts reporting his/her dream immediately after the interviewer gives the question. He/she answers without hesitation.[2]
2   *Rapidity of reporting.* The dream is reported quickly, in one go, without interruptions nor hesitations.

These two characteristics are concerned with the way (time/speech) in which the dream is told. They apparently often coexist: one has the impression that the child is referring to something already lived through and ready to hand that he/she quickly remembers rather than inventing a story on the spot.

The other characteristic can be traced in dream transcription.

3   *Self-definition of the mental experience as dream.* The child self-defines his/her verbal report as a "dream" (not all children do so). The report begins with such expressions as "I dreamed that . . ." and/or finishes with such expressions as "And then the dream ended".

4   *Placement in context of the mental experience in the period of sleep.* The child clearly points out that his/her story occurred during his/her rest or sleep. The child makes such statements as "I have had this dream while I was sleeping" or "Then the dream ended because mother woke me up".

5   *Intrinsic coherence.* The contents of the free dream report are consistent with the answers given to more specific questions about the dream and about the daytime experience the dream refers to.

6   *Good comprehension.* The child gives meaningful and/or original explanations of his/her dream experience that suggest a good understanding of it.

7   *Consistency between dream report and general concept of dream.* The child, in the attempt to give an explanation of dreams in general, refers to his/her dream report and gives elements consistent with it (i.e., he/she provides an example of the general concept); in addition, the explanation of his/her dream experience falls within the known forms of understanding of young children (Piaget, 1926).

8   *Consistency between dream and its recall through a drawing.* After some time, the child can remember the reported dream and draw a picture that appears consistent with the verbal dream report (See Figure 3.1, Chapter 3 and Figure 7.1, Chapter 7).

For the first two indices, "short interval before start of dream report" and "rapidity of reporting", we may assume that children would take more time to begin to answer (interval) and tell (slower reporting) a false dream or an invented story (confabulation) rather than a real dream experience. From this point of view, these two indices should be associated to other indices of credibility in the dream report transcription.

Those children who use the term "dream" to denominate what they are telling (index 3) and those who provide a meaningful explanation of their dream experience (index 6) are likely to have fewer difficulties in *understanding the term "dream"* and to better understand what the researcher means when he/she asks them to tell their dream.

A positive indicator of the *actual dream origin* of a child's verbal report may be the hints given by the child through direct expressions that the mental experience being reported is set in the time/space of rest or sleep (index 4). On this aspect, a previous study found that most children aged 3–7 clearly affirm that dreams appear only in sleep state (Colace, 1991; Colace & Violani, 1993). Additionally, a more recent study showed that children aged 5 and 6 can define the concept of dream, and they defined it as seeing something while sleeping/sleep, something

Table 1.2 Guidelines for evaluating the credibility of children's dream reports

1 Short interval before start of dream report;
2 Rapidity of reporting;
3 Self-definition of the mental experience as dream;
4 In-context placement of the mental experience within the period of sleep;
5 Intrinsic consistency;
6 Good comprehension;
7 Consistency between dream report and general concept of dream;
8 Consistency between the dream and its recall through a drawing

that you think is real but is not, or something like imagination (Eti & Sigirtmac, 2018).

Equally useful for the evaluation of the actual origin of dreams is the investigation on the child's general concept of dream according to Piaget's criteria (index 7). In particular, it may be useful to observe whether such general notion matches or not with the particular dream that the child is telling and that is being evaluated.

For an evaluation of *dream accuracy*, it may be useful to observe how the various aspects of the free report are consistent with the answers given by the child later, during the systematic detailed interview about dream contents and on the daytime experience that the dream refers to (index 5).

The systematic use of drawings, together with verbal dream reports, might offer useful information about their *credibility*. The correspondence of details between the verbal report and the drawing of the dream may suggest that the child is really referring to an "important" mental experience—that is, the dream.

Recently, Sándor et al. (2015; see also: McNamara, 2019) have applied these indices as guidelines for evaluating dream report credibility more objectively, rating dreams on a 0–10 scale (with 0 meaning no credibility/the report is a product of a waking fantasy versus 10 meaning good credibility/report is dream). (See Table 1.2.)

The difficulties in assessing the credibility of childhood dreams are constantly challenging researchers but should not prevent them from continuing this type of research. Two important authors who have dealt directly with child dreams from different perspectives and study methodologies have attributed a degree of credibility to dream reports that encourages future investigation.

Piaget (1945), referring to the need to compare dreams with play, suggests that although children, in telling their dreams, may partly make them up, a sufficient amount of spontaneous dream content always remains, so the attempt to collect their dreams is legitimate.

Foulkes (1993, 1999), who conducted extensive research on child dreams and identified various methodological risks, also suggests that, in general, in children aged 5 and upwards, dream reports may be regarded as believable attempts to describe the dream experience. Furthermore, he claims that, "It must be stressed that there's no absolute way to verify dream reports, whether those of children or of adults" (Foulkes, 1999, p. 24).[3]

Authors have also suggested that the interviewer's experience is very important in the evaluation of credibility of children's dreams: he/she should have developed a certain degree of ability in recognizing credible dream reports—for example, facial mimicry of the child during the interview, content of the dream report, etc. (Colace, 1997; Foulkes, 1982, 1993b; Gartner, 2014).

Notes

1   For a review on literature on the onset of the beginning of dream experiences in children, see Colace (2010), Gartner (2014) and Sándor et al. (2014).
2   For an in-depth analysis of the credibility indices of children's dreams with examples of credible dreams, see Colace (2010, pp. 65–80).
3   Recently Foulkes has seemed less inclined to believe that dreaming is possible in 3- and 4-year-olds. He concluded that "longitudinal sleep laboratory studies have shown that dreaming is basically absent at ages 3 and 4" (Foulkes, 2017, p. 1). However, recent studies found that even young children report kinematic narrative dreams with active self-representation of dreamer, social interaction and emotion (Sándor et al., 2015; Colace, 2010, 2013, 2015; Mari, Beretta, & Colace, 2018).

References

Ablon, S. L., & Mack, J. E. (1980). Children's dreams reconsidered. *Psychoanalytic Study of Child*, *35*, 170–217.

Becker, T. E. (1978). Dream analysis in child analysis. In: J. Klen (Ed.), *Child Analysis and Therapy* (pp. 355–374). New York: Jason Aronson.

Cassi, V., Pinto, G., & Salzarulo, P. (1999). Developmental changes of children's about sleep and dreaming. *Sleep Research Online*, *2* (Suppl. 1), 194.

Cicogna, P. (1991). Il sogno in età evolutiva. In: M. Bosinelli & P. Cicogna (Eds.), *Sogni: figli d'un cervello ozioso* (pp. 328–346). Turin: Bollati Boringhieri.

Colace, C. (1991). *Studio sulla teoria Freudiana del sogno*. M.D. Thesis, Università degli di Roma "La Sapienza".

Colace, C. (1997). *I sogni dei bambini nella teoria psicodinamica: un contributo teorico e sperimentale.* [*Children's Dreams in Psychodynamic Theory: A Theoretical and Experimental Contribution*]. Unpublished Ph.D. Dissertation. Department of Psychology. University of Bologna, Italy.

Colace, C. (1998). Sulla valutazione della credibilità dei sogni raccontati dai bambini: uno studio preliminare. *Psichiatria dell'infanzia e dell'adolescenza*, *65* (1), 5–18.

Colace, C. (2006). Children's dreaming: A study based on questionnaire completed by parents. *Sleep and Hypnosis*, *8* (1), 19–32.

Colace, C. (2010). *Children's Dreams: From Freud's Observations to Modern Dream Research*. New York: Routledge.

Colace, C. (2013). Are wish-fulfilment dreams of children the royal road for looking at the functions of dreams? *Neuropsychoanalysis*, *15* (2), 161–175.

Colace, C. (2015). *Iniziazione ai Sogni dei Bambini*. Roma: Edizioni Mediterranee.

Colace, C., & Violani, C. (1993). La bizzarria del sogno infantile come correlato della capacità di provare sensi di colpa. *Psichiatria dell'infanzia e dell'adolescenza*, *60* (4–5), 367–376.

De Martino, M. F. (1959). A review of the literature on children's dreams. In: M. F. De Martino (Ed.), *Dreams and Personality Dynamics* (pp. 87–96). Springfield: Charles C. Thomas Publisher.

Despert, J. L. (1949). Dreams in children of preschool age. *The Psychoanalytic Study of Child, 3–4,* 141–180.

Eti, S., & Siğirtmaç, A. (2018). The dream concepts and contents of Turkish preschool. Children. In: I. Koleva, H. A. Basal, M. Tufan, & E. Atasoy (Eds.), *Educational Sciences Research in the Globalizing World* (pp. 430–442). Sofia: St. Kliment Ohridski University Press.

Fonagy, P., Gergely, G., Jurist, E. L., & Targe, M. (2004). *Affect Regulation, Mentalization and the Development of the Self.* London: Karnac.

Foulkes, D. (1982). *Children's Dreams, Longitudinal Studies.* New York: Wiley-Interscience Publication.

Foulkes, D. (1993). Children's dreaming. In: C. Cavallero & D. Foulkes (Eds.), *Dreaming as Cognition* (pp. 114–132). New York: Harvester Wheatsheaf.

Foulkes, D. (1999). *Children's Dreaming and the Development of Consciousness.* Cambridge and London: Harvard University Press.

Foulkes, D. (2017). Dreaming, reflective consciousness, and feelings in the preschool child. *Dreaming, 27* (1), 1–13.

Gartner, Y. (2014). *Immature Recall Ability in Dream Reporting with Children Aged 3–5.* MA Dissertation, University of Cape Town.

Goulding, B. W., & Friedman, O. (2020). Children's beliefs about possibility differ across dreams, stories, and reality. *Child Development, 91* (6), 1843–1853. https://doi.org/10.1111/cdev.1338.

Kimmins, C. W. (1920). *Children's Dreams.* London: Longmans, Green and Co.

Kinoshita, T. (1994). Young children's understanding of mental representation: Pretend and dream. *Psychologia: An International Journal Psychology in the Orient, 37,* 3–6.

Mari, E., Beretta, M., & Colace, C. (2018). L'appagamento di desiderio e il ristabilimento affettivo nel sogno infantile: nuove osservazioni. *Psychofenia, XXI* (37–38), 17–28.

McNamara, P. (2019). *The Neuroscience of Sleep and Dream.* Cambridge: Cambridge University Press.

Meyer, S., & Shore, C. (2001). Children's understanding of dreams as mental states. *Dreaming, 11* (4), 179–194.

Piaget, J. (1926). *Le représentation du monde chez l'enfant.* Paris: Alcan.

Piaget, J. (1945). *La formation du symbole chez l'enfant.* Neuchâtel: Delachaux et Niestlé.

Sándor, P., Szakadát, S., & Bódizs, R. (2014). Ontogeny of dreaming: A review of empirical studies. *Sleep Medicine Reviews, 18* (5), 435–449.

Sándor, P., Szakadát, S., Kertész, K., & Bódizs, R. (2015). Content analysis of 4 to 8 year-old children's dream reports. *Frontiers in Psychology, 6,* 534. DOI: 10.3389/fpsyg.2015.00534.

Sharon, T., & Wolley, J. (2004). Do monsters dream? Young children's understanding of the fantasy/reality distinction. *British Journal of Developmental Psychology, 22* (2), 293–310.

Woolley, J. D., & Boerger, E. A. (2002). Development of belief about the origins and controllability of dreams. *Developmental Psychology, 38* (1), 24–41.

Woolley, J. D., & Wellman, H. M. (1992). Children's conceptions of dreams. *Cognitive Development, 7,* 365–380.

Chapter 2

The methodology of this study

This book is based on the dream reports told by my son Marco at home through the years upon waking up in the morning.

My general approach was to give a systematic description of the characteristics of those dreams as they appeared in the verbal report, without proceeding (except in rare cases) with their interpretation. All the observations and descriptions of dream reports that are reported in this study can therefore be replicated by any researcher psychologist (i.e., also non-psychoanalyst) who has some familiarity with the study of children's dreams.

Two systematic collections of dream reports were conducted along Marco's development, from age 4–7 and from age 8–10, during which I was able to collect 126 dream reports.

First collection

The first collection contains the dream reports obtained from my son Marco between 1 May 2012 and 22 June 2015—that is, since he was 4 years and 1 day until he was 7 years, 1 month and 22 days, uninterruptedly (see Figure 2.1). During this long period, all the dreams that he remembered consecutively were collected, without discarding any. A total of 70 dream reports were collected. Most dream reports in this study derived from spontaneous recall.[1] When Marco recalled a dream, I would leave him free to report it without interrupting. The reporting occurred early in the morning and referred to the dream experience of the night before. Marco recounted all his dream reports to his father, his mother, or sometimes us parents together. The mother was instructed not to pressure during the reporting of the dream and to limit herself only to audio recording the spontaneous report. When the child showed that he had finished his reporting of the dream, I asked more detailed ad hoc questions. This last interview was always done by the author. All dream reports were transcribed verbatim (maintaining the verbal expressions and dialect of the child) while they were being reported or were audio recorded and transcribed later. Subsequently, all dream reports were transcribed in a Word document file. The daytime experiences that each dream was possibly referring to (based on the parents' knowledge and also on Marco's

DOI: 10.4324/9781003184874-4

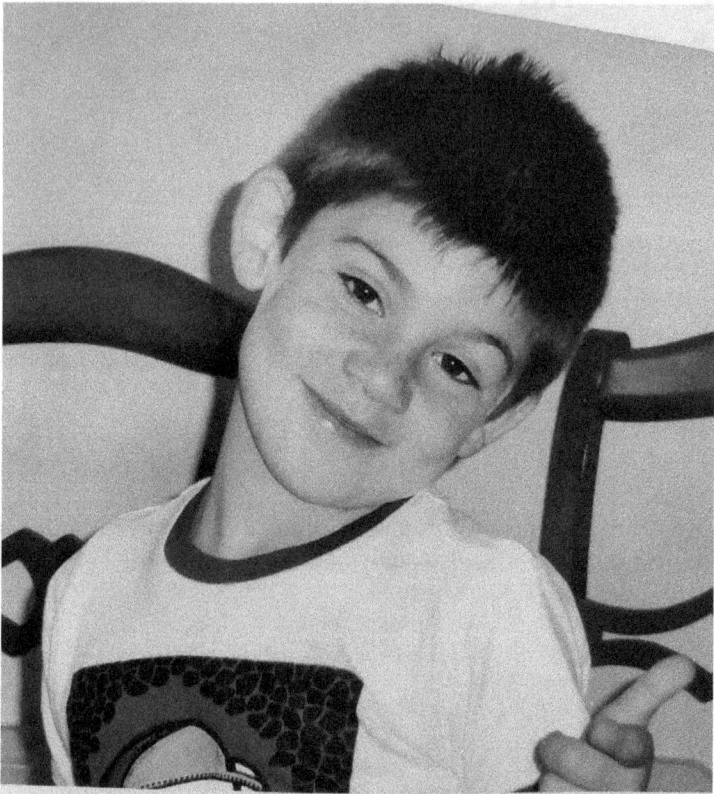

Figure 2.1 Marco at the age of the study

answers to direct additional questions asked by his father) were also immediately transcribed as an appendix to the dream itself. In 7 dream report situations, I even obtained a drawing of the dream.

Second collection

The second collection of dream reports spans between 7 May 2016 and 15 September 2018—that is, since Marco was 8 years and seven days and until he was 10 years and 4 months and fifteen days, uninterruptedly. During this period, all the dreams he remembered consecutively were collected, without any discarded. Dream reports were collected by the same method as the first collection. A total of 56 spontaneous dream reports were collected. An annotation of the waking experiences in relation to the dream was also made; however, in the second collection this was sometimes hindered by the greater complexity and incomprehensibility of the dream, which made it difficult to trace the possible links with daytime experiences.

Dream reports at different ages

For a series of analyses, the 126 dream reports were grouped as follows:

- *36 dream reports* from the *early infantile period*, between the ages of 4 years and 5 years, 11 months (first collection);
- *34 dream reports* from the *secondary period*, between the ages of 6 years and 7 years, 1 month (first collection);
- *56 dream reports* from the *third period*, between the ages of 8 years and 10 years, 4 months (second collection)

The choice of processing dream reports by dividing these into age groups in order to perform certain quantitative analyses is based on the results of previous studies that have suggested differences in various aspects of dreams in these age groups (Colace, 2006, 2010, 2013).

In the past, the changes in the form and content of dreams have been related to the development of the psychic apparatus from the perspective of Freudian developmental psychodynamic psychology (e.g., Freud, 1916–17; Colace, 2010, 2012, 2013) as well as from a Piagetian perspective in relation to general cognitive development (Foulkes, 1982, 1999, 2017; Piaget, 1962).[2]

From the Freudian psychodynamic perspective, the three age periods mentioned previously correspond roughly to major changes in the psychic development and particularly in the formation of the ego (i.e., from instinctual drives to prevalence of thought activity) and of the superego (i.e., identification with parental figures, interiorization of moral norms) as well as in the general mental functioning (i.e., primary versus secondary process). These changes affect the form of dreams (i.e., dream bizarreness) as well as the instigation process of the dream experience (Freud, 1900, pp. 267–268, 1901, pp. 66–67).

From the point of view of cognitive development, as described by Piaget, the major changes that occur between the *preoperational period* (2–7 years, i.e., rigidity of thought, irreversible thinking) and that of *concrete operational periods* (7–11 years, i.e., dynamic and reversible thinking) have consequences for dream characteristics (Foulkes, 1982). Piaget (1962) also described changes in children's dreams by analyzing the influence of development of the symbolic function in dreams and play (e.g., primary vs. secondary symbolism).[3]

As we will see, in Marco's dream repertoire the psychic and cognitive changes (from the perspective of Freudian structural theory of mind) connected with the progress of growing up accompany the evolution and vicissitudes in the *psychic function of dreaming* and sometimes even affect in a direct and evident way the form and content of the dreams. These aspects was already observed in previous studies (Colace, 2010, 2013) and will be dealt with in more detail in the course of this volume, when addressing the differences arising in Marco's dreams according to age as well as in relation to development of ego and superego.

Analysis of dream reports and their diurnal sources

All Marco's dream reports have been evaluated for different aspects related to dream process, dream content and diurnal sources. Some evaluations were based on quantitative measures; others were based on a qualitative analysis, albeit with a classificatory and systematic intent. A description of the main variables considered follows. Other aspects of the dreams and their method of evaluation are mentioned directly in the text.

Dreams

All dream reports collected were firstly classified into *four general categories*: (i) clear wish-fulfilment dreams; (ii) frankly bizarre dreams; (iii) bad dreams and nightmares; and (iv) oedipal dreams. The description of these categories appears directly in the text where appropriate. Within these categories, I then proceeded with *various sub-classifications* based on the characteristics that emerged.

Dream reports were scrutinized for various aspects. I will focus only on the main ones, as follows.

In wish-fulfilment dreams, the following *classification of wishes* was outlined: in relation to content *(phenomenology of wishes)*; in relation to legitimacy or any way of compliance with parental dispositions/rules or admissibility with respect to moral/ethical norms (i.e., simple, disapproved, unacceptable); and in relation to the psychic condition in the mental apparatus (i.e., conscious, subconscious or latent, unconscious). Wish-fulfilment dream reports were analyzed according to *way of fulfilment* (e.g., direct, disguised, symbolic) and *type of wish-fulfilment dream* (*modus operandi*) based on the following classification: dreams of compensation, continuation or anticipation. Furthermore, as we will see, more diversified forms have been identified among wish-fulfilment dreams, such as, for example, *serial dreams, overdetermined dreams* and others.

I analyzed the *bizarreness*[4] in dreams in relation to various aspects. A first general classification concerns the *origin of dream bizarreness* (e.g., neutral or of conflictual/defensive nature) and its possible *triggering mechanisms*. In all those dreams that enacted the fulfilment of an unacceptable wish in a distorted but still recognizable way, I analyzed the various forms of *dream-work operations* that could explain how certain bizarre and incongruous aspects of the manifest dream content were generated (i.e., *dream distortion*). All dreams, including those classified as frankly bizarre (i.e., bizarre dreams in the manifest content of which there is no trace of wish-fulfilment aspects), were also analyzed with respect to the differences in the various *form of bizarreness* (i.e., phenomenology of dream bizarreness) across the age periods.

Dream bizarreness and *the ability of wishes in instigating dream experience* were also examined with respect *to ego and superego development* as a result of the parents' knowledge about the psychological development of the child.

This study found a certain frequency of *bad dreams*. With respect to these, various subtypes were identified and described, also in connection with their diurnal sources.

An in-depth analysis of the *general contents* of the dreams and of *self-representation* in the dream scenario was not the main purpose of this study; however, these aspects may be highlighted in the numerous examples of dreams included in this volume. Furthermore, a quantitative analysis (i.e., percentage frequencies) of some categories of general contents present in Marco's dreams are added in a specific appendix of book (appendix A).

Dream length as an important indirect index of dream complexity was measured through Word's word-count function, applied to the words that the child used to report the dream, excluding all the words that do not give actual information about the dream or comments (appendix A).

Diurnal sources

A detailed analysis covered the diurnal sources of dreams, particularly for direct wish-fulfilment dream reports. In particular, I examined (a) their *type of connection* with the dream content—that is, direct/clear or uncertain/confused; (b) their *nature* (i.e., *motivational/affective*); and (c) their *temporal distance*.

Statistical analyses were made for some of these variables, providing the frequencies, percentages, averages and medians across the age periods.

Dream recall

During the entire first collection, which lasted about 37 months, Marco recalled 70 dreams—that is, an average of 1.8 dreams reported per month. In the *early period*, Marco recalled an average of 1.5 dreams per month. In the *secondary period*, he reported 2.6 dreams per month.

During the second collection *(third period)*, which lasted about 28 months, Marco recalled 56 dreams—that is, an average of 2 dreams reported for month.

It is difficult to directly compare this data with previous studies that have adopted different methods to measure the ability to recall dreams.

However, in line with the results from a previous study, it was observed that 60% or 70% of 3- to 8-year-olds reported at least one dream *in the last month* (Colace, 2006, 2010).

Credibility of Marco's dream reports

Based on my personal long experience in collecting dream reports from young children and also on the basis of the guidelines for evaluating dream report credibility (as mentioned previously), Marco has always given reliable dream reports, except for some dreams that could be emphatically reported as "bad dreams" having the secondary purpose of being welcomed in his parents' bed. During the study Marco was often cooperative and credible in reporting dreams. Questions were asked about his dreams without pressuring him in order to avoid confabulatory answers.

One important aspect is that Marco's dream reports were recalled very closely to the actual dream experience, which prevented or greatly reduced the possible effects of memory distortion in the recall. Finally, I am inclined to consider the clear presence of dream-work operations as well as of certain peculiar bizarreness in some dream reports of Marco (see Chapters 3 and 9) as clear dream-credibility indexes, which help in distinguishing a real dream from an invented story on the spot.

However, as we will see, both these aspects are identifiable only through the comparison of dream contents, the daytime experiences of the child and an in-depth knowledge of the child dreamer.

Limits and strengths of this study

This study is based on the dream reports of *one* child; therefore, each result must be taken with caution and compared with those obtained from previous studies (based on samples or a single child) and/or from future studies to justify any claim of generalization.

This is an investigation that is based on my own son's dream reports; therefore, my indirect influence in the post-reporting *ad hoc* interviews cannot be ruled out. Nevertheless, it should be noted that the dreams were reported freely without any interruption and/or pressure and were entirely audio recorded and transcribed without changes.

One of the strengths of this study, which excludes the possibility of the researcher's subjective criteria in collecting dreams, is that *the collection of dreams took place continuously and consecutively in chronological order*, within specific age ranges, taking into account all the dream reports referred, without discarding any. Furthermore, none of the dreams collected were discarded or selected subsequently (i.e., after rereading and/or assessing them). In this way, the series of dreams collected and analyzed, besides being random, is probably representative of the continuous changes in the dreaming function. However, it should be considered that there is no guarantee that the dream sample collected from Marco is adequately representative of his entire dream repertoire—that is, of all the dreams that a child of his age may experience. In fact, they are mostly dreams that he remembered spontaneously.

To the best of my knowledge, this study is the first longitudinal program that examines for such a long period the *dream reports collected from a healthy child* (therefore not a clinical case) upon awakening and in an at-home setting. Furthermore, a unique and beneficial aspect of this study is the fact that *there was detailed information available and direct knowledge of the daytime experiences of the child* interviewed, as well as of his psychological and behavioural development (being my son). This aspect made it easier to find connections between dream content and daytime experiences. In addition, the certain positioning in time of the dream experience (the night before) made it possible to search, in a more precise and temporally defined way, information about the period of being awake preceding the dream that could be related to the dream content. Finally, more than half of the dream reports collected were included in full version in the book. This allows for a better evaluation of the validity of the theses and conclusions in the book.

Notes

1   At the beginning of the collection, Marco was invited to tell his dream with questions. I would ask, "Marco, did you have a dream tonight?" If Marco replied no, I would say, "Don't worry, dreams can't always be remembered". From then Marco started telling his dream experiences spontaneously.
2   Recently Sandor's research group has begun to investigate the relationships between neurocognitive maturation and dreaming (Sándor et al., 2016).
3   For a more detailed review of Piaget and Foulkes' studies on children's dreams see Colace (2010).
4   Dreams frequently show impossible and/or improbable aspects compared with everyday life experiences, which have been referred as to "dream bizarreness" (Colace, 2003, 2010). For example, we may dream of meeting people we have not seen in years or find ourselves in unknown situations or environments; sometimes the whole plot of the dream is entirely surreal. The first dimension includes those situations that are impossible from a physical and/or logical point of view; the second dimension implies statistical improbability (Colace, 2003). This is one of the most enigmatic aspects of dreaming, which all the most important theories on dreams have tried to explain since ancient times (Colace, 2003, 2010). According to the Freud's disguise-censorship theory, most dream bizarreness is an expression of a motivated effort to disguise unconscious wishes that are unacceptable to the conscience. The dream-censorship agency and, later, the superego functions (in the ego) are responsible for the effort to disguise latent dream contents. In Freud's view, bizarre elements are psychologically meaningful, and dreams do have meanings (Freud, 1900, 1901).

References

Colace, C. (2003). Dream bizarreness reconsidered. *Sleep and Hypnosis, 5* (3), 105–128.
Colace, C. (2006). Children's dreaming: A study based on questionnaire completed by parents. *Sleep and Hypnosis, 8* (1), 19–32.
Colace, C. (2010). *Children's Dreams: From Freud's Observations to Modern Dream Research*. New York: Routledge.
Colace, C. (2012). Dream bizarreness and the controversy between the neurobiological approach and the disguise censorship model: The contribution of children's dreams. *Neuropsychoanalysis, 14* (2), 165–174.
Colace, C. (2013). Are wish-fulfilment dreams of children the royal road for looking at the functions of dreams? *Neuropsychoanalysis, 15* (2), 161–175.
Foulkes, D. (1982). *Children's Dreams, Longitudinal Studies*. New York: Wiley-Interscience Publication.

Foulkes, D. (1999). *Children's Dreaming and the Development of Consciousness*. Cambridge and London: Harvard University Press.

Foulkes, D. (2017). Dreaming, reflective consciousness, and feelings in the preschool child. *Dreaming, 27* (1), 1–13.

Freud, S. (1900). *The Interpretation of Dreams*. S.E., 4–5. London: Hogarth Press.

Freud, S. (1901). *On Dreams*. S.E., 5. London and New York: Norton & Company, Inc.

Freud, S. (1916–1917). *Introductory Lectures on Psycho-Analysis*. S.E., 15/16. London: Hogarth Press.

Piaget, J. (1962). *Play, Dreams and Imitation in Childhood*. New York and London: W.W. Norton & Company.

Sándor, P., Szakadát, S., & Bódizs, R. (2016). The development of cognitive and emotional processing as reflected in children's dreams: Active self in an eventful dream signals better neuropsychological skills. *Dreaming, 26* (1), 58–78.

Part II

The debut of dreaming activity

Infantile dreams (ages 4 to 5)

Chapter 3

The predominance of clear wish-fulfilment dreams

Literature

Previous systematic studies have clearly indicated that dreams, in their early forms—I would say at the beginning—often occur in the form of clear fulfilment of a simple (known) wish that remained unsatisfied (completely or partially) during the daytime (e.g., Colace, 2010, 2013; Mari, Beretta, & Colace, 2018; Kráčmarová & Plháková, 2012). These dreams are simple, short and easily understandable in connection with the dreamer's daytime experiences. Moreover, they rarely show signs of bizarreness. This set of characteristics is the one that best defines this early form of dreaming (i.e., infantile dreaming) that is frequently observed in children up to the age of 5.

In my previous work, I reported hundreds of examples of young children's dreams that fit very well in this description. I always found high percentages of dreams with these characteristics, ranging between 57% and 67% (Colace, 2010), 65% (Colace, 2013) and 80% of dream reports (Mari, Beretta, & Colace, 2018) across my studies.

These results, based on large samples of dreams and/or children, empirically support Freud's original observations on the dreams of young children (1900, 1901, 1916–1917) and indirectly corroborate certain pivotal hypotheses of Freud's general theory of dreams, which in his opinion was substantially confirmed by childhood dreams. I am referring in particular to the following basic assumptions: (a) the dream is a finalized psychic act that has a general and individual meaning; (b) the dream is triggered by motivational impulses (desires, drives); and (c) defensive dream distortion (i.e., bizarreness of dreams) does not appear at the onset of the dream activity but occurs later, along with development.[1]

From an ontogenetic point of view, dreams of direct wish fulfilment are the earliest forms by which the function of dreaming manifests itself in the human being. A simple form that allows us to formulate hypotheses on the dream process, its general and individual meaning and the relationship with waking experiences, without interpretation techniques. Considering that direct wish-fulfilment dreams are so peculiar to early childhood, we can say that the term *infantile dream* can be used as a synonym for them.

DOI: 10.4324/9781003184874-6

It was noted in previous studies that the opportunity to identify these dreams improves when there is detailed information about the dreamer's waking experiences and imaginary world. In fact, a good knowledge of the child who reports the dream allows the researcher to better understand the meaning of the dream content in connection with the daytime experience to which the dream evidently relates (Colace, 2010, 2013; Mari, Beretta, & Colace, 2018). When, on the other hand, there is no such information, identifying these forms of dream may be harder (e.g., Foulkes et al., 1967; Foulkes, 1982; Colace, 2006).

From this point of view, my study on Marco's dreams represented an opportunity for an optimal evaluation of the actual presence of clear wish-fulfilment dreams. First-hand information about his waking experiences, including habits, interpersonal relationships, tastes and preferences and imaginary world allowed me to spot these dreams more effectively and in detail, minimizing "false negative" risks—that is, dreams erroneously classified as non-wish-fulfilment dreams due to the lack of information about the daytime experience that would instead reveal their actual wishful nature.[2]

Clear wish-fulfilment dreams in Marco's early dreams repertoire

The systematic analysis of Marco's dream reports confirms that the earliest form of dreaming, in other words *the debut of (verbally reported) dream activity consists mainly of dreams of open fulfilment of a (known) simple and unsatisfied daytime wish*. These dreams, as we will see, have very clear characteristics that define with precision an *infantile mode* of dreaming, which in certain circumstances can be recurring and can be detected even in adult age.[3]

In particular, in Marco's "early period" of observation—that is, in the first 36 consecutive dream reports collected between the age of 4 and the age of 5 years and 11 months, *26 dreams (72%) were clear wish-fulfilment dreams*. Only in one of them does the fulfilment of the wish fail and is incomplete (see Table 3.1).[4] Furthermore, if we consider the first 16 dream reports collected consecutively—that is, from the age of 4 until Marco reached the age of 5 years and 4 months—almost all dreams are clear wish-fulfilment dreams (14 *n*, 87.5%). This result directly confirms Freud's indication about the high frequency of this type of dreams in young children (Freud, 1901, 1916–1917).

Of the remaining 10 dream reports from this period, 3 seem to be *oedipal dreams*, accompanied by anguish about the death of the father and Marco remaining with the mother. These may also be considered as indirect (i.e., disguised) and symbolic wish-fulfilment dreams, which, however, presupposes a dream interpretation. The other 4 are *bad dreams*, including *anxious dreams* and true *nightmares*, ending with nocturnal awakening.[5] Finally, I observed 5 *frankly bizarre dreams* (two of these are among the bad dreams) or dreams that have elements of impossibility and/or implausibility compared with Marco's daytime experience, without any hint of wish fulfilment. Such a low percentage of bizarre dreams is consistent

Table 3.1 General types of dream reports by Marco between the age of 4 and the age of 5 years, 11 months: frequency and percentage

Clear wish-fulfilment dreams	26 (72%)
Oedipal dreams	3 (8%)
Bad dream and nightmares	4 (11%)
Bizarre dreams	5 (14%)*

*These also include 2 bad dreams with bizarre aspects.

with previous studies (Colace, 2003, 2010; Colace & Tuci, 1996; Colace et al., 1993; Colace, Tuci, & Ferendeles, 1997; Sándor, Szakadát, & Bódizs, 2014). See Table 3.1 for the percentages of these types of dream reports.[6]

All Marco's wish-fulfilment dreams are clear, brief and easily understandable in connection to the child's ordinary daytime experiences and the facts to which they are directly related.

The content of these dreams is immediately intelligible and does not require interpretation and/or deductive reasoning for their comprehension. There is no element of distortion or disguising that prevents them from being understood. In the dream process, an evident transformation that the wish undergoes is *from an original wishful (optative) form to a form of actual hallucinatory fulfilment in the present time* (as already noticed by Freud, 1901). For example, the wish "I wish I was having my birthday party" expressed during the state of wakefulness becomes "It's my birthday party" in the dream. *In this sense we observe that the daytime wish and dream wish coincide.* This is important for understanding the meaning of the dream. In other words, the dream concerns only the fulfilment of the daytime wish and does not contain any other latent psychic material. *The manifest content of dream is the dream.*

Two examples of clear wish-fulfilment dreams follow. Other examples of wish-fulfilment dreams are reported in the following sections, in particular Chapters 4 and 6, where these dreams are analyzed in detail.

The dream of the Befana[7]
M. 05–4;8 (4 years and 8 months).[8] *I dreamed that the Befana brought me a Spider-Man stocking. She left it for me on the sofa.*
(At the end of his dream report, Marco snapped, "I do wish that the Befana comes soon!!")

On the previous evening, we had spotted certain Befana stockings at the supermarket, and he had been particularly attracted by those with a Spider-Man theme. Marco confirmed that the stocking he dreamed about was exactly the one seen at the supermarket. He had asked me to buy one for him, but I had replied, "No, Marco, the Befana is going to bring you one". This had left him a bit disappointed; he had hoped to have it right then. A while before waking up and telling me about this dream, he was smiling in his sleep. This is a typical example of an infantile dream: a short and clear story with a direct link to a known diurnal situation that explains the meaning of the dream with little or no room for error.

The dream of the 'ants' film
M. 31–5;11. *I dreamed that I brought the ants film at school, but then I lost it. In the dream I was watching the film, and then I can't remember. But I remember I lost it.*[9]

Marco appeared serene and smiling while telling this dream. He added that his dream was a pleasant one because he was able to watch the film anyway! He even made a drawing of his dream with himself, his schoolmate N. and the teacher. He said they were in his dream too. The dream was about the popular film *Minuscule*,[10] where all the characters are insects and ants. Marco had not watched that film for a while and had re-watched it repeatedly in the last few days before the dream. He was very pleased about this, also because he likes the soundtrack very much. He had also asked us to buy him all the other DVDs of the film series. On the previous evening, he said he wished he could bring the DVD to school, and we gave him permission. He had already expressed that wish to his mother a few days before. As a matter of fact, on the previous day, while coming down from the school bus, he happily told us that they had a brand-new TV at school, a big flat-screen one (see Figure 3.1).

In some wish-fulfilment dreams, there is a *tendency to exaggerate* in the fulfilment of the wish. See the following example, where Marco satisfies his desire to eat the sweets prepared by his mother two days before:

M. 08–4;9. *I dreamed about the sweets bow, there was a magic door with a hole and I got through it. . . . There was a huge donut* (Marco's favourite dessert), *a tree all made of sweets.*

This effect was known to Freud, who described the tendency to exaggerate as a typical feature of infantile dreams, as an expression of infantile psychic traits such as dissatisfaction and insatiability, as well as of the difficulty for the young child to desist from the satisfaction of a desire (Freud, 1900).

As we will see, this characteristic can occur in the presence of imperative needs and vital desires and/or in certain life circumstances, even in the infantile dreams of adults, such as, for example, dreams about eating in hungry people, and also in dreams about using drugs for drug-addicted patients (Colace, 2009, 2014). (See Chapter 16.) In the infantile dreams of adults, the exaggeration and emphasis on the fulfilment of a wish is due, I believe, to the *urgency of the (unfulfilled) wish that is at the basis of the dream.*

The *transformation of the optative formula* and the *tendency to exaggerate* can be seen as a very early embryonic anticipation of dream-work activity. However, other forms of dream-work operations (see Table 3.2) have been observed in certain dreams that fulfilled multiple wishes together (i.e., overdetermined dreams,

Figure 3.1 The dream of the ants film (# 31). The drawing of the dream shows how Marco is actively present in the dream scenario. We may notice the smiling face of Marco, who is holding the DVD, and of his friend N., confirming the pleasant nature of the dream. The teacher is also portrayed taller than the children. Apart from weighing the reliability of the dream, the drawing of the dream also allows us to perceive the emotions of the dream characters and the level of self-representation of the dreamer. The drawing of the dream gives access to the same dream contents through a different expressive form, enriching them with details that end up providing a perhaps even more realistic idea of the hallucinatory dream experience. From this point of view, it might be desirable that the use of the drawings becomes routine in this type of research (e.g., Colace, 2010; Mari, Beretta, & Colace, 2018).

seen as follows), but in this case, too, these transformations do not hinder the understanding of the dream.

Dreams in which multiple wishes appear

A previous study noticed the presence of dreams in which there are *multiple wishes not in conflict with one another*. These dreams appear to be motivationally over-determined in the sense that they share as a background several wishful forces that find satisfaction simultaneously in the same dream plot and/or scenario (see, for example, Colace, 2010, pp. 186–187). This type of dream was also observed in Marco's dream repertoire. In several wish-fulfilment dream reports (about 27% of these), the wishes represented in the dream are more than one. Alongside what seems to be the main wish fulfilment of the dream, we may notice one or more other wishes:

> *Despicable Me* dream reports
> M. 4–4;7. *I dreamed that there was snow. I went to the amusement park and there was snow. The amusement park was the one from the* Despicable Me *movie. I went there with grandfather and grandmother.*[11]

Marco added that in the dream, he went down along two tunnels, and at the end of the tunnel, he was about to throw up (mimicking the gesture of vomiting with the gesture of bringing his hand to his mouth); he also specified that "he did not vomit" while his grandfather instead "vomited" at the end of the tunnel. I will return to this part of the dream later, discussing the organic stimuli in the dream.

In this dream, there is the *main wish* to go to the *Despicable Me* amusement park and a *secondary wish* to see the snow. The first desire is linked to the fact that Marco, the night before, had watched *Despicable Me* (a movie that he owns on DVD) and was so much impressed by the funfair appearing in the film that he said, "Mom, I want to go to this amusement park!" Marco was very impressed and wanted to go there, and his mother answered, "One day we'll go there". The second wish is about seeing the snow, a wish that dates from a week before. Marco had seen the snow falling in Assisi, a small town in central Italy. With great regret, he had exclaimed, "But why isn't this snow white? Can you see that?" In fact, the snowflakes were small and melted upon touching the ground. This dream also shows that an unfulfilled daytime wish (to see the snow falling) could linger in his latent subconscious state for a long time before finding fulfilment in the dream. This latter aspect is also evident in *serial wish-fulfilment dreams* (see subsequent example).[12]

What we observe in these dreams is an *alliance between two or more (conscious or preconscious) wishes* that join together, setting the conditions for triggering the dream and then finding gratification in them. In its most elementary version, the alliance is between two simple daytime wishes, as in the dream mentioned previously; however, later on, in the dreams from the second period, we observe an *alliance between simple daytime wishes* and the *wishes denied by the parents*, which are stronger in terms of motivational drive and are truly responsible for triggering the dream.

We know that the same mechanism operates in a more elaborated version in the dreams of adults. In this case, the alliance is often between a daytime unrepressed wish and an unconscious wish. The former, unable to trigger the dream on its own, allies itself with the second to grow stronger, receiving greater intensity (i.e., motivational demand) and hence the ability to trigger the dream (Freud, 1900, p. 552).

From the "economic" meta-psychological standpoint, the common element of this mechanism in the infantile version and in the adult version, as described by Freud, is the concept that a *certain minimum wish request* strength appears to be necessary in order to trigger a dream, which is not always reached by one wish alone (Freud, 1900, pp. 552, 560–561). This means that whenever necessary, a single wish that has insufficient motivational drive to trigger the dream may seek and ally with other wishes in order to find its hallucinatory satisfaction in the same dream. This "minimum intensity" of the motivational request for triggering a dream, as we will see later in the dreams from the second and third periods, seems to be increasing in quantity.

The dreams with multiple wishes are important also because in some of them, we may observe the *earliest form of dream bizarreness*. In some of these dreams, the difficulty of having to satisfy two or more wishes in the same dream scenario can give rise to some bizarre aspects (not to be confused, however, with the dream bizarreness of conflictual-defensive origin) that do not hinder the understanding of the dream. I have defined this form of bizarreness as *primary bizarreness*, which is the result of a forced cognitive synthesis that the dream makes in an attempt to find temporal/spatial scenic consistency in the face of multiple motivational requests. Other times, the synthesis succeeds in a harmonious way. I will return to this topic later, in the part on dream bizarreness.

Cooperation between wish and disturbing pre-sleep physiological discomfort in triggering dreams

A particular case of dream overdetermination occurs when the dream is based on both a wish and a disturbing pre-sleep physiological discomfort (and the desire to put an end to it). In these cases, the two stimuli that are *neighbours by thematic association* co-operate together for dream production, to prevent the child from awakening.

> M. 32–5;11. *I had a long, pointed tooth, and it fell out at dinner time, then two other teeth grew and stayed forever* [perhaps he meant that they were adult teeth] *and I had turned into a vampire. We were having dinner (you were there too, Mom and Dad). It was a pleasant dream. I was having fun.*

That evening at dinner, he had enjoyed watching a cartoon, Gasper. His mother had urged him to eat up his dinner, and he had been "bothered" in his watching the movie. Gasper is about a funny vampire, and Marco, in his dream, looked exactly like him. Marco said he had the teeth like the vampire, "downturned" (his upper teeth were pointed and stretched out downwards).

In his dream, Marco resumes the pleasant experience of the cartoon and identifies himself with the main character (wish A); he even reports his experience of growing pointed teeth. At that time, Marco used to talk every day about new teeth sticking out from his gums. Marco couldn't wait for his new teeth to grow like those of older children so he could eat more easily (see, on this theme, also another dream in the following pages): this was a further reason (wish B) for his dream. In this dream, we also observe that a physical discomfort (the teeth growing out from the gums) is transformed into a pleasant and enjoyable experience, and *this is possible through the association of this situation with the fulfilment of a wish*—that is, to be the protagonist of a favourite cartoon. Furthermore, in his identification with the cartoon vampire, Marco exposes his discomfort with his teeth in a *plastic and caricatural way*. This dream-work mechanism, also present in other dreams, represents a playful way to overcome a problem.[13]

Another dream that solves physiological discomfort through the fulfilment of a wish is the *Despicable Me* dream (# 4, mentioned previously). In this dream, we saw that in addition to the fulfilment of a wish, there was the fact that Marco, at the end of his ride down the tunnel, "did not vomit" while his grandfather did instead—an element apparently unclear and not linked to daytime residues. Now, in the film, there is actually a fast descent that causes an upset stomach, and the character Felonious Gru is indeed about to throw up after it. This element of the dream seems accessory and not essential for fulfilling the wish of going to the amusement park; it does not seem to have a precise psychic meaning for the child. There is, however, another daytime event that explains it: Marco and his mother had had a cough in those days, and when he saw his mother coughing, he was under the impression that she felt like throwing up and used to always ask, "Do you feel like throwing up?" fearing that it might happen to him too. This physical discomfort "leans" on a desire to which it is linked by semantic association and is relieved through the fulfilment of the desire to put an end to it by transforming it into a kind of *pleasant and/or caricatural experience*.[14] As if that were not enough, the discomfort is entirely transferred onto Marco's grandfather (who, even in reality, is the one who always solves his "problems") through a very early form of *displacement*. The feeling of nausea is represented scenically by the amusement park ride (i.e., fast descent), which can be categorized with *considerations of representability*.

The transformation of a negative stimulus/experience into a positive solution in dreams was observed by Piaget, who described certain forms of dreams:

"there are dreams in which a painful happening is recalled, but given a happy ending, as in play. For instance, X dreamt of owls in the garden (the owls really were there and frightened her), but hid in her grandmother's skirt to be safe from them" (Piaget, 1962, p. 180).

While in this case, the stimulus is more fearful than annoying, the dream operates with the same purpose—that is, to put an end to it (i.e., negative stimulus) and preserve the state of sleep from a disturbing stimulus, allowing the child to continue sleeping.

Serial wish-fulfilment dream reports

In Marco's dream repertoire, I could find dream reports that always referred to the same wish. These kinds of dreams—that is, *serial dreams*—were also observed in previous studies (Colace, 2010, p. 194; Mari, Beretta, & Colace, 2018; Piaget, 1962).

For example, I reported the dreams of a young girl, Lisa (not her real name), who was interviewed in two separate sessions at 1 year's interval (4 years and 6 months to 5 years and 6 months) and reported similar dreams that had the same "long-time little boyfriend" as their subject (Colace, 2010, pp. 184, 186, 189)

In some of Marco's dreams, I observed that the dreams *concerning the same wish* can occur even months or years after the first dream of the series. These dreams have as their subject the same strong wish of the child in a long-lasting and structured way (e.g., early forms of falling in love). In this regard, I briefly report the following dreams Marco had about his recurring wish to have the Nintendo game console and to be with his sweetheart. As we will see, this latter desire will also remain recurrent in his dreams of the third period.

> M. 14–5;2. *So I had invited M. (his girlfriend). She then had knocked on the door and I had opened it . . . M. went to the television and I was on the sofa. Later I went up to her and gave her flowers.*
> M. 27–5;9. *I dreamed that I was going to elementary school, and there were M. (his ex-girlfriend), G., E. and N. (his best friend), and they were going to the trip.*
> M. 18–5;3. *I had the Nintendo console with the game. I had won it with the fruit juice.*[15]
> M. 34–5;11. *I dreamed that we were staying at the home of Uncle M. and Aunt P. I. (cousin) and I were in the bedroom and were playing with the Nintendo.*

These dreams suggest the strong value of certain wishes, such that they cannot be fulfilled within a single dream or a one-night dream repertoire. In these cases, the desire is really rooted and enduring in children.

Similar serial dreams also appear in the examples reported by Piaget. He reports the series of three dreams about the same desire of having cats (instead of guinea pigs) of young children from 3 years and 7 months to 5 years and 8 months:

"Obs. 98, X, at 3;7 (I) she was dreaming and talking in her sleep:—*Mumcat and Babcat* (the mother cat and kitten belonging to the house), *they're granny and mummy*"—(Piaget, 1962, p. 177)

"Obs. 98, X, at 5;4 (19)—*I dreamt that a cat had eaten the baby guinea-pigs*"—(Piaget, 1962, p. 177).

"Obs. 98, X, at 5;8 (1)—*All guinea-pigs were dead and there were lots of cats in the hen-house* (where the guinea-pigs were. . .)."—(Piaget, 1962, pp. 177–178).

In this chapter, I have focused only on the frequency of clear wish-fulfilment dreams and on their variants, such as *overdetermined* and *serial* dreams. In the next chapters, I will go into detail about the *nature* of these dreams, their *diurnal sources* and *trigger mechanisms* and their *modi operandi*.

Dream-work operations in infantile dreams

In the overdetermined dreams described previously (multiple wishes or wishes plus physiological discomfort), we have noticed the presence of other types of early forms of dream-work operations other than the transformation of the optative formula and the tendency to exaggerate (see Table 3.2). Furthermore, we will see other dream-work operations (e.g., symbolism) in other kinds of dreams in this early period (see Chapter 4 and 7). A list of these dreams is provided in the subsequent table. *These operations are of the same type as those described by Freud in his interpretation of adult dreams (see table), although here they appear in their simplest version.*

The presence, albeit sporadic, of these early forms of dream-work operation proves that they can occur in the dreaming production process even before the establishment of a true dream censorship activity or before they can be used for defensive purposes (i.e., dream distortion): this is in line with the Freudian assumption that dream-work operations are at the service of dream censorship activity but do not coincide with it (Freud, 1900, 1916–1917).

In particular, we note that several of these dream-work operations at this stage of the ontogenetic development of dreaming are at the service of the wish(es) that instigated the dream, in the sense that they work to favour an effective way of satisfying the wish(es). *In other words, they must be considered as the means peculiar to the dream through which it carries out its task.*[16]

Table 3.2 Early forms of dream-work operations in dreams of first period of observation

Dream-work operation	Description
Transformation from optative formula into present time	In the dream, the wishful request is represented as fulfilled in the present time.
Tendency to exaggerate	In some dreams, the fulfilment of the wish occurs in an exaggerated/emphatic way. This can happen both on a quantitative and qualitative level and may facilitate the full satisfaction of the wish. This latter indication also comes from the observation of childhood dreams of adults.
Forcing in cognitive synthesis	In some multiple wish-fulfilment dreams, there is a forcing cognitive synthesis on the space-time plane that generates scenic inconsistency or primary bizarreness.

Table 3.2 (Continued)

Dream-work operation	Description
Condensation	The forcing cognitive synthesis (in some overdetermined dreams) sometimes may be considered as a real elementary form of condensation or tendency to synthesis.
Alliance between two or more simple wishes	The alliance between two or more wishes sets the conditions for triggering the dream and then finding gratification in it. In these cases, one wish alone probably could not have triggered the dream. The alliance of desires is a ploy to make this happen.
Primary form of displacement	A personal inconvenience/discomfort is solved by transferring it to another dream character.
Considerations of representability	A physical sensation of discomfort is represented in the dream by a figure/character who embodies and lives it plastically.
Transformation of something negative into positive	A negative stimulus (discomfort) and the wish to put an end to it are resolved through a pleasant experience linked to the fulfilment of another desire.
Symbolism	Symbolic elimination of the father in oedipal dreams.
Caricatural transformation	Comical/caricatural visual representation of a problem.
Fearful verbalization	The child shows fear or a certain hesitation in reporting the dream when in its content an inadmissible wish appear in open way. The child may apologize for the content of the dream.

Notes

1 I will return later, in Chapter 17, to the implications of childhood dream studies for the question of the empirical controllability of the Freudian dream theory.

2 For example, in my previous studies, I had found about 10%–19% of dreams classified as "dream representing a possible wish fulfilment"—that is, dreams with pleasant contents but with not enough information to establish with certainty the presence of wishes in their content (Colace, 2010, 2013).

3 Infantile dreams represent a truly unique way of dreaming with peculiar and exclusive characteristics. The term was used by Freud (1916–1917) not only for children's dreams but also for certain forms of adult dreams that replicate those of young children and are for this reason called *infantile*. I will deal with these dreams later, in Chapter 16.

4 As noted earlier in the sample studies, dreams of failed wish fulfilment are rare. In previous studies where these dreams were separated from wish-fulfilment dreams, they appeared in about 3%–9% of dream reports in preschool children (Colace, 2010, 2013). In theory, these dreams are to be considered in the same way as wish-fulfilment dreams since they represent a psychic act aimed at the hallucinatory satisfaction of a wish.

5 The scarce presence of nightmares in Marco's earliest period is consistent with the results of previous studies (Simard et al., 2008; Nielsen & Lewin, 2007).

6   The high frequency of clear wish-fulfilment dreams cannot be due to an effect of selective dream recall—that is, the collection of spontaneous dream recall—for at least two reasons: Firstly, the prevalence of this type of dream has been noted in other studies which employed other methods to collect dream reports (i.e., systematic request at home morning awakening, questionnaires on the last dream referred) (Colace, 2010, 2013; Mari, Beretta, & Colace, 2018). Secondly, as we will see in the second and third observation periods, while leaving the collection method unchanged, these wish-fulfilment dreams tend to decrease drastically and to present important changes.

7   The Befana is a good old witch who flies on a broomstick and brings gifts to children on the night before Epiphany (January 6), just like Santa does on the night before Christmas. Peculiar to Italy, the Befana tradition has now spread across the country but was originally restricted to the Rome area. The Befana typically brings stockings full of sweet snacks, chocolates and candy, which in the days preceding Epiphany are usually sold ready-made at cafes and grocery stores.

8   The examples of dreams reported in this book include the progressive number of the dream report in chronological order and the age (the first number is the year and the second number is the month of age) at the time when the dream was recalled and reported. At times, the same dream example may be cited to explain different points/ observations.

9   Although this is a clear wish-fulfilment dream, we see that there is also an unpleasant aspect in the second part of the dream.

10   This is a French animation film, *Minuscule: La Vallée des fourmis perdues*.

11   Other good examples of overdetermined dreams are reported on p. 95 (dream #10, about the swimming pool).

12   Other authors have observed overdetermined dreams. Freud reported the dream of a six-year-old girl about a walk with her father (Freud, 1900, p. 512, see also, 1901, p. 21). Coriat reported a dream in which two wishes are fulfilled (Coriat, 1916, pp. 50–51).

13   Caricatural epilogues—in the sense of *"comical", "funny", "that makes you laugh"*— are also observed in a form of infantile dreams in adults (see Chapter 16).

14   Freud argues that a concern in itself cannot provoke a dream if it does not ally with a wish that acts as the driving force of such a dream (Freud, 1900, p. 511).

15   This dream is reported in full later in Chapter 6.

16   Freud noticed, "At bottom, dreams are nothing other than a particular form of thinking, made possible by the conditions of the stat of sleep. It is the *dream-work* which creates that form, and it alone is the essence of dreaming-the explanation of its peculiar nature" (Freud, 1900, p. 510). From this point of view, the individuation of first dream-work operations in early infantile dreams is a way to study how the dream function develops from being elementary to becoming more complex and mature.

References

Colace, C. (2003). Dream bizarreness reconsidered. *Sleep and Hypnosis, 5* (3), 105–128.

Colace, C. (2006). Children's dreaming: A study based on questionnaire completed by parents. *Sleep and Hypnosis, 8* (1), 19–32.

Colace, C. (2009). Gli studi sull'effetto della frustrazione dei bisogni primari sul sognare e la recente ricerca e teoria sui processi onirici. *Psycofenia, XII* (20), 49–72.

Colace, C. (2010). *Children's Dreams: From Freud's Observations to Modern Dream Research*. New York: Routledge.

Colace, C. (2013). Are wish-fulfilment dreams of children the royal road for looking at the functions of dreams? *Neuropsychoanalysis, 15* (2), 161–175.

Colace, C. (2014). *Drug Dreams. Clinical and Research Implications of Dreams about Drugs in Drug-Addicted Patients*. New York: Routledge.

Colace, C., Doricchi, F., Di Loreto, E., & Violani, C. (1993). Developmental qualitative and quantitative aspects of bizarreness in dream reports of children. *Sleep Research, 22*, 57.

Colace, C., & Tuci, B. (1996). Early children's dreams are not bizarre. *Sleep Research, 25*, 147.

Colace, C., Tuci, B., & Ferendeles, R. (1997). Bizarreness in early children's dreams collected in the home setting: Preliminary data. *Sleep Research, 26*, 241.

Coriat, I. H. (1916). *The Meaning of Dreams*. Gloucester: Dodo Press.

Foulkes, D. (1982). *Children's Dreams, Longitudinal Studies*. New York: Wiley-Interscience Publication.

Foulkes, D., Pivik, T., Steadman, H. S., Spear, P. S., & Symonds, J. D. (1967). Dreams of the male child: An EEG study. *Journal of Abnormal Psychology, 72* (6), 457–467. https://doi.org/10.1037/h0025183.

Freud, S. (1900). *The Interpretation of Dreams*. S.E., 4–5. London: Hogarth Press.

Freud, S. (1901). *On Dreams*. S.E.,. London and New York: Norton & Company, Inc.

Freud, S. (1916–1917). *Introductory Lectures on Psycho-Analysis*. S.E., 15/16. London: Hogarth Press.

Kráčmarová, L., & Plháková, A. (2012). Obsahová analýza dětských snů. *E-psychologie* [online], *6* (4), 1–13 [cit. vložit datum citování]. Dostupný z www: http://e-psycholog. eu/pdf/kracmarovaplhakova.pdf. ISSN 1802–8853.

Mari, E., Beretta, M., & Colace, C. (2018). L'appagamento di desiderio e il ristabilimento affettivo nel sogno infantile: nuove osservazioni. *Psychofenia, XXI* (37–38), 17–28.

Nielsen, T. A., & Levin, R. (2007). Nightmares: A new neurocognitive model. *Sleep Medicine Reviews, 11*, 295–310.

Piaget, J. (1962). *Play, Dreams and Imitation in Childhood*. New York and London: W.W. Norton & Company.

Sándor, P., Szakadát, S., & Bódizs, R. (2014). Ontogeny of dreaming: A review of empirical studies. *Sleep Medicine Reviews, 18* (5), 435–449.

Simard, V., Nielsen, T. A., Tremblay, R. E., Boivin, M., & Montplaisir, J. Y. (2008). Longitudinal study of bad dreams in preschool-aged children: Prevalence, demographic correlates, risk and protective factors. *Sleep, 31* (1), 62–70.

Chapter 4

The nature of wishes appearing in dream reports

Typology of wishes

Marco's early dream reports often contain only the wish that had appeared in the daytime experience, *directly* taken up *("dream wish")* and resolved. In the dream content, no other latent elements are found. From this point of view, the distinction between the manifest and latent contents of the dream makes little sense, and *the study of childhood dreams allows a direct and objective study of the nature of the wishes that the dream deals with.* The situation is only slightly different when multiple wishes appear in the same dream, but their diurnal origin, although with some amount of difficulty, is retraceable.

The wishes that appear in the dreams in Marco's first period can be classified with respect to two basic criteria: (a) type of condition/state of the psychic apparatus (preconscious/conscious vs. unconscious) and (b) parental approval or disapproval (i.e., prohibitions and rules coming from outside). Based on this latter criterion, we distinguish wishes into *simple (unrepressed) wishes* and *disapproved (or denied) wishes*—that is, in conflict with parental rules or dispositions. The latter are wishes that the child should have learned to suppress, or tried to suppress, which nevertheless exist and remain active, ready to re-emerge in the dream. *Simple and disapproved wishes are both known in daytime experience—that is, they are conscious or preconscious.* A third type of wish *(repressed, unconscious, more rarely observed)* is that which is *in contrast with moral/ethical principles* (i.e., inadmissible to the moral conscience). As we will see later, some of these latter wishes may end up being admitted during the interrogation on the dream, so in this sense, they cannot always be properly defined as "unconscious" in the psychodynamic meaning of the term. Furthermore, these wishes appearing in dreams are still understandable in their meaning and in their connection to daytime experiences. A clear example of *unconscious* repressed wishes from this period are the oedipal wishes found in three dreams (see Chapter 7).[1] On the other hand, access to *unconscious wishes* would have required the interpretation of frankly bizarre dreams and perhaps of some complex bad dreams in order to be detected (see Figure 4.1).

DOI: 10.4324/9781003184874-7

In Marco's first age period, dream wishes are predominantly simple wishes that are not in conflict with the parents' rules or dispositions or with moral/ethical principles. They are wishes that the child had manifested openly during the day or, sometimes, wishes that his parents knew about. All those wishes could not be fulfilled in his daytime experience and therefore remained unresolved on the psychic level. However, I observed a dream containing a *disapproved wish* (# 3) and other two containing a *morally inadmissible wish* (#6, #25). In one case, the disapproved wish is directly fulfilled in the dream: Marco goes to the jumping park contrary to his parents' prohibition (see dream of jumping #3, chapter 5, p. 51). In another dream, Marco (at age of 4 years and 8 months) satisfies a somewhat morally inadmissible wish with a sense of shame for having done so, which results in a bizarre effect (dream #6). Finally, in another dream, the fulfilment of morally inadmissible (repressed) wishes takes place in a *direct but anxious form*: Marco replaces his real father with a more permissive family friend who takes him to the park, a wish he could not confess without feeling a certain *fear when reporting* it to his father (dream #25). It is a dream that Marco had at the age of 5 years and 8 months. These latter two dreams are addressed in more detail in Chapter 9.

When Freud described children's dreams, he focused mainly on unfulfilled, unrepressed wishes from the waking life of young children (Freud, 1900, pp. 160–161, footnote 1, pp. 553–554). However, in at least one case, he reported an infantile dream with a wish that I defined as a disapproved wish. He reported the dream of a child under 4 in which he is eating after being punished and denied dinner in his daytime experience:

> A child of under four years old reported having dreamt that he had seen a big dish with a big joint of roast meat and vegetables on it. All at once the joint had been eaten up—whole and without being cut up. He had not seen the person who ate it.[2] (Freud, 1900, pp. 267–268)

Phenomenology of wishes

I will now address the most frequent dream wishes of this period (i.e., simple unsatisfied daytime wishes) while trying to describe them on a phenomenological level.

The wishes appearing in Marco's dream reports are those common to a child of his age and social/economic background (i.e., plausible with the child's expectations.). These are ordinary wishes related to "desired events", "toys— desired objects", "desired games/activities", "desirable people", "wanting to impersonate cartoon heroes" and "doing dangerous and frightening things" (see Table 4.1). Marco's repertory of dream wishes overlaps with those observed in previous sample studies (Colace, 2010, 2013; Mari, Beretta, & Colace, 2018).

I find significant, and worth of further investigation, the fact that in many of Marco's dreams, wishes appear completely similar to those observed by other authors in children who lived in past times and in different social and cultural settings: the wishes to go to the sea and swim, to see the Befana, to pass from kindergarten to elementary school and to have new toys are present in one of the very first systematic studies on children's dreams as much as in Marco's dream repertoire (Doglia & Bianchieri, 1910–1911; De Sanctis, 1899). Even dreams about heroes and/or wearing the costume of the favourite hero derive from environmental situations that are only apparently different: they might have been taken from fairy tales yesterday as they are taken from the TV or from a PlayStation game today (as in Marco's dream reports). For example, Kimmins (1920) described a child who dreamed of impersonating the protagonist of an exciting and adventurous story after having read about it the evening before. Freud described his son Martin, who reported a dream in which he was driving a chariot with Achilles after he read a book of legends about Greek heroes (Freud, 1901, p. 22). In this study, I report Marco's dreams about characters of PlayStation games after having played with it on the previous day.

The studies of Piaget and Freud describe dreams that reproduce wishes in very ordinary daytime situations, similar to the dreams reported by Marco.

See for example the following dreams (for other examples, see Chapter 6):

Marco's dream reports:
M. 02–4;0. *I dreamed about the new movie on the tow trucks* (he is referring to the film *Cars*, where there are tow trucks like the character of Mater). *I was watching the movie.*
M. 18–5;3. *I had the Nintendo with the game.*

Children's dreams reported by Freud:
Last night I went on the lake. (Freud, 1900, p. 129).
I had mentioned the variety of the wishes whose fulfilments are to be found in children's dreams (wishes to take part in an excursion or a sail on a lake, or to make up for a missed meal, and so on). (Freud, 1900a, pp. 160–161, fn. 1)

Children's dreams reported by Piaget:
A child aged 5 years and 8 months: "All the guinea-pigs were dead and there were lots of cats in the hen-house (where the guinea-pigs were)" (Piaget, 1962, pp. 177–178). His explanation: "As a matter of fact X. had for a long time been wanting cats instead of the guinea-pigs" (Piaget, 1962, p. 178).
A child aged 5 years and 10 months: "She dreamt she ate two eggs". "At this time she was not allowed to have eggs, and was constantly asking for them". . . . (p. 178). The same child: "she dreamt that her mother, who was ill, was better and admired one of her games" (Piaget, 1962, p. 178).

Table 4.1 Examples of wishes in Marco's dream reports

I wish I were having my birthday party.
I wish I could watch my favourite movie (*Cars*).
I wish I could go to the jumping park.
I wish I could go to the amusement park.
I wish I got the Spider-Man stocking from the Befana.
I wish I were at school with my friends.
I wish I could see my best friend and we were in candyland.
I wish I had the SpongeBob trolley.
I wish I could go underwater with my new scuba mask.
I wish I were with my girlfriend.
I wish I were at the beach.
I wish I could see Grandpa.
I wish I had the Nintendo game.
I wish I were with Dad chasing the gypsies away.
I wish I could send the evil lady away.
I wish Christmas would come soon.
I wish I could bring my favourite DVD to school.
I wish I could play Nintendo with my favourite cousin.
I wish I could watch my favourite movie.
I wish I could go to the amusement park.
I wish I could go on holiday.
I wish I won the karate fight.

"Age-specific" strength of infantile wishes

The wishes appearing in dreams were of great interest to Marco. Some were strong wishes, objectively or even just subjectively. In the latter case, one must consider the weight that these wishes have on the psyche of a young child. For many of these infantile wishes, the relevance and indispensability of fulfilment can be understood only from the perspective of a young child (whose wishes and daytime experiences must be known). Imagine, for example, asking a child to give up a much-desired toy, or the strong wish to see his beloved grandfather, or even having to give up on his first girlfriend. In his daytime experiences, these wishes failed to reach full satisfaction and were therefore in a state of full or partial dissatisfaction.[3]

In Freud's view (1901), the wishes that are satisfied in children's dreams are only those objectively more important—or that are such, subjectively, for the child. These are intensely felt wishes. Less important daytime experiences do not enter the dream.

After having explained that at the basis of adult dreams, there must still be unconscious wishes, Freud admitted the exception of infantile dreams, where a common unresolved daytime wish may act as dream instigator, and he attributed this ability to the specific weight that the *child's wish* has as wishful impulse in the context of the infantile psyche, "a wishful impulse of the strength proper to children" (Freud, 1900, p. 552). Freud pointed out that for young children, having

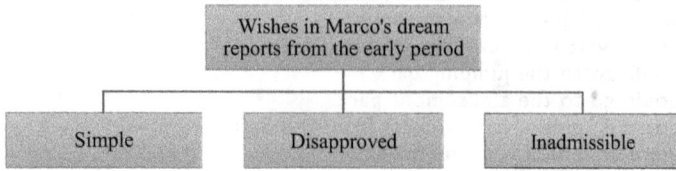

Figure 4.1 Types of wishes in Marco's dream reports

the ability, or "motivational drive", to desist from the satisfaction of the wish and to manage (cope) is more difficult than for adults (Freud, 1901, pp. 66–67).

It is therefore in the context of the infantile psychic apparatus that the specific strength of these wishes is outlined.

Marco's dream reports, collected at different ages, open to the possibility of finding a *range of wishes* with different levels of such dream-instigating ability. Such levels are placed in an ideal continuum that goes from a minimum (simple daytime wish) to a maximum (unconscious wish) in adult dreams. In the second and third periods, we will observe dream wishes characterized by an *ever-greater motivational instigating force* than in the first period. In other words, we will see that a wish of greater intensity will be needed in order to instigate dreams and that sometimes such intensity may be obtained also through an alliance of multiple wishes (as already found in overdetermined dreams).

Notes

1   The above classification of wishes also covers the range of wishes observed in dreams during the second and third age periods.
2   In Freud's view, the *omission* present in this dream is a clear expression of dream censorship (Freud, 1900). See Chapter 11, pp. 119–120 for this argument.
3   Kimmins (1920) also observed that in the child, the wishes that appear in dreams refer to what is most lacking in the daytime life. For example, he observed that poor children had more dreams about toys, gifts and eating than wealthier ones.

References

Colace, C. (2010). *Children's Dreams: From Freud's Observations to Modern Dream Research*. New York: Routledge.

Colace, C. (2013). Are wish-fulfilment dreams of children the royal road for looking at the functions of dreams? *Neuropsychoanalysis, 15* (2), 161–175.

De Sanctis, S. (1899). *I sogni. Studi clinici e psicologici di un alienista*. Torino: Bocca.

Doglia, S., & Bianchieri, F. (1910–1911). I sogni dei bambini di tre anni, L'inizio dell' attivita onirica. *Contributi psicol, I*, 1–9.

Freud, S. (1900). *The Interpretation of Dreams*. S.E., 4–5. London: Hogarth Press.

Freud, S. (1901). *On Dreams*. S.E., 5. London and New York: Norton & Company, Inc.

Kimmins, C. W. (1920). *Children's Dreams, an Unexplored Land*. New York: Longmans, Green and Co.

Mari, E., Beretta, M., & Colace, C. (2018). L'appagamento di desiderio e il ristabilimento affettivo nel sogno infantile: nuove osservazioni. *Psychofenia, XXI* (37–38), 17–28.

Piaget, J. (1962). *Play, Dreams and Imitation in Childhood*. New York and London: W.W. Norton & Company.

Chapter 5

Daytime sources and triggering conditions of clear wish-fulfilment dreams

Wishes and affective states as daytime sources of clear wish-fulfilment dreams

Previous studies have shown that infantile wish-fulfilment dreams are *directly* and *easily related* to the child's daytime experiences (Colace, 2010, 2013; Mari, Beretta, & Colace, 2018). This bodes well for the analysis of the diurnal sources of the dream and its triggering conditions.

In the dream reports collected from Marco, this type of analysis was favoured because of the parents' direct knowledge of the daytime experiences that appeared in the dreams and, of course, the child who reported the dreams. Thus, with Marco's wish-fulfilment dreams, their relationship with his daytime experiences was easily identifiable and recognizable.

The clear and direct relationship between daytime experience and dream content is evident particularly for wish-fulfilment dreams but also for some bad dreams and nightmares.

Based on the observation of Marco's wish-fulfilment dreams, we may establish that the diurnal sources of infantile dreams are essentially reduced to events in which (a) *a wishful experience* was not completed due to various external circumstances (i.e., an unresolved wish or wishes) and (b) *an affective state associated with this experience*, or rather born with this, remained totally or partially (psychologically) unprocessed. The dreams are built directly on the retrieval of memories of unfulfilled daytime wishes and the associated affective states. In cognitive terms, they are reconstructions based on specific facts and/ or events—that is, *episodic memories* (Tulving, 2001).

On a psychological level, the daytime source represents the triggering impulse of the dream. In other dreams Marco had at an older age, such as frankly bizarre dreams, certain bad dreams and certain wish-fulfilment dreams, we will see instead that the diurnal source consists rather of multiple single elements (sometimes disparate) that act as indirect triggers of dream since these are *activators of other latent dream material*, as they often occur in adult dreams.

DOI: 10.4324/9781003184874-8

Underlying daytime experience of wishes

Analyzing the underlying daytime experiences of unresolved wishes corresponds to analyzing dream wishes, as described in the previous chapter. In fact, we have said that *in infantile dreams, the dream-triggering daytime wish and the dream wish coincide*. We can only emphasize once again that since these are wishes that have not reached fulfilment in the daytime experience, they therefore remained unresolved on a psychic and motivational level.

Affective states

In the daytime, the experiences of unresolved wish fulfilment are always accompanied by intense affective states. The most frequent in Marco's experience are *sorrow, disappointment, regret, impatience or frenetic expectation, contentment, surprise* and *excitement*.

Affective states such as sorrow, disappointment, regret or sometimes impatience or frenetic expectation are generally associated with experiences in which wishes were completely unfulfilled in the daytime. On the other hand, affective states such as of contentment, surprise or excitement are generally associated with situations where the wishes had been partially fulfilled but there had been a premature interruption of their fulfilment (see Table 5.1). More detailed examples are given in Chapters 6 and 15.

Table 5.1 The psychological conditions for triggering of infantile dreams

Day residue/day time experience	Daytime wish	Daytime combined affective state	Dream
The night before, as an anticipation of his birthday party that was to take place a few days later, Marco had had a party in a minor tone.	I wish my birthday party arrived soon	Impatience, excitement	M. 01. *I dreamed that we were at my party and my friends were there. We were playing football, and I was shooting with my left.* (Marco often celebrates his parties at a football field near his home.)
He had bought a DVD which was just a short demo version of *Cars* and had watched it the evening before.	I wish I could watch the full version of my favourite movie (*Cars*).	Disappointment, frustration, excitement	M. 02. *I dreamed about the new movie with the tow trucks.* (He is referring to the movie *Cars*.)

(Continued)

Table 5.1 (Continued)

Day residue/day time experience	Daytime wish	Daytime combined affective state	Dream
On the previous evening, we had spotted certain Befana stockings at the supermarket, and he had been particularly attracted by those with a Spider-Man theme.	I wish the Befana brought me the Spider-Man stocking.	Disappointment, impatience	M. 05. I dreamed that the Befana brought me a Spider-Man stocking. She left it for me on the sofa.
On the day before, Marco had bought a scuba mask. He was thrilled about it but was disappointed by the fact that he could not use it at once.	I wish I could go underwater with my new mask.	Excitement	M. 10–5; 2. I dreamed that I was in the swimming pool with my scuba mask.

"Perturbing" character of affective states

In all cases, these affective states, due to the incomplete (full or partial) gratification of the wish, remained in the waking state in a condition of incomplete psychological processing, thus retaining a certain residual amount of *"perturbing" emotional arousal.* It should be emphasized that, as I have already seen in previous studies (Colace, 2010, 2013), the "perturbing" character of the affective state does not necessarily coincide with a negative or unpleasant nature (i.e., sorrow, sadness or disappointment), or at least it is not a prerogative of it: it may also coincide with a positive nature (e.g., excitement, contentment, curiosity or surprise). This suggests that the "perturbing" prerogative of these affective states might have more to do with *quantitative factors* (amount of their failed processing) *than with qualitative factors* (their type). *What these affective states have in common is the fact that they are in a condition in which portions of them have not been processed and have remained active on a psychic-emotional level.*

I will resume this discussion on the perturbing character of affective states in the part relating to the function of the dream (see Chapter 15).

The distance in time of the daytime sources of wish-fulfilment dreams

Day residue

An important aspect of the analysis of the daytime sources of infantile dreams is the evaluation of the distance in time between these and the occurrence of the dream experience. As we will see, this kind of evaluation will be useful also when addressing the function of the dream and meaning of dreams.

Marco's dream reports suggest that the constituting elements of his dream experience—that is, the material that dreams are made of, are mnestic traces of strong and recent motivational and emotional daytime experiences, generally from the day before the dream. In particular, 85% (22/26) of the clear wish-fulfilment dreams of this period go directly back to facts/experiences from the *previous day*, meaning that dreams are based on mnestic traces of these experiences (events, characters, situations). This is a considerably higher percentage compared to what was observed in a previous study (46% day residue), where information about previous-day experiences was indirect and fewer (Colace, 2013).[1]

Among the dreams with evident day residues (i.e., previous day), four also show *other* daytime residues dating back to sometime before (for 1 dream a few days before, for another dream 1 week, for another dream 1 month before, for another dream 2 months before).

Of the remaining 4 dream reports, 2 have daytime sources dating back to two days before, 2 have generic daytime sources that could be not traced with precision.

This suggests that, when collecting dream reports from young children, if we miss the opportunity to gather information about the day before the dream via direct interviews to the parents, the percentage of dreams that report clear day residues might be underestimated.

Actualization

A more detailed analysis of dreams in which appear some aspects that *apparently* do not refer to recent daytime situations but rather to more distant experiences (6 dream reports in total) reveals that 3 dream aspects actually refer to episodes that occurred farther back in time, but mnestic traces of them were somehow re-activated on the day before the dream. In these dreams, an "old" source of the dream that did not occur recently becomes actualized on the day before the dream through an *actualizing experience* (e.g., the old experience is discussed and/or recalled). The *actualization* has been observed in dreams in which more than one wish appears; it may occur in one referred to on the previous day while another refers to an earlier experience but is however re-actualized on the previous day. This phenomenon of actualization of past experiences was also observed in a previous study (Colace, 2013, 167).

See the following example:

> M. 08–4;9. *I dreamed about the sweets bow. There was a magic door with a hole and I got through it. N.* (his best friend) *was there too. We were even able to watch TV. It was a nice dream. There was a huge donut* (Marco's favourite dessert)*, a tree all made of sweets. It was like an amusement park. I wish I could get into that dream for real!*

Marco added that the setting of the dream was that of the *Wreck-It Ralph* movie, which Marco had been very impressed about. There were sceneries with sweets in that movie; however, Marco had watched it about one month before the dream.

In this dream report, we are probably facing the mnestic activation of the previous experience (which occurred one month before) of watching the *Ralph* movie, in which there are sceneries made of sweets. Two days before the dream, Marco and his mother had baked cakes at home (the *actualizing experience*). In this case, the original experience that represents the source of the dream dated back to two days before. However, I have reason to believe that this experience was really exciting, so much that it left a trace even on the day before the dream (e.g., eating the cakes prepared with the mother).

Another example of actualization is given in dream #27, where the content of the dream is a school trip that had taken place a year earlier but that had been subject of conversation on the day before (see Chapter 6).

Indirect actualization. Sometimes the experiences of the day preceding the dream are related to the original experience only *in indirect and more general way*, since the previous day's dream relates to the original because it belongs to the same conceptual category (see Pippi Longstocking dream #46 in Chapter 9).

Daytime sources of children's dreams in literature

The observations on the *nature* and *time* characteristics of the daytime references of Marco's dream reports are consistent with those obtained from previous investigations.

Freud summarized the diurnal origins of these dreams as follows:

> The wishes which are fulfilled in them are carried over from daytime and as a rule from the day before, and in waking life they have been accompanied by intense emotion. Nothing unimportant or indifferent, or nothing which would strike a child as such, finds its way into the content of their dreams.
>
> (Freud, 1901, p. 22)

The dream refers to specific experiences:

> A girl aged 3 years and 3 months: "Last night I went on the lake" (Freud, 1900, p. 129). Explanation: "She had crossed the lake for the first time, and

the crossing had been too short for her: when we reached the landing-stage she had not wanted to leave the boat and had wept bitterly."

(Freud, 1900, p. 129)

In his review on children's dreams, DeMartino also concluded that "the content of children's dreams is often related to experiences of the previous day" (De Martino, 1959, p. 95).

Hug-Helmuth (1919) observed that the dreams of a one-year-old girl reproduced the swimming movements made the previous day in the pool.

Kimmins (1920) reported that most children's dreams contain references to the previous day and show the clear satisfaction of a wish.

Grotjahn (1938) concluded that " dreams would indicate that the child was struggling with strong and strange emotions which could not work through during the excitement and rapidity of reality" (p. 512, cited in Sándor, Szakadát, & Bódizs, 2014).

Dreams related to wishes for situations denied in wakefulness are reported in the review of De Martino (1959), who refers to studies by Kimmins and others (Selling; Gordon). He concluded, for example, that the dreams of children in orphanages were for the most part about "home", "going home" and "life at home".

Conditions for triggering infantile dreams: two examples

My in-depth observations on Marco's wish-fulfilment dream reports suggest that at the basis of these dreams there are always (a) the daytime experiences of strong (age-specific) conscious (or preconscious) partially or entirely unfulfilled (simple) wishes[2] that press to be satisfied[3] and (b) intense affective states associated with them that remain in a condition of inadequate or incomplete psychological processin so that they continue to generate an excessive emotional/arousal state that is likely to be perturbing also during sleep. *Daytime wishes represent the motivational drive and force for the instigation and formation of dreams, and the associated disturbing affective states are the psychologicaly/emotional matter of dreams themselves.* Marco's wish-fulfilment dreams are consistent with Freud's assertion that the dream, in addition to constituting the fulfilment of a wish, is actually generated by the wish itself, which acts as its driving force (Freud, 1900, pp. 560–561).

These are the basic conditions for triggering infantile dreams. Furthermore, as we have seen, these daytime conditions most often occurred on the day preceding the dream.

These criteria may even help predict which daytime experience will enter the infantile dream. As we will see, these concepts will be useful when addressing the function of dream.

For the sake of clarity, I report here two examples of dreams, explaining the relevant day situations in which their motivational (wishes) and emotional triggering conditions arose.

The dream of the SpongeBob trolley

M. 09–5;2. *Last night I dreamed that you bought me the SpongeBob trolley.*

SpongeBob Squarepants is Marco's favourite cartoon. Some time ago, we had promised him this trolley; however, it was hard to find in shops. In the end, we had decided to buy a normal trolley and place a big SpongeBob sticker on it. *The day before* his dream, we had been at the shop to buy the sticker, but it was out of stock. In addition, after reconsidering the dimensions, we decided not to buy the trolley we had thought about initially because its size would not fit. Marco was left annoyed and regretful of the fact that nothing of what had been promised eventually happened (see Figure 5.1).

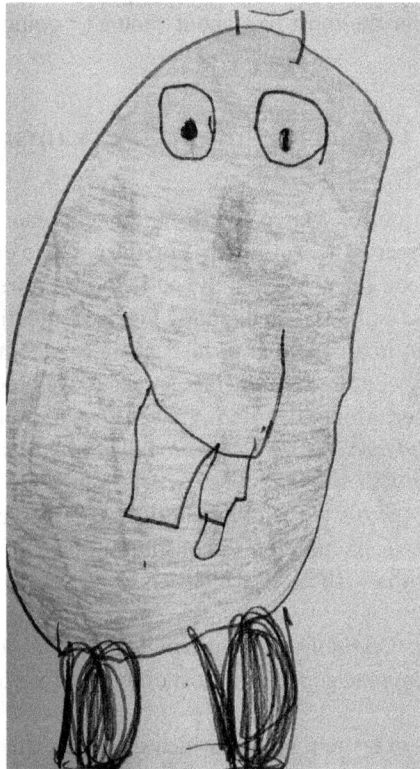

Figure 5.1 Drawing of the dream about the SpongeBob trolley

The diurnal origin of this dream is clear. It is *the unfulfilled wish to buy the desired trolley*, associated with an *emotional regret for not having found it*. It was an affective state that remained unprocessed at a psychological level with a certain amount of perturbing activation (i.e., excessive emotional/arousal).

In this dream, Marco fulfils his desire to own the SpongeBob trolley. Through the wish-fulfilment experience (even if merely oneiric), the dream permits to come to terms with the disturbing affective load (the big disappointment for the missed purchase of the trolley).

The dream of the jumping park

M. 03–4;7. *I went to the trampolines, the jumping park. You* (Daddy) *and Mummy were telling me not to go. But I went there, I jumped a lot, I jumped high, sky-high!!*

A few days earlier, my wife and I had told Marco that he could not jump on the trampolines because it was better for him not to sweat; he had had flu and cough just the week before. Even the *day before* the dream, he had been at the playground but was not allowed to play with the bouncy castle for the same reason.

This dream, too, finds a reference from the state of wakefulness, when Marco could not satisfy his intense *wish to jump* and remained in an affective state of *sorrow* and *disappointment*.

In both the examples previously mentioned, we observe, as daytime source of dream, an experience (from the day before the dream) of a strong (unfulfilled) wish of the child and the affective state associated with it that was prevented from going through its most appropriate psychological processing.

This pattern is always present in Marco's wish-fulfilment dreams and confirms previous observations on the role of wishes and affective states in triggering infantile wish-fulfilment dreams (Colace, 2010, 2013).

In Table 5.1, I report a few examples of daytime wishes and their affective states at the basis of the dreams.

Notes

1   No specific analysis of the daytime sources of infantile dreams had been conducted previously, sometimes due to the methodological limitations of the study (Colace, 2010).
2   As we have seen in this early infantile period, *disapproved wishes* and *morally inadmissible wishes* are rarely observed.
3   This is the standard or minimal condition, but we have seen that there are also wish-fulfilment dreams that are triggered by multiple wishes and dreams that are serially triggered by one same strong recurring wish.

References

Colace, C. (2010). *Children's Dreams: From Freud's Observations to Modern Dream Research*. New York: Routledge.

Colace, C. (2013). Are wish-fulfilment dreams of children the royal road for looking at the functions of dreams? *Neuropsychoanalysis, 15* (2), 161–175.

De Martino, M. F. (1959). A review of the literature on children's dreams. In: M. F. De Martino (Ed.), *Dreams and Personality Dynamics* (pp. 87–96). Springfield: Charles C. Thomas Publisher.

Freud, S. (1900). *The Interpretation of Dreams.* S.E., 4–5. London: Hogarth Press.

Freud, S. (1901). *On Dreams.* S.E., 5. London and New York: Norton & Company, Inc.

Grotjahn, M. (1938). Dreams observation in two-year, four-months-old baby. *The Psychoanalytic Quarterly, 7,* 507–513.

Hug-Helmuth, H. (1919). *A Study of the Mental Life of the Child.* Washington, DC: Nervous and Mental Diseases Publishing.

Kimmins, C. W. (1920). *Children's Dreams.* London: Longmans, Green and Co.

Mari, E., Beretta, M., & Colace, C. (2018). L'appagamento di esiderio e il ristabilimento affettivo nel sogno infantile: nuove osservazioni. *Psychofenia, XXI* (37–38), 17–28.

Sándor, P., Szakadát, S., & Bódizs, R. (2014). Ontogeny of dreaming: A review of empirical studies. *Sleep Medicine Reviews, 18* (5), 435–449.

Tulving, E. (2001). Episodic memory and common sense: How far apart? *Philosophical Transactions of the Royal Society B: Biological Sciences, 356* (1413) (29 September), 1505–1515. DOI: 10.1098/rstb.2001.0937.

Chapter 6

How do dreams act?
The modi operandi of clear wish-fulfilment dreams

Previous studies had suggested that wish-fulfilment dreams act in various ways with respect to the daytime experience that inspired them (Colace, 2010, 2013; Mari, Beretta, & Colace, 2018).

Despite having in common the clear fulfilment of a wish, these dreams differ from one another because they intercept three different situations of the child's daytime experience and respond to these in a characteristic and distinctive way. If we observe the relationship between the wish fulfilment in the dream and the diurnal experience (affective state or event) that the dream refers to, we may notice that *wish-fulfilment dreams differ from one another as expressions of different demands*. Three types of dreams were identified expressing three modi operandi of infantile dreaming processes: *compensation dreams*, *continuation dreams* and *anticipation dreams* (Colace, 2010, 2013).

Marco's wish-fulfilment dream reports confirm the presence of these three types of dreams. Furthermore, from the observation of dreams that report the fulfilment of multiple wishes (i.e., overdetermined dreams), we found the existence of dream that include *more modi operandi together* (i.e., the so-called *mixed dreams*).

Compensation dreams

Compensation dreams derive from a clearly negative affective state and/or experience, such as, for example, the loss of a loved one—that person is still alive in the dream—or another negative situation. *The wish that is represented as satisfied in the dream consists of the occurrence of the opposite of what happened in the daytime* (i.e., the negative situation). In these dreams, compensation is intended in the sense of a true upturning and/or subversion of what happened in reality. Therefore, these dreams in general do not represent only a compensation for what happened in the real life: they actually stage the reality reversed.

> M. 03–4;7. *I went to the playground, to the jumping trampolines. You* (Daddy) *and Mummy were telling me not to go. But I went there, I jumped a lot, I jumped high, sky-high!!*

DOI: 10.4324/9781003184874-9

A few days earlier, my wife and I had told Marco that he could not jump on the trampolines because it was better for him not to sweat; he had had flu and cough just the week before. Even the day before the dream, he had been at the playground but was not allowed to play with the bouncy castle for the same reason.

> M. 18–5;3. *I had the Nintendo with the game. I had won it with the fruit juice. It was a nice black toy. It had the Rabbids game, the one that was on the fruit juice.*[1]

The dream is about the Rabbids game depicted in the cardboard wrap of certain fruit juices, along with the picture of a portable Nintendo console. The day before, at the beach, Marco had asked me, "Daddy, how can we win this Rabbids game? This Nintendo?" I had not replied. In his dream, Marco had this fruit juice and won the Rabbids game and the Nintendo console that he likes very much (both the game and the Nintendo).

His mother also reported that the day before, Marco had told her about this game. We were at the beach, and he asked for a fruit juice and said, "*Mummy, you see, there's the Nintendo!*" And he added, "*I want to win this one! Look, that's the Rabbids game*". And his mother answered, "We'll check on the internet how to sign in for the draw". Marco was very impressed with this game; he even showed it to his cousin J.

Continuation dreams

In these dreams, the fulfilment of a wish consists of the continuation of a generally pleasant daytime experience that was only partially satisfied. In other words, these are wishes that were actually fulfilled in real life, but not completely. The daytime experience may have been interrupted, in which case the dream sort of continues it (i.e., it starts from when it was interrupted), or may have been completed but too soon in the light of the child's expectations, in which case the dream perpetuates the pleasant daytime experience. In continuation dreams, too, we may notice a sort of "compensation"; however, in these dreams, unlike in compensation dreams, there has been at least one initial pleasant situation in the daytime experience.

> M. 13–5;2. *I dreamed I was walking around with a young lizard dinosaur* (to the left in the drawing, brown in colour). *Then I was attacked by pterodactyls* (to the right in the drawing). *They wanted to eat the lizard's tail. Then I fell down under a bridge with the lizard that had torn a building down to pieces, and the pterodactyls attacked it and they wanted to eat all the lizard, so I caught one and threw it in the water and drowned it. I stamped another one down, while the other that was attacking me, I caught it and beat it hard.*

Figure 6.1 The drawing of the scene of the Spider-Man dream; from the left to the right: young lizard dinosaur, Spider-Man-Marco and pterodactyls

The dream ended with me feeding the lizard with all the pterodactyls that I had killed. In the dream I was Spider-Man.
(Marco also added that certain schoolmates of his were in the dream, but he couldn't tell who exactly because he said he didn't remember.)

The dream relates to the child's fancy world. It is a wish-fulfilment dream where the child resumes the adventures of his favourite superhero and impersonates him, fighting against the dinosaurs/pterodactyls (see Figure 6.1).

M. 61–6;11. *There was the stadium of Torino* (football club) *and everybody was cheering with the fans, and that's it. The match was Lazio* (football club) *vs. Torino, but had not started yet. It was a nice dream.*[2]

In the few months preceding the dream, Marco had become a passionate football fan. He also used to play football matches on the PlayStation. He likes the Lazio team. We had been a few times at the stadium and had been watching matches together on TV. Two days before this dream, we had watched a match together, Cagliari vs. Lazio. And I had bought the stadium tickets to go see the next match, scheduled for the coming week. In this dream, Marco goes on entertaining with his passion for football.

> M. 02–4;0. *I dreamed about the new movie on the tow trucks* (he is referring to the *Cars* movie, where there are tow trucks like the character of Mater). *I was watching the movie.*

The dream is about a movie that Marco had actually bought two days before and watched on the evening before the dream. The thing about this DVD is that it contains only one episode taken from *Cars*, so it is much shorter than the original movie, which Marco knows well. The child was probably startled, seeing that the movie didn't last long. He had expected it to last as long as the *Cars* movie. In fact, when questioned, Marco said he was disappointed because the movie was so short and added that it had been longer in the dream. This is a dream that resumes, repeats and prolongs a pleasant diurnal experience.

Anticipation dreams

These dreams represent the fulfilment of a wish that has, as its background, a daytime experience of eagerness for a pleasant event that is supposed to occur in the future. These dreams anticipate the event by making it happen in the present time. This category of dreams also includes those dreams that feature a wish that will be fulfilled on the day following the dream (*dreams of impatience*).[3]

The wishes that these dreams relate to are wishes not fulfilled while the subject is awake.

See the following examples. In both these dreams, we notice the fulfilment of a wish that refers to the anticipation of a desired event that comes true. Both wishes are derived from a real-life situation that may refer to a recent period of wakefulness.

> M. 01–4;0. *Daddy, I dreamed that it was my birthday party. My friends were there, we were playing football at the playing field and I kicked with my left foot.*

A few days later, Marco was to celebrate his birthday with his friends in a place where there is a small playing field (the same place where he had had his party the year before). The evening before, we had celebrated in the family. It is a wish-fulfilment dream that relates to something longed for, that is expected to happen soon.

> M. 53–6;6. *I dreamed of the giant scorpion in the case, the insects' case. I dreamed of the black scorpion* (at that moment, he only had a small yellow scorpion in his collection). *It's the one that's coming out next Tuesday.*

I dreamed there were three little crocodiles around it, in the other compart-ments of the case, and the scorpion was in its compartment. They were fake crocodiles, like the other pieces of the collection.[4]

While reporting his dream, Marco was happy and enthusiastic about the fact that in the dream, he already had the giant scorpion!

He said that was a nice dream. Marco had recently started a collection he was very thrilled about: a series of insect replicas that were sold as weekly issues at newsstands. Each replica had its place in one of the various compartments of a transparent plastic case. The day before the dream, his grandfather had brought him one of those insects and had said that the next issue would be a giant scorpion and was due to come out on the following Tuesday. When Marco came home, he told his mother about the next issue and already couldn't wait for Tuesday to arrive and so he could get the new scorpion.

Marco added, *"I wanted to dream that I had it* (the black scorpion), *but it's just a dream!"* (as if to say, "I can't possibly have it before the date!"). In his dream, Marco anticipated the new issue with the scorpion and had it in his collection already with the other insects. The small crocodiles are an inconsistent element because the series does not include any crocodiles.

In the following dream, Marco expresses anticipation for the Christmas holidays.

M. 22–5;6. *You know, I dreamed it was Christmas.* And then? *That's it.* And were there Christmas presents too? *No. It was a nice dream.*

Marco laughed cheerfully while reporting his dream. In the days before, we had talked about the imminent Halloween as a festivity when there is no school and that comes before Christmas (another festivity with no school). We had also talked about Christmas as holiday time. The dream apparently portrays the achievement of this goal (i.e., staying home from school).

Mixed dreams

We have described dreams that stage more than one wish. In these dreams, each fulfilment of an individual wish may be differently related with the daytime expe-rience and may therefore contain aspects of *compensation, continuation and anticipation* (i.e., more modi operandi together).

M. 27–5;9. *I dreamed I was at primary school. There were M.* (his "ex-girlfriend"), *G., E. and N.* (his best friends) *and we were on a school trip. I had arrived at school with the school bus. Then we were on the footpath, Mum and Dad and me. It was night-time. It was a nice dream.*

The evening before, Marco had played an alphabet game (a game that he liked a lot and had been playing enthusiastically with for several days) and had complained about not being able to write words. We parents had told him he would learn how to write at primary school in the coming year. In the preceding days, he had complained about the fact that his teachers had not taken him again to the primary school visiting day (as they had done once some time before, and Marco had liked it very much). Marco also complained about not having school trips anymore (his school did not arrange any). We told him that their visit to the local theatre had actually been a school trip, and he was disappointed.

Two wishes appear in this dream: the wish to go to primary school (and learn to write) and the wish to go on a school trip. *The dream shows two modi operandi.* On one side, it is a dream that anticipates the fulfilment of the wish to go to primary school; on the other, it is also a compensatory dream as it fulfils the wish to do something that he could no longer do (the trip). Through its mixed mode of action, this dream addresses the state of impatience and excitement for his future attending the primary school (feelings from the memory of his visit to that school on the occasion of the visiting days), and it also faces the disappointment/frustration of not being able to go on a school trip. In this dream, we can observe the phenomenon of actualization. There are in fact direct references to the day before (compilation of the alphabet), and again on the day before, references regarding days past (school trips) had been recalled.

Among the wish-fulfilment dreams from the first period, dreams of compensation, continuation and anticipation are distributed fairly evenly, covering 31%, 19% and 23%, respectively, of clear wish-fulfilment dreams. On the other hand, *mixed dreams* are also present (27%), especially with co-existing aspects of anticipation/ compensation and anticipation/continuation. The category of mixed dreams had not been identified in previous studies, although dreams with more than one wish were noticed since probably their daytime references to different situations had not been fully understood (Colace, 2010, p. 187).

The *compensation dream* described here represents a modus operandi of wish-fulfilment dreams that goes beyond the general concept that all wish-fulfilment dreams compensate what the diurnal experience has failed to grant to the child (Freud, 1901; Kimmins, 1920). Here, compensation is understood more in the sense of a subversion of what occurred in the child's daytime reality.

We have observed that in *compensation dreams*, the wish starts the "real" fulfilment and *its first-time gratification in the dream hallucinatory experience itself.* Indeed, in these dreams, the wish may have been fulfilled at some point, but not recently (e.g., the father breaks his leg and can no longer play fight).

This differentiates these dreams from *continuation dreams*, where the gratification of the wish resumed in the dream had *already started* in the reality of daytime experience. In other words, in *continuation dreams*, the dreamlike scene of wish fulfilment is taken from the daytime experience, where it already really occurred at least once. Nothing new is created. *Anticipation dreams*, too, refer to a wish that was never fulfilled—or in any case, not recently. So, in dreams of compensation and anticipation, there is generally *one more step for the creation of the dream wish or wish-fulfilment scene* compared to continuation dreams.

These difference in the vicissitudes of wish in daytime experience imply that at the basis of *continuation dreams*, there are wishes that may have lost part of their driving and instigating force as they were already partially satisfied in the actual daytime experience, compared to the wishes underlying *compensation* and *anticipation* dreams that appear to be stronger because they were not satisfied at all. From this point of view, the classification of wish-fulfilment dreams into these three types is even more useful. For the moment, I will note that *continuation dreams* disappear in Marco's second period while *compensation* and *anticipation* dreams remain. But I will return on this point in Chapter 8.

The type of wish-fulfilment dreams presented here and their relationship with daytime experiences are similar to the examples reported by Freud and other authors. An example reported by Freud that is close to the ones we have called *continuation dreams* is that of the "trip on the lake" (1901, pp. 20–21) and also that of "driving in a chariot with Achilles" (ibid., p. 22).

One day a girl of three and a quarter made a trip across a lake. The voyage was evidently not long enough for her, for she cried when she had to get off the boat. Next morning she reported that during the night she had been on a trip to the lake, she had been continuing her interrupted voyage (Freud, 1901, pp. 20–21).

> An eight-year-old boy had a dream that he was driving in a chariot with Achilles and that Diomed was the charioteer. It was shown that the day before he had been deep in a book of legends about the Greek heroes (Freud, 1901, p. 22)

In both dreams, the daytime situations that triggered the dream are represented by wishes whose fulfilments were interrupted and therefore not completed. Freud also reported children's dreams of the *compensation type*, as, for instance, the dream of "climbing up the Dachstein" (Freud, 1901, p. 21), which refers to the experience from the previous day in which the child was disappointed and sorry for not having been able to visit Mount Dachstein. Freud also described dreams in which the wish refers to something that will occur on the following day or in the future:

> On another occasion an association which suddenly occurred to him carried us another step forward in our understanding of the dream: "The tree was a Christmas-tree" . . . He had gone to sleep, then, in tense expectation of the day which ought to bring him a double quantity of presents. We know that in such circumstances a child may easily anticipate the fulfilment of his wishes. So it was already Christmas in his dream. (Freud, 1918, p. 35)

Besides, there is also another evident point in the examples of dreams reported by Freud: two forms of wish fulfilment may appear in the same dream, one as "continuation" and the other as "anticipation", described here as mixed dreams.

It is a little girl's dream that refers to the interruption of a hike before reaching the destination because it was too late:

> In a course of walk her father had stopped short of their intended goal as the hour was getting late. On their way back she had noticed a signpost bearing the name of another landmark, and her father had promised to take her there as well another time. Next morning she met her father with the news that she had dreamed that he had been with her to both places.
>
> (Freud, 1901, p. 21)

The little girl then *continued the first hike* and *anticipated the second* by making it.

Other authors after Freud reported examples of wish-fulfilment dreams similar to the types reported here without, however, defining and naming them in three distinct categories related to different daytime situations.

Clear examples of dreams that we have defined as *continuation dreams* were reported by Coriat (1916). He cites for example the case of a child who used a dream to continue an exciting story he had read the day before.

> A five-year-old boy, for instance, after having had a portion of "Alice in Wonderland" read to him, became intensely excited and interested, so much so that it became necessary to discontinue the reading for the day. However, the next morning on awakening, he sat up in bed and spontaneously said: o dear me! I am surprised to see myself in my own bed, because my Teddy bear went down a hole, and I went after him, and then I thought I swam in my own tears. Here was evidently a pure wish dream, a desire to continue the day's excitement caused by story, plus the wish to continue playing with his Teddy bear. (Coriat, 1916, pp. 50–51)

The following is also a great example of what we have called continuation dreams:

> Another boy, age four, who during the day had been at a children's party, betrayed the wish to continue the good time he had at the party by the following dream: Daddy, when I am in bed with my eyes closed, I can see Barbara's party.
>
> (Coriat, 1916, p. 51)

Hill (1926) reports the following example of a compensation dream, referring to a child's passion for tractors. A child had once taken a short ride on the motor tractor and wanted to ride again, but this was not possible, so the child dreamed of driving the tractor:

> On the motor tractor, daddy . . . John (the child dreamer) on it with Oswald and Buddy (his playmates).
>
> (Hill, 1926, p. 11)

Dreams like those that we have defined here as compensation and anticipation dreams were reported by Kimmins (1920). They refer to the absence of the father in the—father who returns home from war—(compensation) and dreams similar to other ones described earlier—that it soon will be Christmas with its presents—(anticipation; Kimmins, 1920, p. 37).

Finally, I am inclined to consider the presence of this plurality of forms of wish-fulfilment dreams as a meaningful indication of the importance of the role of wishes in the instigation of dreams as well as a clear indication that the dreaming is a meaningful and finalized psychic act.

Notes

1   That summer, a popular brand of fruit juices arranged a prize draw: the consumers would log on the juice producer's website and enter the number codes they found printed on the wrap around a pack of 3 fruit juices. The lucky winners would get Nintendo games, plush toys or even Nintendo consoles.
2   This is a wish-fulfilment dream from the second period of Marco.
3   Freud described dreams of impatience in adults as follows: "If someone had made preparations for a journey, for a theatrical performance that is important to him, for going to a lecture or paying a visit, he may dream a premature fulfilment of his expectation" (Freud, 1916–1917, p. 134).
4   This is a wish-fulfilment dream from the second period of Marco.

References

Colace, C. (2010). *Children's Dreams: From Freud's Observations to Modern Dream Research*. New York: Routledge.

Colace, C. (2013). Are wish-fulfilment dreams of children the royal road for looking at the functions of dreams? *Neuropsychoanalysis*, *15* (2), 161–175.

Coriat, I. H. (1916). *The Meaning of Dreams*. Boston: Dodo Press.

Freud, S. (1901). *On Dreams*. S.E. London and New York: Norton & Company, Inc.

Freud, S. (1916–1917). *Introductory Lectures on Psycho-Analysis*. S.E., 15/16. London: Hogarth Press.

Freud, S. (1918). *From the History of an Infantile Neurosis*. S.E., 17. London: Hogarth Press.

Hill, J. C. (1926). *Dreams and Education*. London: Methuen & Co.

Kimmins, C. W. (1920). *Children's Dreams*. London: Longmans, Green and Co.

Mari, E., Beretta, M., & Colace, C. (2018). L'appagamento di desiderio e il ristabilimento affettivo nel sogno infantile: nuove osservazioni. *Psychofenia*, *XXI* (37–38), 17–28.

Chapter 7

Less common forms of dreaming in infancy

In Marco's early dream repertoire, we have seen that most dreams are of the clear and direct wish-fulfilment type. These are the dreams that mainly characterize this period. This type of dreams presents a set of characteristics that define a *way of dreaming* that Freud called "infantile dream" or "dream built along infantile lines" (Freud, 1916–1917, p. 134), which does not refer exclusively to the dreams of young children but is a module that also occurs in adults (under certain conditions). Also, for this reason, the study of children's dreams is of great importance.

The other types of dreams from this period represent a clear minority (*n* 10) that deserve further insight—at least some of them. These dreams appear as forms of dreaming that somehow depart from the forms of infantile dreams and represent early evolutionary changes in the general function of dreaming towards a progressive greater complexity. Some of these (i.e., bad dreams and frankly bizarre dreams) appear in a more predominant way in the dream repertoire from the second and third periods, between 6 and 10 years of age.

Oedipal dreams

In the first period, Marco reported three dreams that may be defined as oedipal. In these dreams, there is an attempt to satisfy, in a slightly symbolic form, an *unconsciously repressed wish* (i.e., to eliminate the father and stay with the mother), which remains in the area of the unconscious and that emerges only in symbolic form in the dream. In these dreams, some bizarre elements also appear.[1] We have already defined these wishes as *morally/ethically inadmissible* because they are in conflict with the child's moral conscience. In these dreams, there is a symbolism that the child uses unconsciously—in Piaget's terms, a secondary symbolism.[2]

These are dreams containing an early form of transformation of latent dream material—that is, the psychic substance of the dream. Therefore, in these dreams, it becomes necessary for the first time to make a distinction between latent and manifest contents of the dream. It is interesting to note that at this age, Marco, given the overwhelming presence of simple and direct dreams without inherent transformations, still has the potential to carry out these early

DOI: 10.4324/9781003184874-10

symbolic transformations. Moreover, we have previously addressed the early repertoire of *dream-work operations* which these symbolic transformations are part of. I will return to this topic when addressing the evolution of *dream work*.

At the age of 4 years and 8 months, Marco reported a dream that can be considered the first dream of this type.[3] Here, too, we are dealing with dreams that depart from the dream pattern intended as a plain and direct fulfilment of a wish.

> M. 07–4;8. *I dreamed that you, Dad, were dead. You had fallen from the balcony. I was at home with Mummy. She called the ambulance. I was sad. I cried so much in the dream. The men came and put you on the stretcher and took you away (but you were dead, though). I waited at home with Mummy. In my dream, you did like this: you fell backwards from the balcony* (he gestures to show me how).

While telling this dream, Marco appeared upset and anguished. He said, "I don't want to lose my dad!" In his dream, the father dies even if it is not Marco who kills him directly. In this way, he can remain alone with his mother. The dream is accompanied by anguish. Another dream of anguish triggered by an oedipal desire was reported at the age of 5 years and 5 months.

> M. 23–5;5. *I had a bad dream. I dreamed that the gypsies had hit you* (Daddy) *and slammed you against a piece of iron (Daddy died). I cried.*
> (Marco remaining at home with his mother was not part of the scene, though).

In this dream, the father is killed by the gypsies while Marco is home with his mother.

The last oedipal dream was reported at the age of 5 years and 10 months. We may see, in this regard, that Marco's dreams never stage the death of the mother.

> M. 29–5;10. *We were at the restaurant with M. and I.* (girl schoolmates). *You were there* (Mummy) *and Daddy, and we were watching a play of big puppets (they were as big as window dummies). Daddy got up to go open the door. There was a thief. He shot at you with his gun and you died, and I broke into tears.*

In this dream, the father is killed by a thief. The dream resumes certain elements from different diurnal episodes placed at various distances in time. The dream seems to take its cue from the "game of shooting at each other with toy guns" played during the day by father and son and perhaps replicates the attempt in that game and then in the dream to elaborate unconscious guilty feelings for the oedipal drive to eliminate the father (see the drawing of this dream, Figure 7.1).

Figure 7.1 Drawing of Marco's dream report (dream report # 29), the dream of the thief with the gun). Left to right: door of restaurant, father, thief with gun, puppets, girl schoolmate and Marco. The use of dream drawings to compare with verbal reports can be of great use to discern some nuances of the dream content, the characters, the scenario and the self-representation in dream, as well as to evaluate the credibility of the dream. Marco rarely provided a drawing of the dream. However, when he did, it was of great use for the comprehension of the dream content.

In the first dream, the father dies accidentally, while in the other two, he gets killed. *In the second period, starting from the age of 6, oedipal dreams disappear*[4] even if oedipal themes can be hypothesized in some *bad dreams*. I will return to this point later, when discussing the relationship between superego development and dreams. We can see that the symbolism used by the child in these dreams is already at the service of dream censorship, which, starting between about half the age of 4 and the full age of 5, appears to start functioning at least in some dreams (e.g., see dreams #6 and #25, Chapter 9).

Early bad dreams and nightmares

In Marco, bad dreams appear more frequently along with his development of dreaming abilities, towards the end of the first half of his fifth year of life. From this point of view, the bad dreams seem to be the prerogative of a more advanced phase of the ontogenetic development of the function of dreaming. On the other hand, the scarce presence of nightmares in Marco's first period is in line with the low prevalence of these dreams in pre-schoolers (Simard et al., 2008; Nielsen & Levin, 2007).

I included in the category of bad dreams all those that were defined by Marco as "bad" or "ugly" dreams and in which unpleasant emotions such as sadness, fear, anguish or worry were mentioned in the verbal report of the dream, and/or appeared in his feelings during the report, and/or were expressed when answering to further questions about the dream content.

Marco's early bad dreams (only four in this period) concern "being abducted", "being shot at" and "fear that daddy goes away". Of these, only one may be defined a nightmare. Later, when bad dreams' frequency increases (periods II and III), I will focus more on various types of bad dreams and their contents.

Marco's first bad dream dates back to the age of 5 years and 4 months (#20). It was a bad dream that caused abrupt awakening:

M. 20. *I dreamed that the gypsies wanted to take me. I was near you* (Daddy). *I wrapped my arms tight around your neck, you shoved like this* (he made the gesture) *and they went away.*

The dream has a connection with the previous day: Marco was frightened because when he got out of the car, at a shopping mall, he lost sight of me (the father) for a moment (his mother sometimes warns him that if he does not stay close to his parents, the gypsies will come and kidnap him).

Here a specific fear episode circumscribed in space and time gives rise to a more general and deep-rooted fear "of gypsies", a fear that the dream somehow allows to overcome and process (the father sends the gypsies away). *The diurnal residue in this case does not resume directly in the dream but acts as an indirect trigger of other psychic material.*

In other words, in this dream, the diurnal residue activates some latent (sub-conscious) psychic material that is the true reason for the dream. It is therefore a completely different type of diurnal residue with respect to those that originate wish-fulfilment dreams, where the diurnal residue is itself the direct and explicit theme of the dream—and probably its only trigger.

My previous studies were not specifically focused on nightmares and bad dreams (Colace, 2010); however, some indications can indeed compare with this study.

In a previous study conducted with a similar methodology (collection of dreams at home), the dreams falling into this category were less than 5% (Colace, 1998, 2010).[5]

In a questionnaire-based study, it showed that dreams rarely show "aggressive action" and "anxious themes" (18% between 3 and 5 years of age) in their content (Colace, 2006). In the same study, the vast majority of parents reported the absence of nightmares. Only 14% of the parents reported that they showed up "sometimes" (3–5 years), and only 1% reported that their children "often" had nightmares.

On the other hand, while reporting the dreams, the children (3–5 years) frequently appeared quiet or glad (78%) and more rarely anxious (18%) and gloomy (4%) (Colace, 2006).

Marco's first frankly bizarre dreams

Several studies, even conducted with different methodologies and using different content scales of the dream bizarreness, converge towards establishing that young children's dreams are rarely bizarre (Colace, 2003, 2010, 2012; Colace & Tuci, 1996,; Colace et al., 1993; Colace, Tuci, & Ferendeles, 1997).

For example, a previous study found that at least up to 5 years and 6 months, *frankly bizarre dreams*—that is, dreams with content that is senseless, inconsistent and bizarre—are no more than 15%, and dreams with "some strange effects and incompatible with common everyday experience" are 17% of the dream reports collected (Colace, 2010). Foulkes (1982) observed that children's REM dreams (3–5 years) are not "terribly bizarre" and do not show "deviations from the physical laws characteristic of everyday reality" but refer to family situations of the children's everyday world (ibid., p. 67). Foulkes found that the dreams of younger children do not show any unfamiliar characters or settings. Resnick et al. (1994) found that only 34% (14/41) of the dreams of younger children showed at least one element of bizarreness (i.e., implausible/impossible elements: "inconsistency", "uncertainty", "discontinuity"). (For review, see Colace, 2003, 2012; Sándor, Szakadát, & Bódizs, 2014.)[6]

Marco's dream reports confirm these data. *Frankly bizarre dreams are rare in the first period.* Marco only reported 5 (14%) dreams that fall into this category.[7]

In these dreams, it is difficult to detect links with the waking experience, and the dream contents are scarcely compatible and/or plausible with respect to the child's daytime experiences. These dreams apparently show no trace of wish fulfilment, and their meaning remains obscure. These dreams therefore differ from those that, while showing early signs of dream distortion and bizarreness, do not prevent us from seeing in them the fulfilment of an underlying "illegitimate" wish (i.e., dreams in which a disapproved wish is fulfilled in a slightly distorted way) (see Chapters 8 and 12). Unlike these latter dreams in these bizarre dreams, it is therefore difficult to discern the dream-work operations and dream-distortion work, but they remain useful too in describing some phenomenological aspects of dream bizarreness (see Table 7.1).

It is very likely that in previous studies, when information on daytime experiences and on the dreamer was scarce, a dream could be wrongly judged as *bizarre* due to the presence of some aspects whose origin was unknown to researcher (Colace, 2010). In Marco's dream repertoire, since I had a lot of information that helped me understand every aspect of the dream contents, it was easier to reveal the meaning of some dream reports.

In Marco's dream repertoire, the first example of dream bizarreness that cannot be explained by the concept of *primary bizarreness* (see Chapter 3) appears in

Table 7.1 Phenomenology of bizarreness appearing in Marco's early frankly bizarre dreams

Characters' condensation	One dream character brings together characteristics of different real-life characters
Incongruous characters	Impossible or improbable characters
Incongruous space and/or time overlaps	Things and objects are placed in places that are not the usual ones. Actions are carried out at different times than during the day.
Strange and improper actions	A dream character performs improbable actions that he/she would not perform in reality.
Vagueness	Vague description of a character or situation

the case of dream #11, when Marco was 5 years and 2 months. It is a dream that escapes understanding, has no clear connection with any daytime experience and does not show any apparent wish-fulfilment justification.

> M. 11–5;2. G. (Marco's best friend) *shoved me, I shoved him back against the car, and behind there was a curtain for a puppet show, and then when I shoved G., he smashed the car to pieces. The puppets were in the car, and we were doing a show. He wrecked all Uncle C.'s car.*
> (When I asked, "But was it Aunt E.'s car or Uncle C.'s?" Marco answered, "Actually it was neither of their cars. In my dream, they had parked their car wrong because they had Grandpa Tore's car.)

In these very first bizarre dreams, the whole repertoire of bizarre aspects that can be observed in the dreams of adults and older children appears (Colace, 2003). The elements appearing in the dream are *intrinsically bizarre,* in the sense that they are implausible and impossible in the waking experience (for example, the mother pooping by the pool, dream # 19). Almost all these elements start from real daytime references that in the dream are however *distorted in their original and usual meaning* and *in their spatial/temporal collocation.* As in early bad dreams, and perhaps even more so, for these dreams, we may say that the diurnal references act as indirect triggers of other psychic material, the meaning of which we miss most of the times. Therefore, the diurnal references of bizarre dreams and of some bad dreams seem to act as triggers of latent material, which is probably the real motivational drive of the dream and its psychic substance. So, *bizarre and bad dreams are early examples of dreams tied to the concept of latent dream contents, like oedipal dreams.*

In the following dream example, there is a wide repertoire of bizarre elements. Characters appear in which various characteristics and aspects of real-life characters are *condensed*; there is an *incongruous space and time overlap*.

There are also *indeterminate characters*, and *bizarre actions appear*. The most typical bizarre elements are in roman.

> M. 17–5;3. *I dreamed that there was a dummy on the roof,* and we were in a house (a new house) with the garden. It wasn't this house of ours, *and I was with Grandpa Tore and Grandma Graziella* (I had left him at his grandparents' house that day). *Then there was* someone on the roof, a guy dressed like a chick. *He was wearing a scarf and a hat and was dressed in a chick costume. I had seen his shadow. Then, as I was watching TV, I thought it was the antenna. I said* (the antenna that was fluttering) *so I went up to the roof and there was no one. There was someone, N.* (Mr. N. is the janitor of our building), *who was fixing it. We discovered that afterwards,* that he was fixing the antenna and then he was a chick who had stolen everything from us including our spyglass.

The sources of the dream appear to be the following: One is the idea of moving to a new house with a garden that Marco would have liked. I don't know what the chick refers to. Often, when we want to turn off the television, we tell Marco that the antenna does not work or that the janitor has turned it off. However, these elements do not clarify the meaning of the dream. The situation is very different from wish-fulfilment dreams, where the diurnal source explains the dream—that is, its origin, its probable triggering event and its general and individual meaning. The character dressed as a chick is a bizarre element in itself. There is a character who brings together various characteristics (chick, scarf, hat). The other bizarre element is the unusual action of climbing onto the roof.

Regarding the fact that the chick steals our spyglass, the only general reference during the day is the idea of moving house. Note that a character like the chick has no connection (as other fantastic characters do) with daytime events, such as a cartoon, a video game or others, which would have made it a plausible element.

In these dreams, there are forms of bizarreness that appear in adult dreams, although in greater quantity in the latter (see Table 7.1). This means that even a child of this age may have a repertoire of *cognitive abilities potentially capable of producing bizarreness (scenarios, plot, characters, etc.) on the mental level and reporting it verbally.* Moreover, this is in accord with the existence of various dream-work operations observed in wish-fulfilment dreams (Chapter 3). We suppose that these same dream-work operations may have been employed in these bizarre dreams for the purpose of a defensive distortion of latent material resulting in a bizarre manifest dream content.

Ultimately, in this age period, other forms of dreams appear, albeit in minority, such as those mentioned previously, which show the potential possibility for a 4- or 5-year-old child to produce more complex dreams. This suggests that, at these ages, *the simplicity and ordinary aspects of most dreams are not due to the lack of the cognitive and verbal skills needed to produce and/or report dream bizarreness nor to the absence of dream-work operations, ready to eventually produce distortions, but rather to a real major production of simple wish-fulfilment dreams.*

I will return to this topic in my attempt to describe the (theoretical) essence of those aspects of intrapsychic development that are correlated with a greater presence of dream bizarreness during development.

From a timeline perspective, the bizarreness (similar to that of adults' dreams) of these frankly bizarre dreams is preceded by what we have defined *primary bizarreness* that occurs in certain *multiple wish-fulfilment dreams* and in one dream, at age 4 years and 8 months, where there appears a bizarre aspect attributable to a defensive distortion (#6, Chapter 3). We have seen that in that case, the bizarreness is mainly of a cognitive type and can be found in space-time overlaps in the dream and/or in the temporal location of the characters and situations in the dream. It may be attributed to a need for dream synthesis. Note that in these multiple wish-fulfilment dreams, in contrast to early frankly bizarre dreams, the connection with diurnal experiences and their meaning remains open and understandable (i.e., wish-fulfilment nature of the dream). I will return to the difference between types of bizarreness in Chapter 9.

Daytime sources of minority forms of dreaming

As we have seen, the daytime source of frankly bizarre dreams and of certain bad dreams is often harder to identify. They remain more indirect and sometimes obscure. To understand them, one must start making hypotheses and deductions. It is a type of connection that is substantially different from what is observed in clear wish-fulfilment dreams. In these minority forms of dreams, more elements of daytime life are taken up and put together to compose a dream plot and scenario. Nor is there a specific experience and/or event that is picked up in the dream and developed. We have seen how sometimes a specific daytime fear can trigger more general and more deeply rooted fears.

In both bad dreams and bizarre dreams, we can say that the daytime references trigger other (latent) psychic material, the meaning of which is, most of the time, obscure. Instead, in wish-fulfilment dreams, it is the wish itself that is the object of the dream, its psychic material.

In two *bad dreams*, the *day residue is uncertain with respect to the distance in time* and does not explain the dream content and meaning. In two other bad dreams, the *day residue is clear and direct*, but only in one case does it explain the meaning of dream, while in the other, the day residue activates a thematically related stimulus.

In *frankly bizarre dreams*, the daytime elements are taken up only in some aspects or details that appear in a disparate way in the dream plot. Therefore, their sense and meaning are not at all clarified by the daytime experiences, which seem to provide only an input for a dream of obscure meaning. These characteristics of daytime residues (i.e., unclearness) complicate the assessment of their distance in time from the dream experience. In one of these dreams, the elements resumed from the state of wakefulness date back to the previous day, in another they are older, and in another they are uncertain.

In *oedipal dreams*, there are references to the previous day. However, the dream does not reproduce the daytime scene/experience but activates something similar thematically. So when addressing these dreams, it is necessary to proceed with some interpretation.

Notes

1   In several occasions, Freud observed that children's dreams may present symbolic aspects (Freud, 1900, 1910).
2   According to Piaget (1962), there is a "conscious or primary symbol" (pg. 171) when the child knows the meaning of symbols and "a secondary or unconscious symbolism" (171) for those symbols "whose significance is not understood by the child himself" (171).
3   Kimmins (1920, p. 40) reported the presence of repressed unconscious material in the dreams of young children at 5 years of age.
4   This is in line with the hypothesis about the evolution of oedipal stage along the psychological development of the child.
5   This percentage included "bad dreams" or unpleasant dreams but also neutral dreams or pleasant dreams that were not classifiable as wish-fulfilment dreams (see Colace, 2010, pp. 158–159).
6   More bizarreness was found in the dreams of young children that present with a psychological disease (Freud, 1909; Foulkes et al., 1969).
7   These also include 2 bad dreams with bizarre aspects (see Chapter 3).

References

Colace, C. (1998). Wish-fulfillment in dream reports of young children. *Sleep*, *21* (Suppl. 3), 286.
Colace, C. (2003). Dream bizarreness reconsidered. *Sleep and Hypnosis*, *5* (3), 105–128.
Colace, C. (2006). Children's dreaming: A study based on questionnaire completed by parents. *Sleep and Hypnosis*, *8* (1), 19–32.
Colace, C. (2010). *Children's Dreams: From Freud's Observations to Modern Dream Research*. New York: Routledge.
Colace, C. (2012). Dream bizarreness and the controversy between the neurobiological approach and the disguise censorship model: The contribution of children's dreams. *Neuropsychoanalysis*, *14* (2), 165–174.
Colace, C., Doricchi, F., Di Loreto, E., & Violani, C. (1993). Developmental qualitative and quantitative aspects of bizarreness in in dream reports of children. *Sleep Research*, *22*, 57.
Colace, C., & Tuci, B. (1996). Bizarreness in children's dreams. *Journal of Sleep Research*, *5* (Suppl. 1), 38.
Colace, C., Tuci, B., & Ferendeles, R. (1997). Bizarreness in early children's dreams collected in the home setting: Preliminary data. *Sleep Research*, *26*, 241.

Foulkes, D. (1982). *Children's Dreams, Longitudinal Studies*. New York: Wiley-Interscience Publication.

Foulkes, D., Larson, J., Swanson, E., & Rardin, M. (1969). Two studies of childhood dreaming. *American Journal of Orthopsychiatry, 39*, 627–643.

Freud, S. (1900). *The Interpretation of Dreams*. S.E., 4–5. London: Hogarth Press.

Freud, S. (1909). *Analysis of a Phobia in a Five-Year-Old Boy*. S.E., 10. London: Hogarth Press.

Freud, S. (1910). *Leonardo da Vinci and a Memory of his Childhood*. S.E., 11: 59–137. London: Hogarth Press.

Freud, S. (1916–1917). *Introductory Lectures on Psycho-Analysis*. S.E., 15/16. London: Hogarth Press.

Nielsen, T. A., & Levin, R. (2007). Nightmares: A new neurocognitive model. *Sleep Medicine Reviews, 11*, 295–310.

Piaget, J. (1962). *Play, Dreams and Imitation in Childhood*. New York and London: W.W. Norton & Company.

Resnick, J., Stickgold, R., Rittenhouse, C., & Hobson, J. A. (1994). Self-representation and bizarreness in children's dream reports collected in the home setting. *Consciousness and Cognition, 3*, 30–45.

Sándor, P., Szakadát, S., & Bódizs, R. (2014). Ontogeny of dreaming: A review of empirical studies. *Sleep Medicine Reviews, 18* (5), 435–449.

Simard, V., Nielsen, T. A., Tremblay, R. E., Boivin, M., & Montplaisir, J. Y. (2008). Longitudinal study of bad dreams in preschool-aged children: Prevalence, demographic correlates, risk and protective factors. *Sleep, 31* (1), 62–70.

Part III

The decline of infantile forms of dreaming (ages 6 to 7)

Chapter 8

Changes in dream repertoire and developments in wish-fulfilment dreaming

The decline of the infantile module of dreaming

The collection of Marco's dream reports over the years allowed me to develop observations and hypotheses about the changes that gradually occur in the development of the dreaming function from an ontogenetic point of view.

The early way of dreaming, defined as infantile or direct wish-fulfilment dreaming, was the one frequently observed in Marco from the age of 4 up to almost full 5 years of age.

In fact, dreams of clear wish fulfilment are essentially concentrated in the first 36 dreams told consecutively. As we will see, this form of dream does not disappear completely: it continues to exist, although less frequently and with major differences (types of wish, modes of fulfilment, increase of bizarre aspects in dreams), also in Marco's second and third age periods.

Many of the changes that appear in dreams in the course of dreaming development are framed as "deviations" from this primary infantile form of dreams. Although Freud did not specifically investigate the dreams of older children, he claimed that already between the ages of 5 and 8, there is the possibility of seeing some dreams that have characteristics like those present in adults. It is plausible to think that precisely in this age period of Marco's (6–7 years) and in the following (8–10 years), there is the possibility of identifying the changes that prelude the shifting from a simple form of dreaming to the more complex forms found in adults, by analyzing the manifest content of the dream and, when necessary, thoughts and latent material that may be understood thanks to a direct knowledge of the child and of his daytime experiences.

Already in Marco's early infantile period dream repertoire, and sometimes precisely in some clear wish-fulfilment dreams, I could identify certain early variations going in the direction of a greater complexity of dreaming. For example I observed, albeit in a few dreams, the possible manifestation of early dream-work operations (not yet a censorship activity) and some primary forms of symbolism and bizarreness aspects.

DOI: 10.4324/9781003184874-12

In this chapter, I deal with the analysis of the early changes in child-hood dreams in chronological order—that is, starting from when the change occurred for the first time in the development of the dream process. Therefore, when necessary, I may also review some dreams that, chronologically speaking, belong to the first period. In fact, some of these changes take place starting from the dreams of the second period, but others, although more evident in this phase, saw their onset in certain dreams of the first period. In other words, I will describe the dreams more from the point of view of the development of the dreaming function, whose changes sometimes do not follow the clear distinction between the two age periods. In this part and in the fourth, I will try to describe those processes and changes that precede, and perhaps *prepare*, the real adult dream.

Changes in Marco's dream repertoire

Before going into the details of the changes in the dream content, let's see the differences in Marco's dream repertoire—that is, the changes in the distribution of the frequency of general type of dreams in the second period (6 years,–7 years, 1 month). The most evident change is represented by the fact that *clear* wish-fulfilment dreams decrease sharply. On the other hand, bad dreams and frankly bizarre dreams—that is, without any recognizable reference to a wish—increase. Oedipal dreams are not observed in this period (see Table 8.1).

If we consider the proportion of *clear wish-fulfilment dreams* versus the remaining *non-wish-fulfilment dreams*, the difference between the first and second age period is evident and statistically significant (see Table 8.2). This indication, along with previous studies, confirms that the "golden age" for the observation of direct wish-fulfilment dreams in large quantities gradually comes to an end at around 5 years of age (Colace, 2010, 2013). In particular, previous studies suggested that starting from the second half of the fifth year, dreams of direct wish fulfilment and without bizarre elements become less likely to be encountered (Colace, 2010, pp. 118, 119, 159).

Table 8.1 General types of Marco's dream reports between 6 years and 7 years, 1 month

Bad dream and nightmares	22 (65%)
Bizarre dreams	13 (38%)*
Clear wish-fulfilment dreams	8 (24%)**

*Bizarre dreams also include 9 bad dreams with several elements that are scarcely compatible and plausible compared to Marco's everyday experience and/or less clearly associated with an everyday experience.
**One of these is to be considered a failed wish-fulfilment attempt.

Table 8.2 Variation in frequency of clear wish-fulfilment dreams in dream repertoire between the first and second age periods

	1st period	*2nd period*
Clear wish-fulfilment dreams	26/36 (72%)	8/34 (24%)
Other dreams, in which no wish fulfilment is evident	10/36 (28%)	26/34 (76%)

$X^2 = 16,59$
df 1, p = 0.000

Changes in wish-fulfilment dreams

The differences observed in the distribution of the various general types of dreams is a clear indication of a change in the variety of Marco's dream repertoire. A more detailed analysis of dreams, however, shows *precise lines of change in the dream*, of which there are some sporadic anticipations in the previous period, showing an evolution of the dream function towards greater complexity and diversification.

In the second period, wish-fulfilment dreams change in the sense that they decrease in frequency and start to become more complex. In wish-fulfilment dreams, *the direct gratification of a simple daytime wish becomes infrequent. We are faced with the fact that 4 out of 8 of these dreams refer to repressed wishes* and show the fulfilment of desire in more indirect ways (although the dream remains understandable). While repressed wishes are present in the 50% of wish-fulfilment dreams in this period, in the first period of Marco they are only present in the 12% (3/26) of wish-fulfilment dreams.

Some early motivational conflicts appear in the dream contents, including those of moral nature, and indirect ways of satisfying wishes and new dream-work operations also appear as well as new types of dream bizarreness (i.e., phenomenological categories). These changes imply that the meaning cannot be understood as easily as in the previous infantile dreams, and we need to introduce the concept of latent dream material.

In the 4 dreams that seem to satisfy simple daytime wishes, we see the wish to eat (following a fast the night before), the wish to leave for the upcoming beach holiday, the wish to have a collectible scorpion as soon as possible (its issue being imminent) and the wish to go to the stadium to see a football match.

I am reporting in the following sections an in-depth analysis of dreams in which the *indirect fulfilment* of wishes in contrast with parental rules/dispositions (i.e., *disapproved wishes*) or in contrast with moral/ethical principles (i.e., *inadmissible wish*) appears. Compared to the simple infantile form of the dream, the following changes have been identified, occurring in chronological sense:

a   fulfilment of two wishes in conflict with each other, one of which is the expression of moral conscience;

b   open but timorous fulfilment of a wish, which is somehow conflicting with the moral conscience;
c   fulfilment in indirect form (implicit/allusive) of a latent *disapproved wish*;
d   indirect and symbolic gratification of a physical need (in the *disapproved way of its manifestation*) through the fulfilment of a simple wish;
e   fulfilment of a *disapproved wish* in conflict with another egosyntonic wish;
f   disguised fulfilment of a wish in contrast with rules, with the support of a fulfilment of a simple daytime wish

Fulfilment of two wishes in conflict with each other, one of which is the expression of conscience

We saw already that an early form of motivational (manifest) conflict appears in a dream from the first period (#06),[1] producing a bizarre aspect in the dream content (i.e., Marco's sad facial expression that clashes with his being happy). I will now provide a few more details about this dream.

Dream of returning to school

> M. 06–4;8. *I dreamed I was at school and had a sad face. I had a sad face because mummy was not there.* Were you sad or cheerful? *I was happy. All my friends were there, but in the end, I closed my eyes again and I was with mummy. That's it.*

This dream shows a fight between two wishes that struggle against each other for fulfilment and then reach a *compromise*. On the one hand, the dream fulfils Marco's wish to go back to school, to his schoolmates he has not seen for a while because he's on holiday; on the other hand, there is the wish to stay home with his mother. In the first part of his dream, Marco stages the fulfilment of the former wish but in a *strange way*: he is happy but has a sad face at the same time. In this dream, homesickness and the pain of leaving his mother are expressed by the "sad face", while the happiness of getting back to his friends is expressed by the words "I was happy" (affective state). The wish to go back to school (and meet his schoolmates) is somehow in contrast with the child's conscience, which requires him not to give displeasure to his mother and remain with her. In the "second part" of the dream, the longing for the mother prevails, and Marco returns to her.

The strange bizarreness aspects in this dream are given by the overlapping of two wishes that express motivationally different demands of the child and that are manifested by the contrast between the pleasant tone of the dream and the sad face of the dreamer and by a *sudden space-time discontinuity in the plot* of the dream, or the sudden passage from school to home.

This can be considered the first dream that shows a bizarre aspect attributable to dream distortion (see Chapter 9).

This dream report is very important because it shows an example of an embryonic psychic conflict in the dream experience (that the child is not clearly aware of) between two different forces, one of which represents the demands of consciousness. At the basis of this conflict, there is perhaps an early sense of "shame" for having preferred his friends to his mother. *This conflict can be considered the simplest version, or the prototype, of those that appear in adult dreams between unconscious wishes that fight to find fulfilment while censorship acts in the dream as the result of an indirect and disguised fulfilment* (i.e., disguise-censorship model of dream distortion).[2]

If this reading is correct, the bizarreness of this dream is in line with what emerged from previous systematic studies where we found a clear statistically significant correlation between degree of dream bizarreness and measurements of moral conscience development (Colace, 2010).

Dreams about the open but timorous fulfilment of a wish that is somehow conflicting with the moral conscience

A dream about an *open but timorous fulfilment of a wish* that *is not entirely admissible* (i.e., somehow conflicting) *by the conscience* appeared at the age of 5 years and 8 months (first period):

> M. 25–5;8. *I dreamed that Mummy was married to uncle C. Mummy kissed him on the mouth. Daddy was already married with Aunt B. and his son was G.* (who in reality is the son of C. and B), *and he was older* (he was 5) *while I was younger* (in his dream, Marco was the son of Uncle C. and his true mother), *and I was sitting in G.'s lap. We were at the restaurant, and we had finished dining. It was a nice dream.*

"Uncle" C. ad "Aunt" B. are friends of ours. G. is their son and Marco's best friend. The day before the dream, C. and G. had paid an unexpected call on us, and we had gone to the playground all together. Marco had had a very pleasant time; he is really fond of C. and G.

While telling this dream, Marco was somewhat timorous, as if he feared I might get annoyed because in his dream he "replaced" me with Uncle C. He smiled and put on a cunning face. Recently Marco had had a daydream of similar content and had told it to his mother. He specified that in the dream, he was 1, while G. was 5 years old, and G. was holding him. After telling his dream, Marco hugged me as if to say, "*I'm sorry that you were not my dad in the dream*".

Marco probably would have liked to have, at least for one afternoon, Uncle C. as his dad instead of me, because Uncle C. seemed more inclined to take him to the playground than his true father. Marco attempts a sort of "deformation" in order to "sugar the pill", by making me appear as the father of his best friend, but he cannot hide the true "conflicting" desire in his dream. In fact, Marco had some *hesitation in reporting this dream* and apologized to his father for having replaced him in the dream.

In other words, Marco feared that his desire and its fulfilment might cause displeasure to the father and was therefore timorous in reporting his dream.

In this dream, we see the signs of an initial activity of *internal censorship* (superego activity) that apparently becomes explicit in the fact that Marco, having failed to suppress and/or disguise his "inadmissible" wish, fears that he may be discovered and scolded by his father.

In these two dreams (#6 and #25), we are therefore faced with inadmissible wishes that the child suppresses or tries to suppress, which are *in contrast with the moral conscience*. In the first case, we may assume that at the basis of dream-distortion work, there is a sense of shame (wanting to be with friends rather than with the mother); in the second, it seems to us that the timorous dream reporting may be based on feelings of guilt for having replaced the father. Shame, even before guilt, may be counted among the first reasons of moral conscience for *dream censorship activity* and *resistance to dream reporting*. These dreams belong to Marco's early period and testify to some of the dream-change beginnings that will develop later.

Fulfilment in the indirect (implicit/allusive) form of a latent wish disapproved by parents

In the following described dream described, a direct fulfilment of a simple strong wish—that is, to participate in the karate competitions—implicitly refers to a second wish, opposed by the parents (i.e., to go to the sea and bathe), the existence of which is admitted *with some hesitation* only after reporting the dream. This second wish is not approved by the parents, who directly warned not to talk about the beach and bathing in the sea because it wasn't possible at that time.

The dream of the karate competition

> M. 39–6;1. *I dreamed I was fighting with a 16-year-old kid. He was older than I was, and I won. I did the karate moves. We were at school. It was a nice dream.*

Immediately at the end of his report, Marco snapped, "Daddy, is it true that in three days, there's the karate competition and I'm going to win the belt? Can we go to the beach after that? Grandpa said he is waiting for us. Can we bathe in the sea?"

It is worth noting that this dream was reported on a May 27, when it was hot already (in Italy), but not enough to bathe in the sea as Marco would have liked to.

The dream relates to the imminent karate competitions that Marco was about to join and that we had been talking about on the day before the dream. It also relates to his unexpectedly interrupted watching of the film that was Marco's then favourite: *The Karate Kid*. The dream was triggered by multiple simple wishes (i.e., the wish to be already at the karate competitions, the wish to impersonate the film character),[3] but it also hints at a *denied wish* (i.e., the wish to go to the beach and bathe) that Marco himself expressed upon awakening from the dream. This is something that Marco longs for but dares not to ask for fear of a negative answer: *the wish to go to the beach and bathe* was something that had already been asked and *not permitted, because it wasn't the right season yet and it was cold.* Marco knew that after the competitions, we would move to our summer house; we had even talked about this the day before the dream. Marco therefore does not dare to directly satisfy the denied wish *but only hints* at it since *he knows* that it is contrary to his parents' will, so much so that, once awake, he asks his parents directly for the possibility that this can be achieved. In this request, there is *the search for parental approval in the form of a question* regarding this wish. This request is an expression of the same dream censorship, preventing the direct (undisguised) fulfilment of a disapproved wish in his dream. In certain dreams that we will see later, this *"authorization to proceed"* for some disapproved or illegitimate wishes will come through *"the authorizing parent"*, who appears as a dream character in the dream plot. This represents a trick to circumvent dream censorship or an expression of a *permissive* censorship. *This dream may be regarded as the first clear example of indirect or "disguised" wish fulfilment.* We note the existence of latent dream material only revealed through a direct question asked by the child to the parent, seeking permission for something that the child knows to be "forbidden" and that during the dream experience is internally censored, so much so that in fact it does not appear in the manifest dream content. However, this psychic latent material it *is not properly unconscious*: it rather acts on subconscious level and is then detected during the reporting of the dream. This psychic material can emerge in the dream in a mildly disguised form and/or when the child is asked questions *if the right psychological conditions are created*—for example, if the child has positive feedback from the parent during the dream report, that reassures him, or he feels at ease when expressing his dreams to the father or mother or requests (once again) approval himself by making a question.

In this dream, a *simple wish* acts as an activator of another *suppressed latent wish* that rests on the first one, giving strength to it on the level of its motivational drive and, at the same time, finding partial implicit gratification through it (in the form of allusion).

This mechanism by which a simple desire and its fulfilment find space through alliance with another (denied) wish can be seen as the *prototype* of what normally happens in adults' dreams, when a diurnal desire triggers a repressed unconscious wish that finds space, although disguised, in the dream. In this dream, for the first time we observe an *alliance between a simple wish and a repressed wish*.

We may assume that in this dream, the simple daytime wish, *to win the competitions,* triggered the dream only because it was strengthened by the more powerful one (opposed by parents), *to go to the sea for a swim.*[4] The dream's true wishful instigation impulse would be the latter, which appears explicitly only at the end of the dream report.

As we will see, in this period and in the third (from 6 years onwards), Marco's dreams seem to require an ever-greater motivational force for their triggering. A simple unresolved daytime wish is not always sufficient. In this dream, the presence of the fulfilment of a wish in an indirect way is accompanied by other aspects not directly understandable, for which deductions are required in order to get their probable meaning: first, the fact that the combat occurs in an unusual place (at school), and second, the fact that Marco said that the child in the dream is not the one who appears in the film. The presence of the school can be explained because some of the fights that take place in the film are staged in a school or right outside the school entrance. For the second aspect, we can assume that Marco's wish is to win against "the bad guys" in general (in the dream, the elder child is the bad guy). The dream, however, proposes again the same age difference between the fighters.

Indirect and symbolic gratification of a physical need (in a disapproved way of its manifestation) through the fulfilment of a simple wish

Here Marco reported a dream that portrays a situation quite similar to the one previously mentioned (i.e., indirect gratification). However, in this case, unlike in the previous one, the dream does not allude to a wish but more properly to a need—that is, the need to drink *by night*—and here the link with the simple wish is not allusive but rather symbolic.

The bathtub dream

> M. 44–6;3. Marco mumbled something unintelligible in his sleep. I went to his bed, he woke up. I asked, "Were you dreaming?"
> *Yes, I dreamed I was taking a bath. I was here at home in the bathtub.*
> Immediately after, Marco added, "Daddy, I'm thirsty!" I gave him water and he drank a lot, then slept again.

The evening before, at dinner, Marco had eaten salty food. We had dined out at a restaurant, where he had eaten salty food (a pack of potato chips, salami, ham). It is quite possible that he was thirsty at the time of going to bed.

This dream seems to be triggered by thirst. However, the need to drink, unlike what usually happens in these cases, is not represented directly in the dream (drinking); on the contrary, it is accomplished *symbolically* by bathing in the bathtub, which Marco usually fills up with water. It is probable that the great amount of water he puts into the bathtub is a good indication of his wish to drink plenty of water. The dream tries to prevent the thirst stimulus from interrupting sleep but succeeds only for a while. So far, there is nothing new. However, two aspects make this dream important. Why should the satisfaction of the desire to drink need to be expressed indirectly and/or symbolically disguised? And why does Marco choose (among the many possible ways) to represent water in the dream precisely through a bathtub? We must then wonder why Marco does not satisfy his wish to drink explicitly. Yet this is a seemingly legitimate basic need. Looking more closely, we notice that this basic need at night-time is expressed in the wish that one of the parents bring him a drink directly at his bed. Recently, Marco had been told many times that he should drink before going to bed, and if he gets thirsty during the night, he should get up and drink on his own *without waking up his parents*! We are therefore faced with the need to drink, which Marco has not yet learned to satisfy at night by himself (drinking from the bottle placed next to his bed), and for this reason, he has been scolded several times by his parents because he wakes them up every time in the heart of the night. Marco is therefore aware of his parents' possible reproach and is learning not to wake them up: this is the reason why his need cannot be expressed directly in the dream. If this assumption is right, then the fulfilment of the need to drink *must* occur indirectly (i.e., symbolically).

The second important aspect of this dream is that the choice of a bathtub for the fulfilment of the need to drink is not by chance. In fact, it seems likely that "taking a bath" is one of Marco's strongest wishes, which could not be satisfied at that time because the bathtub was broken.

A simple unsatisfied wish (to bathe in the tub) joins thirst (nocturnal stimulus) and the related (disapproved) wish to drink by having a parent bring him some water at night, triggering a dream of what the disapproved wish is, reaching a hallucinatory fulfilment in a symbolically disguised way. However, the dream failed, hence the awakening and the actual satisfaction of Marco's need to drink (with the water brought by the father).

In this dream, therefore, we are faced with a *disguised fulfilment of a disapproved (repressed) wish* that takes place through the fulfilment of another simple daytime wish in which the disapproved wish finds a way of satisfaction. We may also notice how the simple daytime wish makes its way towards triggering the dream only thanks to its alliance with the much stronger repressed wish to drink with "dad and mom bringing me water to bed". It is only through this alliance that the dream can be triggered, and it is only through symbolic transformation that Marco's desire to drink finds the way of hallucinatory satisfaction.

Finally, we notice that if we hadn't had information about the experience from the day before, this dream would have seemed to be a wish-fulfilment dream of a simple wish (the wish of "taking a bath"). This dream expresses well the Freudian concept according to which a dream has multiple levels of meaning/ interpretation.

In both the dreams mentioned previously (# 39, #44), the fulfilment of the repressed wish takes place through the direct fulfilment of a second simple wish connected with the first. In the first dream, the connection between the two wishes is based on the fact that the child knows that after the competitions during the weekend, we would go to the seaside (as it usually happens). In the second dream, the child ignores the nature of the connection between the simple and the repressed wish. *In other words, in the first dream, we observe a veiled, almost*

conscious, allusion, while in the second, there is a relationship between the sym-
bolized object and the symbolizing content which the child is not aware of (i.e., we
have the unconscious repression of a disapproved wish, or secondary symbolism
in Piaget's terms).

These two dreams show how the disguising of the latent content of the dream
(i.e., the dream distortion activity) can be obtained with *a similar mechanism that
can operate on different levels of awareness.*

These two mechanisms are the beginning of a path that starts from direct wish
fulfilment and will arrive at the complex dreams of adults, where the fulfilment of
an unconscious wish is verifiable only after its complex interpretation in a psychoanalytic setting. These dreams represent an important opportunity to know these
early changes since it is relatively easy to identify those wishes that, although not
expressly mentioned in the manifest dream content, claim their specific action
(hallucinatory satisfaction). By studying these cases, we can perhaps identify further elementary dream-work operations which, when implemented with increasingly complex psychic material, are at the basis of adult dreams. The study of
these dream-work operations and the discovery of the latent contents of dreams
are possible only thanks to the direct knowledge of the child, his diurnal experiences and his desires, including those that are denied by the parents.

Fulfilment of a repressed wish in conflict with another egosyntonic wish

In dreams like the following one, told by Marco at the age of 6 years and 4
months, we observe the appearance of dream distortion and consequent bizarreness, *caused by the dream-censorship activity*—i.e., dream distortion of conflict-
ual/defensive nature that can be inferred from daytime events (a moral/aesthetic
conflict). This is unsurprising, as we have already seen at the age of 4 and 8
months (dream # 6, *Dream of returning to school*) an example of the interiorization of the rules and of early dream-censorship activity that produces bizarre
aspects in the dream content.

The tooth dream

> M. 47–6;4. *I dreamed I was at Grandpa's house, in the small bathroom, and
> Grandpa pulled my tooth away* (one of Marco's teeth was then starting to
> loosen), *and I said, "Oh my gosh, now I can't eat anymore! Now I'm going
> to remain toothless!" I moved my tongue like this* (he mimicked the gesture
> of pushing the tongue against the tooth). *I tried to touch it but could not feel it
> anymore. I can't tell if it was a nice dream or a bad dream.*

The day before, while he was eating a sweet in his grandfather's house, he had
to stop because his tooth had started bleeding (a baby tooth that was about to fall
off), so he went to the bathroom to spit the sweet and the blood in the sink. His
grandfather offered to pull the tooth off, and Marco was scared about that. He was

also disappointed for not having been able to eat his sweet. Later, his grandfather gave him another sweet, and this time he could eat it. The grandfather's attempts had continued with a trick when they were at the playground: while playing ball, he would say to Marco, "Throw it up high so it falls on your mouth and you'll get rid of that tooth!"

I had to ask additional questions to Marco in order to understand this dream, which presents certain apparently illogical aspects. On the one hand, Marco said, "*I wish the tooth fell off so I would not have to think about it anymore*", but on the other hand, he said, "*I'd be sorry because if the tooth falls off, it would be bad*" (the aesthetic reason of "I'd look ugly" plus "I would no longer be able to eat sweets"). Marco also reveals his desire that the tooth would fall and/or *that Grandpa would finally pull it out so it would no longer be "torture" during the day*. However, he said, "*Yes, I would like the tooth to fall off so I wouldn't think about it anymore, but then I'd look ugly*". In saying this, Marco appears worried about the (conflicting) question. *This dream represents a wish that goes beyond what Marco is willing to admit* and that, however, if looked more closely at, he ends up admitting. We may note the difference from previously mentioned dream #39, where, although with some qualms, the wish was immediately revealed after telling the dream ("Shall we go to the sea, Dad?").

This dream clearly shows the coexistence of two conflicting wishes that are pressing to be satisfied, one of which is rejected (at subconscious level) by the child's ego for (conscious) aesthetic needs. The fulfilment of wish (a), *that the tooth falls soon*, tends to be partially suppressed because it conflicts with *the child's aesthetic needs*, or with wish (b), *to be good-looking and not "toothless"*. It is therefore a matter of two conflicting forces. Wish (b) presents itself as ego-syntonic, or a wish that is part of the predominant tendencies of the ego (to have no problems when eating and to be good-looking). The legitimacy of these arguments is also based on the possibility of seeing my son Marco daily fixated on these issues and on my knowledge of his sensibility towards wanting to look good and not toothless. The child shows impatience and distrust in that his baby tooth will eventually be replaced by a permanent tooth. The wish that the tooth falls soon and/or that Grandpa removes it soon is also the wish that "everything is resolved as soon as possible". In fact, he knows that sooner or later, the tooth will fall off (it jiggles a lot).

In my view, the presence of these conflicting forces increases the complexity of the dream. From a developmental point of view, *we can hypothesize that the early forms of conflict in dream processes simply consist of a contrast between two wishes*, one of which is egosyntonic. Thus, the ontogenetic development of dream distortion and bizarreness might also be viewed as the result of *a progressive increase in the conflicting situations of individual wishes that compete for satisfaction* and make dreams increasingly harder to understand.[5] We can note that, in this dream, the conflict derives from a wish whose fulfilment involves and offends the aesthetic needs of an ego ideal that is being formed. *The first reasons that I found at the basis of early dream deformation and censorship in Marco's dreams are the sense of shame, feeling of guilt and certain aesthetic needs.* This gives proof of the progressive completion of a fully functioning superego in the child's psychological development. These indications are consistent with the results of previous systematic studies. Particularly, certain correlational data suggest that that dream bizarreness is clearly influenced by the development of the superego functions of children. Thus, bizarreness in dreams becomes more probable only in children who show a more complete development of the superego, evidenced by the appearance of the ability to experience a sense of guilt (Colace, 2010, 2012).

Disguised fulfilment of a wish against the rules, supported by the fulfilment of a simple daytime wish

Dream of returning to kindergarten

> M. 52–6;5. *I was back in my kindergarten class with N., and I was with teacher P. and E., and teacher P. told us, "Stay still!" It was a beautiful dream.* (He didn't mind that he was ordered not to move.)

After reporting his dream, Marco mused sadly about the fact that teacher P. would not come back because she had moved to another place and said, "Now I can't see her anymore!"

This dream apparently satisfies only the simple daytime "wish to go back to kindergarten" and "see his kindergarten teacher again" (Marco had started attending elementary school for a few weeks then). However, the strange detail of the dream—that is, the teacher saying, "Stay still!"—should suggest us that there is more to it than its manifest content. A closer look proves that "Stay still!" is actually the most frequent request that Marco was hearing from his elementary school teachers, who were trying to discipline children to the new rules of elementary school. In this dream, Marco not only satisfies his desire to return to the more permissive setting of kindergarten and to see his beloved teacher P.: through *person replacement*, he also accepts that it is P. herself who gives that annoying order. In this way, Marco satisfies with a compromise the (denied) wish "to be able to move freely" by returning (in the dream) to kindergarten (i.e., a freer and more playful setting) and, at the same time, by accepting the order to "stay still", but only on the condition that the order comes from his beloved teacher.

The six situations described previously date back to the age range between 4 years, 8 months and 6 years, 5 months. They are all related to the earliest forms of the complicated way in which wishes are satisfied in dreams, which are no longer plain and directly understandable as in most dreams from Marco's earlier age. We also notice that some of these dreams require asking a few questions to Marco about them. For all these dreams, it is necessary to introduce the concept of the content/latent meaning of the dream, since the meaning of the dream is not in its manifest content alone. In these dreams, multiple wishes are often fulfilled; however, unlike in the multiple dreams from the early period, where multiple *simple wishes* appeared, we are observing here an alliance *between simple daytime wishes and disapproved wishes.*

Modi operandi of dreams

In wish-fulfilment dreams, we note that 4 (50%) are *compensation dreams*, 3 (37%) are *anticipation dreams* and one (13%) is a mixed (continuation/anticipation) dream. *The dreams that we have defined, continuation dreams, triggered by partially satisfied daytime wishes, disappear at this stage.*

The power of wishes and the triggering of dreams: from childhood to adult dreams

Marco's wish-fulfilment dreams show that, as we grow up, dreams require more and more powerful wishes in order to be triggered (see also dreams of the third period). At first, simple unresolved daytime wishes are sufficient; later we find dreams based on the presence of multiple simple wishes that create an alliance of wishful impulses/requests. Subsequently, along with age and psychic development, this is no longer enough: stronger wishes are needed in order to trigger dreams—such as, for example disapproved wishes, wishes that clash with moral/ethical principles (more rarely observed), which are suppressed or that the child tries to suppress, and also certain recurring wishes (e.g., to have a little brother/sister). All these types of wishes precede, chronologically and gradually, the unconscious wishes present in adult dreams (the most powerful in terms of dream triggering).

In this context, for example, the absence of continuation dreams in the second period might be due to the fact that these are based on partially satisfied wishes, which therefore have a lower ability to instigate dreams. *In this sense, the distinction between the three types of wish-fulfilment dreams (i.e., compensation, continuation, anticipation) may give direct indications about the strength of the underlying daytime wish, higher in compensation and anticipation dreams and lower in continuation ones.* This is in line with Freud's assertion that the dreams of adults, compared to those of children, require, in order to be triggered, a desire that has a greater triggering force. This reflects the fact that in adults, the presence of an unconscious desire (or in any case, an alliance between simple and unconscious desires) is necessary for triggering dreams.[6]

In Marco's dreams, we rarely found properly unconscious wishes. On the other hand, these would have required the use of dream interpretation, which I did not undertake. However, we assumed the existence of unconscious wishes at the basis of oedipal dreams and of some bizarre dreams. We observed disapproved wishes and moral/ethical illegitimate wishes which were repressed or that the child attempted to suppress, which remained latent but were identified through investigation and additional questions. These wishes can emerge in the dream in a mildly disguised form and/or when the child is asked questions, if the right psychological conditions are created (see dream #39, mentioned previously). If we consider as a whole the dream wishes in Marco's dreams between the ages of 4 and 7 in terms of their ability/possibility to trigger dreams, these can be classified as follows, as in an *ideal line that goes from a minimum to a maximum of dream-triggering capability*:

- *simple* (unrepressed), known wishes *partially fulfilled* (but not enough for the child) in the daytime experience;
- *simple* (unrepressed), known wishes *not fulfilled* at all in the daytime experience

Both these wishes can trigger dreams on their own, but only in young children. In older children, they must ally with other wishes; otherwise, they cannot find expression in the dream.

- *Combination of wishes*. A group of two or more wishes can ally to find together the ability to trigger a dream. This alliance can occur *between simple wishes* and also *between simple and disapproved wishes or wishes inadmissible to the conscience (latent or properly unconscious) or between two or more disapproved and/or inadmissible wishes*. The latter alliance appears only in the third period.
- *Recurring*, very strong (known) wishes that retain an important motivational strength over the years. These wishes may be at the base of *serial dreams* (see Chapter 3). These also include the child's *historical* wishes. Sometimes these wishes can be part of *simple* wishes; other times they fall into the group of *disapproved* ones (see Chapter 12).
- *Disapproved wishes*. These are wishes that are in contrast with parental rules or dispositions). They are wishes that the child should have learned to suppress or try to suppress but that nevertheless exist and remain active, ready to re-emerge in the dream.
- *Moral/ethically inadmissible* (repressed, unconscious) *wishes*. In some cases, these wishes cannot be properly defined unconscious since can be directly detected when the child is asked supplementary questions about his/her dream report (i.e., without the aid to free associations techniques). Other times, these wishes are rejected unconsciously and often remain in the area of the unconscious; this is the case of supposed sexual desires in oedipal dreams but also of repressed wishes supposed at the base of plainly bizarre dreams. However, dream interpretation is necessary in order to support this latter assumptions with evidence.[7]

On the other hand, as we will see in Chapter 11, the dream-triggering capability of a wish is also linked to the development of the ego and superego.

Wishes' ability to instigate dreams and dream complexity

In the past, I have found myself wondering what happens at a certain point in the development that involves a transition from simple infantile dreams to more complicated dreams. What happens to straightforward wish-fulfilment infantile dreams? A plausible answer based on Marco's dream reports is that *dreams change, in form and understandability, because simple daytime wishes are no longer sufficient to trigger dreams.* When the onset of the dream requires *multiple simple wishes* (with *primary bizarreness*), *repressed wishes* that need disguised fulfilment, *older recurring wishes* that do not find confirmation in current day residues or *alliances of different kinds of wishes (simple and disapproved or inadmissible)* with the intervention of defensive transformation (i.e., dream distortion), we go towards more incomprehensible and bizarre dreams. The dream is no longer explained in its entirety by its manifest content: we need to resort to the concept of latent dream content, or in any case of latent psychic material that may be verbalized at a later time, after the dream is told, when asking more specific questions about the dream.

I believe that this major change in the wishes' ability to instigate dreaming may be a first simple key to explain the gradual change from infantile dreams (simple and understandable) to adult dreams (bizarre and apparently incomprehensible).

Through the interpretation of adult dreams, Freud noticed that bizarre dreams are instigated by an unconscious wish that cannot be expressed directly: the transformations (i.e., dream distortion, dream censorship) to which such an unconscious wish must submit in order to reach a disguised fulfilment generate what we see as a bizarre dream (i.e., the manifest dream content). Through the observation of Marco's dream reports, we can directly show that, as the child grows up, dreams become more complicated, exactly because they no longer originate from one simple daytime wish. While the dream content apparently refers to simple wishes, it is actually made up of other latent material—that is, older wishes, disapproved and/or inadmissible wishes that find expression in the dream but in a more complex way.

The winding path of the connection between these latter wishes and the simple wishes and its connection with the daytime experiences that becomes indirect and uncertain make dreams increasingly incomprehensible: this process preludes to the bizarreness and obscureness of adult dreams. From this viewpoint, the dreams in this age range (6/7 years and up) may be considered as the missing link in the transition from infantile to adult dreams.

Daytime sources

In the dreams from this period, which satisfy simple daytime wishes, the connection with diurnal residues is still clear and direct, with a reference to a precise daytime experience in which a wish manifested itself.[8]

On the other hand, in dreams that satisfy disapproved or inadmissible wishes or make alliances between these wishes and simple daytime wishes, the reference to the diurnal experience remains quite direct, but only with regard to the simple wishes present in the manifest content of the dream, while for disapproved wishes (that emerge only from the "interpretation" of the dream report), the daytime reference is unknown: these latent wishes refer to situations of the past—probably those in which these wishes arose and those in which they are (unconsciously) repressed.

The dream may take its cue only from one daytime episode, which then develops differently in the dream plot. Instead, in the first period, the daytime experience (unresolved wish) is resumed identically in the dream plot. Furthermore, while in the dreams from the first period, the waking experience was taken up directly in the dream—that is, it was itself the core of the dream—in this period sometimes the diurnal experience that the dream refers to only acts as a stimulus *activating one or more latent wishes.*

Sometimes, in an overdetermined dream, it is possible to clarify an aspect of the dream related to a wish, but not all the rest. Thus, in some dreams, such as #44, the connection, although direct (day residue), is not exhaustive for understanding the full dream content, since in addition to the direct fulfilment of a clear wish (i.e., the wish to take a bath), it also evokes a second more latent wish (i.e., drinking with the parents' help), which is discovered later. In other words, the daytime experience acts as a direct source for wish (a) and as an indirect source for wish (b).

In dream #39 (the dream of the karate competition), the content clearly refers to some diurnal experiences (day residue), but for other aspects, there is no confirmation in the diurnal experience that directly explains that dream element.

In dreams whose manifest content (or at least part of it) clearly refers to waking experiences, it can be observed that the diurnal residues in *5 out of 8 dreams (62%) date back to the previous day* (e.g., #45, the following dream report) while in another dream to two days earlier; in another, the temporal distance is uncertain, and finally in another, it is understood that the dream dates back to the previous day, but only after its content has been somehow examined and interpreted, thus going back to the diurnal experiences that underlie it. See the following of day residue in dream:

M. 45–6;3. *I was sitting at the table in the school cafeteria with N.* (Marco's best friend), *and we were waiting for lunch when a small spider came out of a piece of furniture nearby.*

The night before, after preparing Marco's favourite food, sausage, his mother realized that it had gone bad, and therefore, right when Marco was starting to eat it, he had to leave it.

In dream #47 (mentioned previously, the dream of the tooth), the diurnal reference to the previous day is clear; however, the dream is not easy to interpret, and some additional questions must be asked. The dream does not resume and replicate a daytime experience but only takes a cue from it.

In dream #52 (mentioned previously, the dream of returning to kindergarten), there is apparently the fulfilment of a simple wish, but there is no precise daytime source and a rather vague connection to a general situation.

The dreams from this period, similarly to those from the first period, refer to *affective states* such as *impatience, disappointment, frustration* and *excitement*; yet it is plausible to hypothesize that their intensity is greater than the same affective states from the first period, as they were affective states often associated with disapproved latent wishes that remained dissatisfied.

Notes

1 Dreams #6 and #25 have already been mentioned in Chapter 3. Here I return to these dreams by analyzing them in detail.
2 This dream highlights an aspect known to Freud—that is, the possibility that the satisfaction of one wish occurs at the expense of the satisfaction of another (Freud, 1900, p. 530).
3 The wish to impersonate the boy protagonist of *The Karate Kid*, who fights against his senior and wins, and to watch the film again is proved by the fact that in the morning and afternoon of the day preceding the dream, Marco had watched this film repeatedly and had enjoyed it very much.
4   Freud (1900, p. 553) said that (in adults) a conscious wish can trigger dreaming only by arousing an unconscious wish with a similar tenor, thus gaining power.
5 Boag (2006, 2017) rightly highlighted how in Freudian dream theory, there is an alternative account for dream bizarreness based on Freud's theory of mental conflict and the instinctual drives (i.e., competing motives attempting to find equilibrium). Dream bizarreness arises, in part, through an interdrive competition preventing the direct expression of wishes.
6 On this argument, see Freud (1900, pp. 552–553, 560–561).
7 Even when we have been able to glimpse, without interpretation, the repressed wishes in dreams, they have rarely been of this type.
8 Unlike the first period of observation, in this second period, the analysis of the diurnal sources of wish-fulfilment dreams is based on a few dream reports.

Reference

Boag, S. (2006). Freudian dream theory, dream bizarreness, and the disguise-censor controversy. *Neuropsychoanalysis*, *8* (1), 5–17.

Boag, S. (2017). On dreams and motivation: Comparison of Freud's and Hobson's view. *Frontiers in Psychology*, *7* (January 6), Article 2001, https://doi.org/10.3389/fpsyg.2016.02001.

Colace, C. (2010). *Children's Dreams: From Freud's Observations to Modern Dream Research*. New York: Routledge.

Colace, C. (2012). Dream bizarreness and the controversy between the neurobiological approach and the disguise censorship model: The contribution of children's dreams. *Neuropsychoanalysis*, *14* (2), 165–174.

Colace, C. (2013). Are wish-fulfilment dreams of children the royal road for looking at the functions of dreams? *Neuropsychoanalysis*, *15* (2), 161–175.

Freud, S. (1900). *The Interpretation of Dreams*. S.E., 4–5. London: Hogarth Press.

Chapter 9

Development of dream bizarreness and dream-work operations

General development of dream bizarreness in Marco's dream reports

In some of Marco's dreams from the first period and continuing throughout the second, changes begin to occur that call for the introduction of the Freudian concepts of *latent dream content, dream-work operations, dream distortion* and *dream bizarreness*, for the first time in the development of the dreaming function.

The development of dream bizarreness may be analyzed on a *quantitative level* by observing the frequency of bizarre dreams among the *entire dream repertoire* while the subject grows up. Previous studies (Colace, 2010, 2012) and Marco's dream reports have shown that complex and bizarre dreams are more likely to be found starting from the fifth or sixth year of age. Indeed, we have observed an increase of proportion of frankly bizarre dreams and bad dreams and a decrease of simple wish-fulfilment dreams from the first to second period.

However, my study of Marco's dreams, with me having full access to their daytime sources, direct knowledge of the child and the opportunity to ask the child about his dreams, allowed me to also perform a useful *qualitative analysis of bizarreness in dreams*—that is, its origin or nature—as well as to analyze the early functioning of *dream-work operations*, moving on from the infantile module of dreaming to more complex dreams. In previous chapters, I have dwelt on explaining some bizarre aspects and the dream-distortion work that could explain them, whenever they appeared in the examples of dream reported. In this chapter, I return to these aspects of the dream *by attempting an in-depth and systematic description of the evolution of dream bizarreness and its underlying mechanisms*.

From a quality perspective, in Marco's dream reports, there are at least two different types of dream bizarreness that follow one another chronologically along the course of his development. I am referring here to a classification with respect to the *nature* and *causes* of dream bizarreness.

A very early form of dream bizarreness, already observed in certain overdetermined dreams from the first period—that is, *primary bizarreness*, expresses a difficulty in the scenic/cognitive synthesis of the dream when several *non-conflicting wishes* are satisfied simultaneously.

DOI: 10.4324/9781003184874-13

A second form of bizarreness is the product of *defensive dream distortion* and of dream censorship demands. In some of Marco's dreams, we observe this bizarreness as a simple expression of a compromise between two mutually excluding motivational requests. This type of bizarreness also includes those based on an *ethical/moral* conflict. It is the most evident form in the dreams of adults at the basis of which it is supposed the action of a psychic agent (censorship activity) contrasts the open fulfilment of unconscious repressed wishes and permits their satisfaction only in distorted and disguised forms.

On the other hand, we may notice that certain dream-work operations (e.g., considerations of representability) can produce autonomously (i.e., regardless of the dream censorship) a "neutral" (i.e., non defensive) distortion of the meaning of the dream. For example, the primary form of *displacement* and the *considerations of representability* may be used in dream work as a way to solve a personal inconvenience/discomfort by transferring it to another dream character who embodies and lives it plastically. This dream work may sometimes produce a neutral or "by default" bizarreness in dreams (see Figure 9.1).

Primary bizarreness

One first aspect that marks a change in the formal plainness of dreams is the appearance, in some of these, of a very early form of "bizarreness" that we have defined as *"primary bizarreness"*. This is in fact the earliest form of bizarreness that occurs more diffusely in dreams rather than conflictual/defensive bizarreness (i.e., censorship activity). This kind of bizarreness may also be defined as "neutral bizarre effect" to distinguish it from *conflictual/defensive bizarreness*. It can be observed in *some* dreams that we have called "overdetermined dreams" on a motivational level—that is, those dreams that satisfy simultaneously two or more wishes—both admissible to the conscience and not in conflict

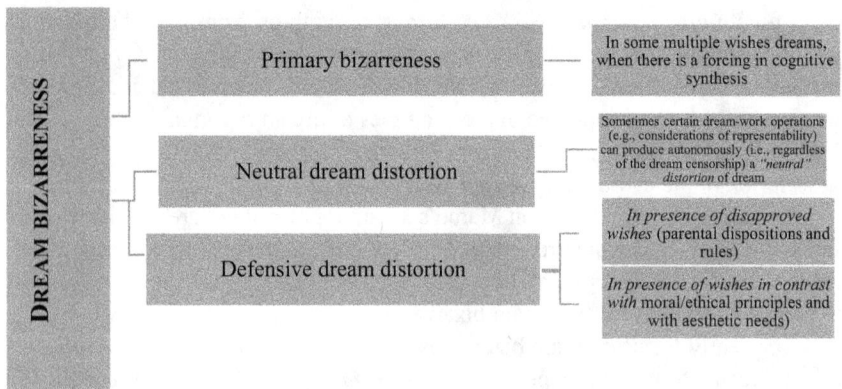

Figure 9.1 Types of dream bizarreness

with one another within the same dream scenario (see Chapter 3 for example of these dreams). In these dreams, sometimes we may observe some *forced cognitive overlapping* of themes in the same dream setting that causes a "bizarreness effect" (e.g., the dream setting is inconsistent or incoherent). However, we note that *this bizarreness does not preclude at all the comprehension of the wish-fulfilment nature of the dream.* This operation of cognitive forcing evokes the more complex one present in adult dreams that Freud called "a kind of necessity to combine all the sources which have acted as stimuli for the dream into a single unity in the dream itself" (Freud, 1900, p. 202), later known as *dream condensation.*

In fact, in these dreams, several wishful requests, although clearly distinguishable, are somehow condensed together into the same dream plot and scenarios.

In my view, this is another sign of how the dreaming process is subordinated to and guided by the child's wishful drives, to which logical and cognitive principles are sacrificed. In other words, the wishful pressures generate the dream scenario, sacrificing logical/cognitive consistency.

Primary bizarreness appears for the first time in dream report #04, at 4 years and 7 months of age (see Chapter 3). The dream, reported as follows, occurred later; however, primary bizarreness can be seen quite clearly in this one.

M. 10–5;2. *I dreamed I was in the swimming pool with my scuba mask, and in the water, there were the whale, the jellyfish, the shark and the fishes. Grandma Concetta and Grandpa Antonio were watching me from up out of the water, and I was playing hide-and-seek in the water with the fishes and the jellyfishes. There were the rocks, the houses made of water, the sky made of water, the sun made of water, the moon. Grandpa Tore and grandma Graziella were also close (beyond the glass walls of the pool) and were telling me, "Go, Marco, go!"*

On the day before, Marco had bought a scuba mask; he was thrilled about it but disappointed by the fact that he could not use it at once. He even asked permission to wear it at home. In fact, on the afternoon preceding the dream, Marco had played with it at home with his friend. As a matter of fact, that week we had planned on going to the beach on the weekend, but then we decided to stay in town. And when we told Marco that maybe, as an alternative, we might go to a swimming pool in town, he asked permission to bring his mask along.

This dream is based on multiple daytime wishes, resumed and fulfilled in the same dream scenario: *the wish to go to the beach and wear the scuba mask* and *the wish to go to the swimming pool, to play hide-and-seek* and *to see all his grandparents together* (Marco holds the concept of family very dearly!). The simultaneous fulfilment of all these wishes in the same dream is not an easy task at the cognitive level: there is some search for consistency, but it is forced. He wears a scuba mask in the swimming pool (something unusual), and he is with his grandparents all together, which is almost never the case, neither at the beach nor at the pool. Grandma Concetta is usually with us at the beach. One wish of Marco (never fulfilled) is that Grandpa Antonio would come and watch him swimming. There are sea creatures (fishes and others) that normally would not be found in a swimming pool. He plays hide-and-seek in the water! (see Figure 9.2).

In other words, this dream is a triumph of wishes all put together in a single setting that can hardly remain consistent at spatio-temporal and cognitive level.

An important aspect that these dreams seem to suggest is that at the basis of bizarreness, even in this early form, there still seems to be *some competition between two or more wishes* that press to be satisfied immediately and that generate a cognitive/representational problem in the formation process of the dream scenario. In these dreams, however, the easy connection with daytime experiences, the clear presence of wish fulfilment and the understandability of the dream itself are all there. *We can observe that the first appearance of bizarreness in dreams, in the ontogenetic development of dreaming, is due to the presence of several wishes* (not in conflict with each other) *that force the cognitive construction and synthesis of the dream.* These overdetermined dreams with primary bizarreness may have led, in the past, to erroneously attribute the presence of conflictual/defensive bizarreness also to the first infantile dreams, therefore overestimating the presence of this kind of bizarreness also in the dreams of young children.

Figure 9.2 The drawing of the swimming pool dream. Left to right: the shark, the whale (dark blue), the crayfish (orange), the jellyfish (pink) and the turtle (green)

Defensive dream distortion and bizarreness

We have already seen *frankly bizarre dreams* that do not fit into the concept of primary bizarreness in a few examples from Marco's first period. It should be pointed out that unlike *overdetermined dreams*, in these dreams, there is no trace of wish-fulfilment.

In particular, the first example of a frankly bizarre dream that cannot be simply explained with the concept of "primary bizarreness" appears in the case of dream #11, when Marco was 5 years and 2 months. It is a dream that has no clear connection with any daytime experience and does not show any apparent wish-fulfilment intent. Another bizarre dream from that period is #17, which he had at 5 years and 3 months (see Chapter 7).

However, in these frankly bizarre dreams Marco had, *we can only assume that bizarreness is founded upon certain unconscious repressed wishes that would require defensive distortion,* but we do not have the possibility to establish this with certainty without interpreting the dream.

According to the following Freud statement, we should assume that these dreams are the first that originate from a truly unconscious repressed wish of Marco, which finds expression in dreams only in disguised form. Freud concluded:

> We have learnt, lastly, from numerous analyses that wherever a dream has undergone distortion the wish has arisen from the unconscious and was one which could not be perceived during the day. (Freud, 1900, p. 552)

These dreams are important because they show that, potentially, children at the age of 5 are already able to experience and report more complex dreams than the simpler (infantile) ones prevalent at that age. What changes along with age is the frequency with which these dreams occur (more and more often), but the basic conditions for producing them are already present in young children. Incidentally, it must be said that the presence of these dreams is another proof that the frequent simplicity of children's dreams cannot be considered an artifact—that is, it cannot be attributed to a supposed inability to produce and report more bizarre dreams. While in these dreams we can observe forms of bizarreness on a *phenomenological level, we cannot observe those possible dream-work operations that would have generated the defensive distortion of the latent elements of the dream with the final bizarre effect.*[1]

On the contrary, in some wish-fulfilment dreams analyzed in the previous chapter, with a slight deformation of disapproved wishes, we can detect *the reason for their bizarreness* with no need for interpretation techniques. So these dreams might help us find the dream-work operations that generated them. In these dreams, we are able to observe and explain the early forms of defensive dream distortion and bizarreness in the Freudian sense.[2] I will now briefly return to these dreams, highlighting the reasons for the intervention of dream-work distortion.

The first form of dream bizarreness that does not fall within the concept of primary bizarreness but seems to be the result of a defensive distortion may be represented by those dreams that attempt to satisfy two self-excluding wishes. This is, in other words, a variant of an overdetermined dream that does not present, as it often happens, wishes that are equally egosyntonic, but it is distinguished by the presence of one of these wishes that can be defined as *egodystonic*. This is the case of a previously mentioned *dream of returning to school* (#6) that Marco had at 4 years and 8 months. As we noted in the analysis of this dream, we observe a *moral conflict* that is based on a sense of shame for having preferred to go with his friends for a moment instead of staying with his mother. The effect of this conflict is the bizarreness consisting of a facial emotional expression (negative) that does not accord with the tone of the dream (positive/pleasant). It is a latent but understandable conflict in the dream, even without interpretation, that generates a bizarre aspect.

Another example of a *moral conflict* appears in a previously mentioned dream (#25) Marco had at the age of 5 years and 8 months. Here Marco fulfilled openly in dream a wish conflicting with his conscience: the repressed "illegitimate" wish of replacing his true father with another who is more permissive and accommodating. The bizarreness lies in the fact that impossible (but desired) events occur in the dream and in the fact that the dream is described and experienced as pleasant while it is verbally reported with a *strangely timorous* attitude.

The previous example suggests that already between 4 and 5 years of age, we may observe dreams, albeit in small numbers compared to the general repertoire, which present aspects of defensive distortion that produce bizarre aspects, or dreams that are accompanied in their reporting by fear, shame or guilt since at their origin there are *illegitimate repressed wishes*. This authorizes us to suppose that an internal dream censorship is operating, acting on the basis of the interiorization of parental norms and ethical/moral principles (i.e., the moral conscience or superego).

In the previously mentioned dream of the karate competition that Marco had at 6 years and 1 month (# 39), the forbidden wish finds indirect fulfilment in the dream but only in a latent and implicit form (i.e., the plain wish, to be already at the karate competitions, hints at the disapproved wish, to go to the beach and bathe). Here the defensive distortion in the dream worked perfectly, as the wish does not appear in its manifest content. However, it is the psychological essence of the dream acting at a latent level. There is no direct fulfilment of this wish in the dream; it becomes known only after the narration of the manifest dream content, when the child, taking courage, asks for parental approval directly (i.e., the external request for authorization to proceed). This latter circumstance reflects the assumption that these desires, although repressed, are not strictly unconscious but latent or subconscious, ready to be recovered without resorting to free associations.

The same thing happened at 6 years and 3 months in the "bathtub" dream (dream #44), where the wish to drink had no direct expression in the dream, but its existence was understood only upon awakening when the child asked for water—a dream that disguises its true nature. *In this dream, the operation of defensive distortion is unconsciously symbolic*, and we may assume that there is a connection between the simple wish—bathing in the bathtub—with the forbidden latent wish to drink by having the parents bring water at night.

At 6 years and 4 months, in the "tooth-loss dream" (#47), conflicting emotions are present. A positive satisfaction of the wish that the tooth falls off at once generates apparently unjustified and incomprehensible concerns, the cause of which is understood only later, when Marco questions himself about the dream. Here, too, we discover that the conflict rests on the fulfilment of wishes that contrast with other psychic situations. The fulfilment of the wish that the tooth falls soon tends to be partially suppressed because it conflicts with the child's aesthetic needs—that is, to be good-looking and not "toothless". However, in dream #6 (the dream of returning to school), the contrast was between two separate desires, one of which is egosyntonic (i.e., the primordial core of censor agent) and the other egodystonic; *here the wish conflicts, more generally, with an ego ideal regarding the aesthetic intrapsychic component*. Ultimately, these dreams have allowed us to observe the conflictual reasons supposedly at the basis of the dream's defensive distortion and bizarreness.

Repertoire of dream-work operations

Defensive distortion and bizarreness in dreams is supported by a series of dream-work operations. We mentioned these when examining some example of dream reports. Here I will try here to describe these operations systematically *with respect to their consequences for dream bizarreness and dream understandability*.

We had already noticed some dream works in some dream reports from Marco's first period. In particular, these were the operations of *transformation of the optative, exaggeration, forced cognitive synthesis, condensation, displacement, considerations of representability, comical/caricatural transformation, transformation of something negative into positive* and even *unconscious symbolism* in some evidently oedipal dreams.

The *transformation of the optative* (optative clauses, Freud, 1901, p. 24) consists of the transformation that the dream makes of the wishful formula into an immediate (hallucinatory) lived experience. It does not involve an impairment of the comprehensibility of the meaning of the dream nor its greater complexity and bizarreness.

Exaggeration should be understood, on the one hand, as the *peremptory expression of a wish* and, on the other hand, as *an action of the dream-work activity* to satisfy that wish as completely as possible. This aspect, although not very frequent, is in my opinion a typical sign of the infantile way of dreaming. This aspect does not preclude the understanding of the dream, nor does it increase its complexity. Exaggeration is also present in the infantile dreams of adults (see Chapter 16).

The earliest examples of *condensation* and *displacement* in dreams are quite understandable, and while giving the dream a certain bizarreness, they do not affect its understandability and meaning. In other words, although these mechanisms are the same as we observe in adult dreams, *they can present themselves in a more elementary and essential way*. Both dream-work operations may appear initially in overdetermined dreams and give rise to *primary bizarreness, but afterwards, we note that they can also be at the service of dream censorship*.

The *consideration of representability* is one of the most easily identifiable dream-work operation in Marco's dream reports (e.g., the amusement park dream, #4). *The child represents an abstract concept or a physical sensation through a person/character who embodies and lives it plastically*. This mechanism can also be used when necessary for the cause of dream censorship.

The *comical-caricatural representation* is a very interesting way to solve, for example, a problem occurring in the daytime experience, to help overcome the dilemma of something requested (e.g., by the parents) but that one would rather avoid doing. This dream-work operation may or may not be at the service of the censorship function (see the *amusement park dream #4* and the *Gasper dream #32*). This dream-work operation sometimes serves to another work of dream— that is, the *transformation of something negative into positive*.

In infantile dreams of adults, caricatural epilogues—in the sense of being "comical", "funny" and "that makes you laugh"—are also observed as the expression of an attempt to prevent the epilogue of a repressed and forbidden desire (see Chapter 16).

The same *symbolism* can be present very early in dreams. When moderate, as in the case of Marco's oedipal dreams, it leaves the understanding of dream meaning open from a Freudian point of view.[3]

Another form of dream-work operation observed in previous studies on children's dreams but not in Marco's dream reports is the *omission* of some elements from the dream content. The omissions can lead to a more difficult understanding of the dream as well as to bizarreness. This phenomenon was also observed by Freud (1900, pp. 285–286) and described in my previous study (Colace, 2010). In Freud's view, it is a clear form of dream-work distortion and a direct expression of the dream-censorship function (Freud, 1916–1917, Lecture 9).

See the following example reported:

Dream #13: child aged 6 years and 3 months

A girl who visited a castle during the day dreams of going there with her Prince Charming (a schoolmate).

> I dreamed I was the princess, and then I did like Cinderella I lost my slipper and then, then . . . then came Prince Charming" [laughs]. [Where were you in this dream?] "In the castle." [But do you really know this castle or not?] "Yes." [And where is this castle?] "The castle is in Rome. I saw it and

then dreamed of it. Because daddy once took us to see it and then afterwards I dreamed it." [And who was the Prince Charming?] "He was a kid at the nursery school that I like." [How was this dream?] "Beautiful. I was happy.
(Colace, 2010, p. 174)

In this dream, a little girl reveals what she had initially omitted only when questioned about the dream (while laughing).

The significant aspect of these dream-work operations is that they can already occur, albeit infrequently, in 4- or 5-year-old children. This suggests that the greater presence, in this age range, of clear wish-fulfilment dreams is not to be attributed to the cognitive impossibility of producing more complex dreams but rather to the fact that the dreaming function works and deals with simple and unresolved daytime wishes, the fulfilment of which does not require nor involve the need for defensive dream-work operations.

On the other hand, we can confirm that these dream-work operations appearing in early dreams and—as Freud noticed—in adult dreams *are not necessarily associated with dream-censorship activity.* They are expressions of the ways in which dream processes work. Some of these (e.g., condensation) seem peculiar, at least in this ontogenetic stage of dreaming development, of those dreams where different wishful requests must be put together.

In Marco's dreams from the second period, the elements of transformation mentioned previously are confirmed, and other dream-work operations can be observed due to the presence in the dreams of *disapproved* and *inadmissible wishes*, the fulfilment of which requires transformations that underlie their indirect satisfaction and are somehow disguised. *The new dream-work operations appear at the service of censorship activity* (see Table 9.1).

A mechanism observed in several dreams is that of implicit fulfilment based on an *allusive disguise* (dream #39, the karate competition). The forbidden latent wish does not appear in the manifest content of the dream but reaches fulfilment through an *allusion* between the simple daytime wish and the forbidden one—*an association that the child himself may reveal when questioned after reporting his dream.*

The fulfilment of a latent wish can occur through the totally *unconscious use of a symbol*, whose link between the symbolizing and the symbolized is unknown to the child and unclear to him even at the moment of reporting the dream (the bathtub dream #44). In this dream, the fulfilment of a simple wish acts in the sense that it disguises the true meaning of the dream (I'm thirsty and I want my parents to bring me water), which in the end is understood only because it manifests itself upon awakening (the child asks to drink).

In both these cases, the dreams do not have a bizarre aspect in themselves but show a deformation with respect to the true meaning of the dream, or rather their *manifest content distracts from the latent content* through the fulfilment, in the dream, of a simple wish. In these latter dreams, unlike in childhood dreams, it makes sense to start speaking of *psychic latent material as the real substance of*

Table 9.1 New dream-work operations in the dream reports from the second period

Allusive disguising	A legitimate simple wish disguises another illegitimate wish by guaranteeing gratification through an allusion of the former with the latter.
Unconscious symbolism	A repressed wish reaches a symbolic fulfilment through something legitimate that represents it, where the child is unaware of the connection. It is already present in the first period in oedipal dreams.
Direct dream-censorship activity	Dream-censorship activity is directly evident in some forms of conflict between an egosytonic wish vs. an egodystonic wish. However, an early sign of the presence of dream censorship is also evident in two dreams from the first period.
Strategic alliance between wishes	A *simple* wish joins an illegitimate *repressed* wish, and together they activate the dream.
Displacement (replacement of person)	One person is replaced by a second who performs actions proper to the first.
Authorization to proceed	In a *verbal report* of dream, the child asks for permission to fulfill a disapproved wish found in the latent content of dream.

dream. In fact, in dreams like #44, where the meaning could be apparently understood, we find that we reached new contents of the dream that do not correspond with the reported manifest content and its meaning.

We noticed that the symbolism and allusive nature of the previous dreams are completely personal; *the symbolizers and the elements that allude to other dream contents are strictly personal* and can be understood only if one is directly familiar with the child.

Both these two mechanisms explain how the dream creates, when required by the circumstances, *"opportunistic" (i.e., strategic) alliances between wishes* in order to facilitate dream-censorship activity. An example of opportunistic alliance is also present in the dream of returning to kindergarten (see Chapter 8, #52), where a wish in contrast with the rules is fulfilled by hiding behind the fulfilment of a simple wish.

In consideration of the fact that even in *multiple dreams* (i.e., overdetermined dreams), the dream creates the conditions for satisfying several desires together, I must believe that opportunism is a general peculiar characteristic of the dream, even in the child. Furthermore, this mechanism can also serve the sole purpose of reaching the conditions of triggering the dream through a strategic alliance between *simple* desires which allows them to reach the hallucinatory state.

In another dream (#47, the tooth dream) that Marco had when he was 6 years and 4 months, an unconscious conflict between two wishes, one of which is egosyntonic, well represents *an embryonic form of defensive dream-censorship activity*. Although in the previous dreams, there is a conflict too, in the "tooth dream", it is even more evident which are the *opposing motive forces*. The result is that this dream that expresses the fulfilment of a simple wish (that the tooth finally falls off) is not experienced as a pleasant event as one would expect. It clearly appears from the questions (after the dream report) that this is due to the fact that Marco wants to be good-looking. In this dream, the general mechanism of dream censorship can be observed in an elementary way in the conflict between two wishes, one of which tends to reject the direct expression of the other or allows it to the detriment of the presence of anxiety, since it is the one that most represents the core of thoughts most important to the person (ego and superego tendencies). In this case, it is the aesthetic sense.

In the previous dreams, there is the first clear evidence of the fact that at least one form of dream distortion/bizarreness clearly arises from a conflict between the motive forces of the ego and the wishes rejected by it, and that when an effective deformation is not achieved, this causes anxiety. Specifically, the cases of dreams #06, #25 and #47 tell us that the first needs of the ego (particularly the superegoic and ego-ideal aspects) on the basis of which an attempt is made to reject a wish might be those related to the "sense of shame", "feelings of guilt" and the "aesthetic needs" of the child.

In a dream report from this period, I also observed a form of *displacement*, while in a dream from the first period, I had found a personal inconvenience/discomfort solved by transferring it to another dream character. In the dream of returning to kindergarten (#52), we observe a *more complex* displacement through the *replacement of a person*: the most permissive kindergarten teacher takes the place of the stricter elementary school teacher, and in his dream, Marco *transfers upon his kindergarten teacher* the authority to order to "stand still".

Beyond the dream operations aimed at preventing moral illegitimate wishes from finding direct expression in the dream, there are also dreams in which the wish escapes deformation, but the child has some fear in reporting them, or he requires an apology for the wish expressed in the dream (both noticed in a dream from the first period, dream #25). In other cases, it is also possible that there is *an explicit request for approval of the disapproved wish* from the parent to whom the dream is being told (dream #39). Both are expressions of *resistance to report the dream*. The latter action may also appear, in the same form, in the dream content (i.e., as an internal psychic operation) in which the authorizing parent appears, a plastic way of representing the "*authorization to proceed*", scenically an operation that is also an expression of the considerations of representability in the dream. I will return to the latter aspect when discussing certain dream reports from the third period.

The dream-work operations described previously, although infrequent and in their most elementary expression, are *of the same type as those identified and described by Freud* through the interpretation of the *dreams* in adults (i.e., displacement, condensation, symbolism, considerations of representability, etc.). The dream-work operations in Marco's dreams were directly confirmed through the analysis of the manifest dream content. In Marco's dreams, dream-work operations can be better studied because the material they rely on is known, permitting me to understand what operations have affected that material. In fact, in the case of adult dreams, we recognize the (latent) material on which the operation took place only *ex post*, after having learned it via dream interpretation. On the contrary, in Marco's dreams, we can recognize the effects of dream-work operations from the (known) material on which the deformation is carried out.

As we have seen, certain dream-work operations can be independent and autonomous in respect to censorship demands. Furthermore, what we observe in some of Marco's dreams is that certain dream-work operations are also at the service of the simple wishes themselves, acting so to *facilitate and/or amplify* their fulfilment in dreams. So dream-work operations are not only at the service of the censor agent but also at the service of the needs or of the power of the wish.

The dream-work operations are the most distinguishing of the process of dreaming. Their study allows us to observe how the dream acts. They represent the very essence of the dream, that is, as the dream works. Also in this case, the children's dreams allow us an advantageous look to deepen our knowledge of the dream.

Frankly bizarre dreams of the second period

When we cannot understand the nature of the underlying wish in the dream—that is, in frankly bizarre dreams—analyzing the origin of the bizarreness becomes difficult, if not impossible. However, these early *frankly bizarre dreams* are still useful since they allow us to view closely, from a *phenomenological perspective*, certain elements of bizarreness that are also typically present in adult dreams, such as, for example, *intrinsically bizarre characters*, *strange actions*, *indeterminate characters* and *space-time overlaps*, here inserted in the context of a less complex dream scenario and narrative and therefore easier to analyze. In the second period, Marco reports 13 dreams that fall into this category (although 9 of these are also configured as a bad dreams; see Table 8.1, Chapter 8). In Table 9.2, I report the types of bizarreness found. Here are some examples. A very bizarre dream reminiscent of, in its complexity, those of adults is the following:

> M. 46–6;4. *A young lady had put me in jail, and I cried because I wanted my mum. I was so sad because they had put me in jail all alone. It was a very bad dream, because I called Mummy and she did not come. Then the dream ended that they let me go to Mummy. They freed me from jail and let me go (so the dream was a little nice, too). The jail was like the one in the Pippi Longstocking film. I was in that jail. The lady in the dream was the same as the hostess on the plane, I mean the plane to Greece.*

The jail in the dream relates to the Pippi Longstocking movie that he had watched the evening before. In the film, Pippi's father is in jail, and there are two pirates who go talk to him in jail. The lady reminds Marco of the flight attendant on a plane. Marco recalls the one who was on the plane to Greece the year before,

Table 9.2 Types of bizarreness in frankly bizarre dreams from the second period*

Bizarre characters	Inherently improbable characters
Overdetermined characters and/or situations as a direct expression of condensation (dream-work operation)	A dream character brings together characteristics of multiple real-life characters. A situation has an emotional connotation that is not proportionate.
Incongruous superposition of space and time	Things and/or objects are placed in places that are not the usual real-life ones. Actions are carried out at different times from what happens in real life.
Sudden space-time discontinuity	The dream scene suddenly changes incongruously.
Strange and improper actions	A dream character performs unlikely actions, which he would not do while awake.

*Although there were very few bizarre dreams in the early period, the types of bizarreness described here were also present in Marco's early bizarre dreams.

but it might be that he is mistaking her for the flight attendant on the plane to Dublin that we took in winter and where Marco was seated away from his mother. He called her and cried, but she could not sit next to him because the seat was already taken. It is very likely that the dream lady looked like that flight attendant. We had flown about a week earlier, and it was a very nice experience for Marco.

In this dream, as well as for several bizarre dreams, we are far from the direct and easily understandable connection to daytime experiences in early childhood dreams. In this dream, *which is also configured as a bad dream*, the motivational origin of which is unclear, we can perceive the action of the daytime residues in activating other latent material—that is, the fear about sitting on the plane away from his mother, experienced recently and that probably relates to deeper fears, is represented plastically in the dream with the "prison scene" (from the film he had watched the evening before). In this dream, therefore, we can understand the mechanism that causes the bizarre effect (but not the psychic reason)—that is, the representation, through a scene (out of context and apparently without connection to the daytime experience of the child) symbolizing a real past situation of fear. This mechanism is a clear example of what Freud called "consideration of representability".

The following dream (#48) also shows an unprecedented complexity, as well as a *sudden discontinuity* in dream events. The presence of bizarreness is so evident that it is commented on by the dreamer himself. In this dream, the meaning is obscure, unlike in the one previously mentioned, where in the end, the presence of fear is understood.

M. 48–6;3. *I was with Grandpa, and we were going to Villa Lazzaroni* (a park in Rome)*, and there was one man. Then a pole fell on us, and we were almost* *hit, and then we stopped because there was a person feeling ill. It was a girl. She had fallen to the ground and was feeling ill, and there were the police and the ambulance, and then you where there too, Daddy. (You had heard that the girl was dead). I said, "Yuck!" I said, "This thing makes me want to puke". Then you, Dad, you said, "Then it was you! You made her feel sick!" I was in the car with Grandpa, then they handcuffed me and took me to jail. Then I opened my eyes and I was scared. Why? Because I thought I was in jail for real. Because dreams make you believe that they are true, you see!* Then, about the dream, he added, *It happened at Circeo* (a seaside place south of Rome).*

Then what has Villa Lazzaroni to do with it? *But dreams are like this!* You mean you first were at Circeo and then you found yourself into Villa Lazzaroni? *Of course!*

About his dream, Marco said, "*It seemed so real, I was disgusted by the vomit and woke up all of a sudden*". (He actually went to sleep with us in the big bed). In the afternoon on the day before, we had been to the cinema. Marco was about to drink from a bottle of water and had said that it smelled like vomit. Strangely enough, it really smelled bad and we threw it away. On the day after the dream, Marco said he had never seen anyone feeling sick. "Maybe it was the father of the Viking, who dies in the dragon trainer film?" Marco said, "Yes, maybe it was that". "Or maybe the mother of the Viking in dragon trainer?" (In the film, this character feels ill and falls several times while fighting). About this possibility, Marco also said, "Yes, it could be". Marco said he had never seen anyone feeling ill at Villa Lazzaroni, nor has he ever felt ill himself. The dream has a bizarre aspect (*sudden discontinuity*) because it takes place first at Circeo (a seaside area in Lazio) and then at Villa Lazzaroni (in Rome).

In this dream, the diurnal sources are disparate and come from different waking situations. They are put together and stand there to represent something that is not known in the state of wakefulness, and this gives the dream a strange and bizarre aspect.

Analyzing the *daytime sources* of these bizarre dreams is generally difficult because they are *vague* and *uncertain*, and they hardly help to understand the meaning of the dream (we analyzed the daytime sources of bizarre dreams also configured as bad dreams in the next chapter).

We can notice directly from the dream transcript that the previously mentioned frankly bizarre dreams (#46, #48) are, at the same time, considerably longer than the previous ones of a clear wish-fulfilment nature. This confirms an effect known in the literature—that is, the positive correlation between bizarreness and length of the dream (Colace, 2003).

In conclusion, in Marco's frankly bizarre dreams, some *types* of bizarreness can be described that are the same ones observed more markedly in adult dreams (see Table 9.2).

Notes

1   This would have required, in fact, the work of classical dream interpretation, which was not in the scope of this study.
2   According to the disguise-censorship theory, most dream bizarreness is the expression of a motivated effort to disguise unconscious wishes that are unacceptable to the conscience. The dream-censorship agency and, later, the superego functions (in the ego) are responsible for the effort to disguise latent dream contents. Bizarre elements are psychologically meaningful, and dreams do have a meaning. Based on his experience in adult dream interpretation, Freud observed that the strangeness, senselessness and implausibility of dream contents (i.e., all the bizarre aspects of the dream) always correspond to a given amount of dream work and distortion. This aspect of the classification refers to a quantitative difference: in short, different degrees of dream distortion/bizarreness (three categories) of manifest dream content apparently reflect different quantities of dream work. Children's dreams differ in the fact that they introduce a lower level of distortion and dream-work activity (Freud, 1901, pp 18–20; see also Colace, 2010, pp. 34–35, 117).
3   Freud and Piaget both find the symbolism in the dreams of very young children (Freud, 1900, pp. 379, 383–385; Piaget, 1962, pp. 169–171).

References

Colace, C. (2003). Dream bizarreness reconsidered. *Sleep and Hypnosis*, *5* (3), 105–128.
Colace, C. (2010). *Children's Dreams: From Freud's Observations to Modern Dream Research*. New York: Routledge.
Colace, C. (2012). Dream bizarreness and the controversy between the neurobiological approach and the disguise censorship model: The contribution of children's dreams. *Neuropsychoanalysis*, *14* (2), 165–174.
Freud, S. (1900). *The Interpretation of Dreams*. S.E., New York: Basic Books.
Freud, S. (1901). *On Dreams*. S.E. London and New York: Norton & Company, Inc.
Freud, S. (1916–1917). *Introductory Lectures on Psycho-Analysis*. S.E., 15/16. London: Hogarth Press.
Piaget, J. (1962). *Play, Dreams and Imitation in Childhood*. New York and London: W.W. Norton & Company.

Chapter 10

Bad dreams

With Marco, bad dreams appear more consistently only later in the development of dreaming, towards the end of the first half of his fifth year. From this point of view, they seem to be the prerogative of a more advanced stage of the ontogenetic development of the function of dreaming. In the second period, these dreams account for about 65% (22/34 of dream reports).

This is a high frequency of this type of dreams. It must be taken into account that some bad dreams had between the age of 6 years, 7 months and 6 years, 10 months coincide with two aspects that have influenced Marco's life in that period: the moving to a new home and the illness of his grandfather, which also reduced the time and attention that his parents could dedicate to him. Furthermore, it is quite possible that at least a part of the nightmares and bad dreams of this period may have been unleashed by the fact that, at that time, Marco's schoolteachers were discussing the theme of fears and how to deal with them.[1]

Themes

I included in the category of bad dreams all those that were defined by Marco as "bad" or "ugly" dreams and in which he is explicitly present in the dream (consistently with their content) and/or feels an unpleasant emotion such as sadness, fear, anguish or worry, or Marco crying (prolonging in wakefulness the affective state of the dream) while he reports the dream.

Most of Marco's bad dreams concern "being kidnapped", "his own death", "the fear of being alone" (e.g. his parents die and/or abandon him) and other themes of anguish and fear (see Table 10.1).

Types of bad dreams and daytime sources

In Marco's repertoire of bad dreams, different types were found. A first general criterion of distinction in bad dreams is *whether the dream is interrupted or not, with awakening* in the middle of the night. More than half of Marco's bad dreams (14/22, 64% of bad dreams) were interrupted by nocturnal awakening, in fear and/or anguish, and are therefore close to the definition of true *nightmares* (Sandman

DOI: 10.4324/9781003184874-14

Table 10.1 The content of bad dreams and nightmares

Leaving a desired place
The parents no longer being there
Fear of having to go to the summer camp
The parents disappearing
Fear of bubbles and blood from a mosquito bite
Being chased by "skeleton characters" (fearsome but attractive game)
He and his parents dying because the house is on fire
Being hit by a car and dying
Being abducted
Being put in jail
Thieves in the house
Being alone and hearing the alarm ring
Falling into a labyrinth
Ugly child (from a film)
Dad leaving with his suitcase
Soldiers shooting each other
Ugly lady dressed in black
Being killed in war
Having the face deformed

et al., 2013; Levin & Nielsen, 2007; Valli & Revonsuo, 2009; Simard et al., 2008). Among the remaining dreams (*n* 8), there are mostly moderately bad dreams.

Many bad dreams do not originate, at least apparently, from actual daytime fear or frightening experiences and *concern general fears*. These dreams have no clear daytime references (i.e., uncertain, generic). Others bad dreams, on the other hand, were *caused by a very specific frightening daytime stimulus*—for example, a big fright—which is then resumed in the dream. In this case, daytime sources often go back to the day preceding the dream (i.e., day residue).

Finally, unexpectedly, several dreams (about 30%) emerged which should be considered rather as "anomalous" bad dreams or *false bad dreams*. These are dreams that are only apparently "bad" and present unsuccessful attempts to satisfy the wish to challenge a fear and win over it—that is, to dispel it. These have frequently clear day residues too. *In the end, in bad dreams (all), we find that about 50% have residues from the day preceding the dream.*

In *false bad dreams*, we observe a dangerous attempt to stage an experience of fear to satisfy the pleasure of risk and an attempt to dispel such fear that gets out of hand. This situation can be understood through observing Marco's diurnal behaviour towards a stimulus that is as much desired as it is scary. Marco wants to watch the trailer of the horror film *Child's Play*, but at the same time, he is afraid. He insists on watching this trailer that his friends have heard about. While watching the video, objectively scary, Marco oscillates between enthusiasm and fear, between seeking and escaping the stimulus. Similarly, this situation may be reproduced in some bad dreams. However, while in the state of wakefulness, the child has control of the situation—for example, by closing his eyes at the

appropriate time—this cannot happen in the dream. These dreams might reproduce the desired frightening stimulus, but in the hallucinatory experience of the
dream setting—where, due to the condition of sleep, one cannot run away from
the frightening situation—the only way out is waking up. In these dreams, when
in the daytime experience the fearful stimulus has in some way been sought in the
form of a (pleasant) daring challenge, the dream takes up this stimulus and stages
the attempt to overcome the fear (in this sense, it configures as a wish-fulfilment
dream of the continuation type) and/or represents the wish (with a bad ending) to
play with fear. These dreams do not arise as true bad dreams but become such during the dream experience in their final outcome. These are dreams that therefore
concern fearful and yet sought-after themes, even in the daytime experience.[2]

The observation of Marco's false bad dreams are consistent with certain conclusions by Piaget. This author also noted that some types of nightmares should rather
be regarded as challenges of disturbing experiences and/or characters with a "desire
for liquidating" them, similar to what happens in certain game situations. The difference lies in the different controls of these stimuli that, in the dream, can make
the disturbing, scary aspects prevail (see Piaget, 1962, p. 180).[3] On the other hand,
Freud also claimed that children's play (Freud based his observations in this respect
on his grandson's spool-throwing game) allows one to *master and abreact* the fear
and control of a situation (Freud, 1920–1922, pp. 16–17). However, in the dream
there may be a bad ending: the child does not succeed in over winning his/her fear.

Here are some examples of different types of bad dreams (see Figure 10.1).

An example of a bad dream that starts from a precise and identifiable daytime
fright that triggers a more general fear is the first bad dream that Marco reported
at 5 years and 4 months (#20), about gypsies (see chapter 7).

A *bad dream with nocturnal awakening* but without a precise daytime reference
is the following (from the first period):

M. 26–5;8. *I was younger, and you* (Daddy) *were holding me in your arms.
S.* (Marco's cousin) *was also there. There was a thief who wanted to take me
away. It was a bad dream. We were at Hydromania* (an amusement park in

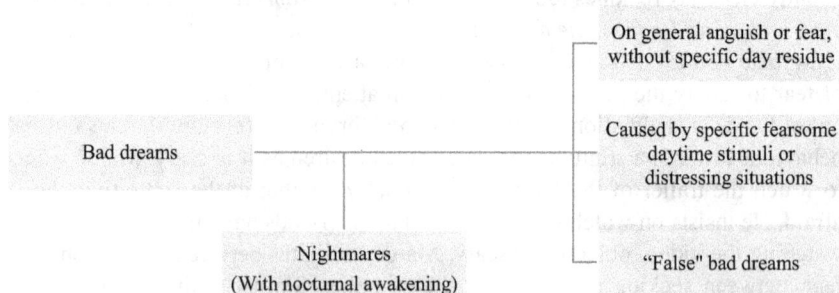

Figure 10.1 Types of bad dreams

Rome), *then we went back home and the thief went away. Mummy, Uncle D. and Aunt A.* (the cousin's parents) *were also there.*

It is a dream of anguish with awakening; Marco, in his sleep, called "Daddy" and then woke up and hugged me tight. The dream contains bizarre elements (the fact that he was younger) and the fear of thieves that Marco also has occasionally in daytime life. It should be noted that there is also a wish in the background of the dream setting (i.e., going to the Hydromania water park).

A bad dream with awakening on a general fear without any clear day residue is the following one:[4]

M. 57–6;9 (dream recalled in February). *I had a bad dream. I dreamed that a man took me away in his arms and put a hand over my mouth so that I could not speak.*

Some bad dreams are dreams in which Marco is moderately sad or frightened by something, for which *it is easy enough to find a connection with the daytime experience* (i.e., a direct day residue, a sudden scary stimulus) without particular elements of bizarreness, such as the following dream:

M. 50–6;5. *I dreamed I had a mosquito bite here on my calf that became a blister and then a scab and I got all scratched. I was scared and nauseated by the blood flowing out from the scab.*

Marco reported that D. (a school bus friend) yesterday showed him a mosquito bite, which he then scratched and the blood came out, forming a scab. Marco said, "When we got off the bus yesterday, he showed me his wound [blister], and the blood came out, up to here". "And you got scared?" "Yes." Marco added that it was a giant mosquito bite.

Marco reported that the day before, D. had shown him a scab that was bleeding. D. had told him that the windows were open at school and mosquitoes came in, and Marco was a bit impressed.

See also the following dream:

M. 70–7;1. *My whole face was deformed. My face was swollen cheeks with blisters and pimples. Long neck, deformed nose and mouth. It was a bad dream. I got scared.*

Marco spontaneously draws the dream (see Figure 10.2).

A bad dream (with nocturnal awakening) with a direct daytime stimulus is the following:

M. 63–7;0. *I dreamed of the ugly girl* (the one with the crooked teeth). *It was a bad dream.*

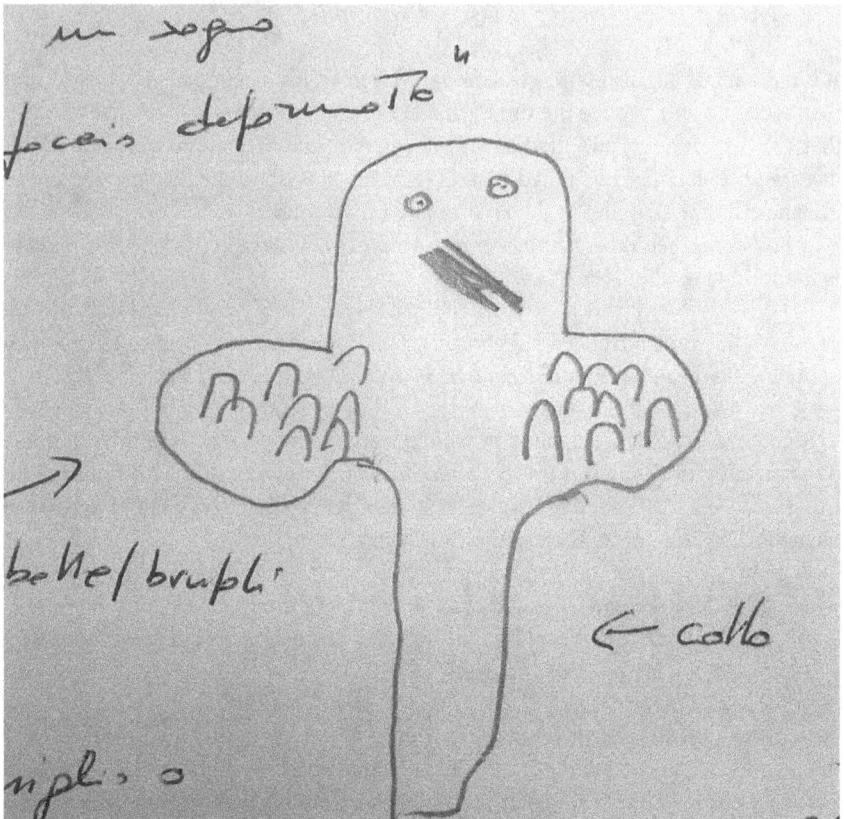

Figure 10.2 The dream of Marco's deformed face with some pen notes

The girl in the dream appears in the trailer of a film that Marco had caught a glimpse of the evening before. The very scary and creepy image was seen for a moment by Marco. The girl's face in the film gets transformed. She becomes a monster with very sharp teeth and a particularly gruesome mouth. Upon seeing that scene, Marco was visibly shaken. In this case, the dream was probably triggered by a sudden emotional state of fright that may have remained unprocessed because it was too close to the onset of sleep.

By an unfortunate coincidence, two days later in the evening, Marco again happened to come across the trailer of the film with the ugly girl, without however seeing the scene directly. He reported the following dream:

M. 64–7;0 (in an agitated tone). *I dreamed of the ugly girl* (the one with the crooked teeth). *It was a bad dream.*

The previously mentioned bad dreams (#63, #64) were clearly caused by scary stimuli incurred (unpredictably) just before going to sleep.

In other bad dreams, some bizarre aspects appear, as in the following example of a dream with anguish[5]:

> M. 43–6;3. *I dreamed that you* (the parents) *had disappeared. You were younger. Then you returned normal, as you are now. In the dream, Mummy was running and did not wait for me. I found myself alone and I was frightened. Then the dream was over and I woke up.*

Marco said it was a bad dream. He woke up in fear, climbed off his bed and came to our room. He had this dream while falling asleep. That time Marco had been put to bed in a mobile home (we were camping out) when he was already asleep, so his mother could not kiss him good night. Upon falling asleep, Marco had not had his parents close to him, so he may have felt upset upon awakening because he was in an unfamiliar environment (not at home). This is, however, a dream with bizarre elements (e.g., young parents who change and then return as they were, the mother running).

In the months preceding his seventh birthday, Marco had a few nightmares (close in time) on the theme of thieves, thefts and his abduction or death. This period coincides with the installation of an alarm system at home.

Examples of *false bad dreams* are the following:

> M. 69–7y;1. *I was at war and I was a grown-up, but they stabbed me with a knife and I died.*

It was a dream with an abrupt awakening.

That evening, before going to sleep, Marco had been watching a short bit from the Transformers film, where there was a violent scene: soldiers were shooting in the desert against the Transformer. Marco would have liked to watch this film but I didn't, so I had switched to another channel.

The interpretation of this dream is complex. On the one hand, it can be seen as a wish-fulfilment dream (i.e., false bad dream, *continuation dream*, to watch the film and be the protagonist); on the other hand it can be seen as a nightmare.

In the middle of the night, Marco wakes up and tells the following dream:

> M. 54–6;6. *I was walking alone along the streets of New York, then there were skeletons following me, so I got into a house where there were Grandpa, Grandma and Aunt, and they hid me.*

The negative characters of this dream are people halfway between skeletons and zombies, protagonists of a scary game that Marco desired.

In some dreams of anguish, the daytime source is an experience of fear that is recalled even after some time, through a more recent (and more modest) frightening experience that acts as an instigator of the dream (see the Pippi Long-stocking dream #46, Chapter 9).

We have seen that in some of Marco's wish-fulfilment dreams, there is an alliance between wishes (also of different type) in order to trigger the dream, just as it happens in adults, where daytime wishes can give rise to unconscious impulses. Now we observe that in some bad dreams, too, even the most recent and perhaps less important fears can arise and make room for the representation of deeper fears. What these two situations have in common is the same dream-triggering mechanism: *a recent stimulus (wish or fear) which, although insufficient to trigger the dream, acts by activating a stronger unconscious stimulus.*

The drama in some of Marco's bad dreams appears even clearer and more vividly in Marco's drawings of them. The following bad dream (# 28 from the first period) is useful, as Marco provides a scenic representation in which we see very well the threatening tone of the characters and the scary nature of the plot. Even in the case of nightmares, as already noted for wish-fulfilment dreams, the drawing of the dream can provide valuable information on the emotional aspects of the dream scenario (see Figure 10.3).

M. 28–5;9. *Dad, I had a very bad dream* (Marco cries as he tells it). *We were at the carousels and I was in a car* (like a bumper car). *I was with Mom in one of these cars and you were alone in another. Then there were dark men* (he

Figure 10.3 Dream of the carousels. Left to right: (in the car) Marco, black men with gun, broken glass of the car.

means black men) *who wanted to shoot us, and then we went home. The dark men were in the bumper cars, and they shot us with guns but they didn't catch us* (we didn't die).

The percentage of bad dreams Marco has had, even if comparisons are not always easy, is higher than the one found in previous systematic studies.

In a previous study, conducted with a methodology similar to the one described here ("at-home dream collection"), the dreams that fall into the bad-dreams category in a group of children aged 5 to 7 did not exceed 35%[6] (Colace, 2010).

In a questionnaire-based dream study, dreams rarely show "aggressive action" and "anxious themes" in their contents (23% among the 6 to 8 age bracket), and while reporting their dreams, the children were rarely "anxious" (25%) or "gloomy" (5%) (Colace, 2006).

With regard to real nightmares, in the same study, only 16% of parents (in the 6 to 8 age bracket for children) reported the presence of nightmares "sometimes" and 1% "often", while the overwhelming majority reported "no nightmares".

Notes

1   Several studies indicate that bad dreams and nightmares are more frequently reported during intense life stress (for review see Nielsen & Levin, 2007).
2   A confirmation of the presence of these *false bad dreams* also comes from a recent online survey on childhood dreams during the period of full lockdown due to the Covid-19 pandemic, where, despite the considerable presence of real bad dreams, these forms have also been observed (Colace, unpublished collection).
3   On this mechanism of dreams, see also dream #32, Chapter 3.
4   The dreams with anguish of the December–February period coincide with a difficult and extraordinary period for Marco. In fact, in addition to moving to a new home and encountering the first difficulties at school (bad notes from his teacher), he also felt deprived of our attention due to the illness of my father (his grandfather) that diverted his parents' time.
5   As we have said, several bad dreams are also considered very bizarre dreams (see Chapter 7, Table 7.1).
6   But this percentage also included neutral dreams and other dreams, see Chapter 7, endnote 5.

References

Colace, C. (2006). Children's dreaming: A study based on questionnaire completed by parents. *Sleep and Hypnosis, 8* (1), 19–32.

Colace, C. (2010). *Children's Dreams: From Freud's Observations to Modern Dream Research.* New York: Routledge.

Freud, S. (1920–1922). *Beyond the Pleasure Principle.* S.E., XVIII. London: Hogarth Press.

Levin, R., & Nielsen, T. A. (2007). Disturbed dreaming, posttraumatic stress disorder, and affect distress: A review and neurocognitive model. *Psychological Bulletin, 133* (3), 482–528. DOI: 10.1037/0033-2909.133.3.482. PMID: 17469988.

Nielsen, T. A., & Levin, R. (2007). Nightmares: A new neurocognitive model. *Sleep Medicine Reviews, 11*, 295–310.

Piaget, J. (1962). *Play, Dreams and Imitation in Childhood.* New York and London: W.W. Norton & Company.

Sandman, N., Valli, N. K., Kronholm, E., Ollila, H. M., Revonsuo, A., & Laatikainen, T. (2013). Nightmares: Prevalence among the Finnish general adult population and war veterans during 1972–2007. *Sleep 36* (7), 1041–1050.

Simard, V., Nielsen, T. A., Tremblay, R. E., Boivin, M., & Montplaisir, J. Y. (2008). Longitudinal study of bad dreams in preschool-aged children: Prevalence, demographic correlates, risk and protective factors. *Sleep, 31* (1), 62–70.

Valli, K., & Revonsuo, A. (2009). Sleep: Dreaming data and theories. In: W. P. Banks (Ed.), *Encyclopedia of Consciousness* (pp. 341–355). Amsterdam: Elsevier Publisher.

Chapter 11

Ego and superego development and changes in dreaming

The Freudian structural model of the mind and dreaming

In the Freudian theory of dreams, the theme of the transition from "infantile" dream production to more complex dreaming in adults is addressed with *two complementary explanatory models* which refer to his *structural theory of the human mind*. The first model is linked to the *general development of the ego*, or the progressive domination of thought over drives. The second and more specific model concerns *the completion of the superego development*—that is, the need/possibility to repress wishes that are inadmissible to the dreamer's conscience. This latter model attempts to explain those forms of dream bizarreness caused by defensive distortions of an ethical/moral nature and is closely linked to the disguise-censorship theory.

Development of ego, dreaming and dream bizarreness

The former model arises from the perspective of how dreams change according to the type of wishes that originate them and in relation to the development of the dreamer's ego. We may call this model the "*dominant and inhibitory influence of the ego*" on the dream (Freud, 1901, pp. 66–67, 1900, p. 552). This model refers to the development and maturation of the ego, which, being related to voluntary motility and consciousness, has the ability to discern and, based on the direct influence of life experiences, allows adults as well as older children to become aware of the "uselessness" of hallucinatory wish fulfilment.

According to Freud, older children and adults try to postpone the fulfilment of the wish through the progressive domain of thought over wishful impulses, finding gratification by changing the external reality. Following the development of the ego, simple daytime wishes progressively lose the degree of interest and urgency that they have in younger children (who are unable to give them up) and that have the power of triggering dreams specifically and exclusively in the infantile psyche. In this first explanatory model, there is also a direct reference to

DOI: 10.4324/9781003184874-15

the *inhibitory influence of the ego* towards all those *infantile wishes that are now considered useless to life in the course of development*. In this case, the repression of the wish is motivational (but not for reason of ethics and moral order) and seems to concern *survival and adaptive advantage* (in a Darwinian sense). I believe that this broadens the range of grounds for which a censorship activity would be required. It is also plausible to think that these factors, related to the concept of survival, are those that first require the suppression of certain wishes in a developmental perspective even before of the repression based on ethical, moral and social pressure. With respect to this first model, *Freud states that the infantile form of dreams becomes rare in the healthy adult*.[1]

> Adults . . . have also grasped the uselessness of wishing, and after long practice know how to postpone their desires until they can find satisfaction by the long and roundabout path of altering the external world. In their case, accordingly, wish fulfilments along the short psychical path are rare in sleep too; it is even possible, indeed, that they never occur at all, and that anything that may seem to us to be constructed on the pattern of a child's dream in fact requires a far more complicated solution. On the other hand, in the case of adults . . . a differentiation has occurred in the psychical material, which was not present in children. A psychical agency has come into being, which, taught by experience of life, exercises a dominating and inhibiting influence upon mental impulses and maintains that influence with jealous severity, and which, owing to its relation to consciousness and to intentional movement, is armed with strongest instruments of psychic power. A portion of the impulses of childhood has been suppressed by this agency as being useless to life, and any material of thought derived from those impulses is in a state of repression.
>
> (Freud, 1901, pp. 66–67)

This model implies that, with the development of the ego, simple wishes (the only ones that produce simple dreams) are no longer suitable to generate the dreams, and the possibility/necessity increases that the triggering of the dream is more frequently caused by several wishes joined together (also of repressed type) and, in the adult, by unconscious repressed wishes, the only ones that have a stronger motivational force (dream triggering power/capacity). These are the same wishes that then, in the dynamics of the dream process, *need to be deformed in order to get a disguised gratification until the typical dream bizarreness is produced.*

Development of superego and dream bizarreness

The second explanatory model analyzes the progressive presence of bizarre elements in its manifest content, which Freud attributes to an action of defensive distortion of the latent dream material. This model refers directly to the development of the ability and the need to remove wishes that are not admissible to the conscience, as they are no longer tolerated by the ego on an ethical/moral level. Here Freud refers to the development of moral consciousness and the superego (see Freud, 1900, pp. 267–268, 1925, p. 46)—in other words, the influence of education on the progressive internalization of moral and ethical rules. Freud referred to this model when explaining the progressive presence of bizarreness in children's dreams, attributing most parts of dream bizarreness to the dream distortion engendered by dream censorship, the same one acting in adults' dreams (see Colace, 2010).[2]

In Freud's view, it is only the development of superego functions that makes it possible—and necessary—to dissimulate those wishes at the basis of dreams that, again due to the development of these functions, have been removed and now return in the form of unconscious wishes in the dreams. Thus, in young children who have not yet developed superego functions, dreams are mostly simple and free from defensive distortion (which is unnecessary). Where these conditions are not present (i.e., children who have not yet developed the superego functions), dreams are mostly free from distortion. Thus, the dreams of young children are frequently clear and simple because children lack those intrapsychic conditions that enable and require the disguising of the dreams' latent content. Freud gave the following example of this process:[3]

> A child of under four years old reported having dreamt that he had seen a big dish with a big joint of roast meat and vegetables on it. All at once the joint had been eaten up—whole and without being cut up. He had not seen the person who ate it.
>
> (Freud, 1900, pp. 267–268)

Freud attempted to explain the bizarre element of the dream—that is, that "he had not seen the person who ate it":

> Who can the unknown person have been whose sumptuous banquet of meat was the subject of the little boy's dream? His experiences during the dream-day must enlighten us on the subject. By doctor's orders he had been put on a milk diet for the past few days. On the evening of the dream-day he had been naughty, and as a punishment he had been sent to bed without his supper.
>
> (Freud, 1900, p. 268)

In this dream, Freud attributed the bizarre element of the dream to the fact that the child had started the development of the interiorization of moral norms, particularly to obey the prohibition of dining by his parents. Therefore, the child supposedly performed a minimum dissimulation—that is, he removed from the manifest content of the dream the person (i.e., the dream-work operation: omission) who ate the meal.[4]

> He had been through this hunger-cure once before and had been very brave about it. He knew he would get nothing, but would not allow himself to show by so much as a single word that he was hungry. Education had already begun to have an effect on him: it found expression in this dream, which exhibits the beginning of dream-distortion. There can be no doubt that the person whose wishes were aimed at this lavish meal—a meat meal, too—was himself. But since he knew he was not allowed it, he did not venture to sit down to the meal himself, as hungry children do in dreams. (Cf. my little daughter Anna's dream of strawberries on p. 130.) The person who ate the meal remained anonymous.
>
> (Freud, 1900, p. 268)

This is an explanation that falls within the more general model of the *disguise-censorship theory of dream* and concerns the dream bizarreness caused in adult dreams by the masking of unconscious desires which are inadmissible on an ethical/moral level (the biggest part of bizarreness in adult dreams). We also note that in Freud's view, the omission in dreams is a clear expression of dream-censorship activity.

Statistical correlational data supporting the model

Systematic studies have shown how the model of the influence of superego development on dream bizarreness can be controlled empirically in children by making its assumptions operational (Colace, 2010, 2009, 2012). Freud's theory that dream bizarreness in children is correlated with the development of super-ego functions has received empirical support. In particular, three studies on children's dreams show *statistically significant positive correlations between dream bizarreness measures and indices of superego function development* (e.g., "ability to experience sense of guilt", "acquisition of moral rules", "adaptation to reality and social environments"—comprehension subtest-WPPSI/WISCR[5]: Colace, 1997, 2010, 2012; Colace & Violani, 1993; Colace, Violani, & Solano, 1993) (See box 11.1.) These results suggest that the bizarreness in dreams becomes more probable only in those children who show a more complete development of their superego. In these children, there are intrapsychic conditions that enable the possibility/need to disguise the dream's latent content. Conversely, where these intrapsychic conditions are not present (i.e., in children who have not yet fully developed superego functions), dream reports are more simple than bizarre. These data make even more sense since the same measures of dream bizarreness adopted in these studies conversely were not affected by the development of several cognitive abilities, such as, for example, short- and long-term memory, visuospatial memory, descriptive ability of visual stimuli and locquacity/imaginative ability (Colace, 2010).[6]

Box 11.1   Stories about feelings of guilt

These are stories about transgression administered to children with the purpose of measuring the development of their ability to experience a sense of guilt (Colace, 2010). These stories measured the sense of guilt in children, which related to different transgressions. Story A shows a transgression consisting of an aggressive action that, to a certain extent, might well be considered unintentional. Story B shows a transgression consisting of the voluntary disrespect of a parental "order" (see the subsequent stories). Both stories allowed us to identify three levels of development of the ability to experience a sense of guilt.

Story A

A boy/girl called Angelo/Anna is playing on a lawn. There are also other younger boys/girls with Angelo/Anna, and Angelo/Anna knows that younger children are not so steady and that one needs to watch out so that they do not fall. However, Angelo/Anna starts running very fast and pushing the others, so a young child falls, gets bruised and starts to cry.

Story B

A boy/girl called Stefano (Paola) goes to play with his/her friends. Then his/her friends decide to buy ice cream, but Stefano (Paola) is not supposed to have one because his/her mum and dad have prohibited him/her to eat sweets and ice creams. However, Stefano (Paola) decides to have the ice cream on the sly, together with his/her friends.

At the first level, there are children who, in their answers, did not show any uneasiness or any fear of their parents for what the protagonist did, or "for themselves" in the place of the protagonist. At a second level, there are children who at first did show a certain uneasiness and fear or worry for the possible consequences of their action, such as, for instance, punishment from the parents, but who, in any case, did not show a clear sense of guilt. At a third level, there are children who said the protagonist would repent for what he has done, feel mean and/or guilty and try to help the victim. Uneasiness in these children is due to the awareness that the action committed is wrong in itself.

These results provide direct support to the assumption that the presence of at least a part of dream bizarreness (i.e., those due to defensive distortion activity) is specifically influenced by the development of the superego.

The previous data are consistent with two major Freudian deductions on dream bizarreness, namely (1) bizarreness cannot be considered as intrinsic to the nature of the dreaming process and (2) bizarreness cannot be considered a common feature of all dreams (Freud, 1910, p. 34, 1916–1917, pp. 128, 143).

Variation in Marco's dream repertoire in relation to his psychic development

Although this study does not provide specific measurements of psychic development indicators, the opportunity to observe my son daily in his behaviours and attitudes allowed me to draw a picture of his psychic development.

Marco at around 4 to 5 years of age (i.e., when first dream reports are collected), like all children of his age, still did not perform well-structured rational thinking that helped him desist from and give up the fulfilment of his daytime desires and requests; various instances of impulsiveness prevailed. At around 5 years, Marco moved on to developing a central aspect of his ego and personality. The ego becomes more and more an organizing and planning instance, keeping contact with reality. At the same time, Marco's language and thought (functions of the ego) became consolidated (i.e., logical thinking) and allowed for a better reconciliation of the instincts (i.e., emotional regulation). Impulsiveness now appeared more contained and controlled.

At about 5 to 6 years, the superego is increasingly defined in the ego, as the result of the interiorization of moral and social norms (i.e., parental influences, cultural/social impositions). This involves an increased sense of responsibility, and the appearance of a sense of guilt observable in Marco's daytime experiences (i.e., greater development of moral conscience). Self-observation and self-evaluation behaviours were also more present in his daytime experiences.[7] Marco also paid strong attention to his aesthetic aspect (i.e., development of ego ideal).

These important changes in the structuring of the psychic apparatus have influences on the development of the dreaming function. Major changes observed in the kinds of dreams experienced by Marco and in dream instigation and the process between the first and second period may be analyzed in relation to Marco's psychic development as well as in the light of the Freudian theorical models mentioned previously.

I found in Marco's repertoire of dream reports a *decrease in clear wish-fulfilment dreams* (dreams that refer to simple [unrepressed] wishes) in the second period and a higher frequency of dreams referring to more important and stronger wishes (recurring [repressed] wishes, long-time [repressed] wishes, disapproved latent wishes, repressed morally or ethically inadmissible wishes) in the second and third period. These results are consistent with the previously mentioned model about the "dominant and inhibitory influence of the ego" on dreams, according to which older children and adults are inclined to give up to the hallucinatory fulfilment of a simple wish, finding gratification by changing the external reality.

The development of the ego makes simple daytime wishes ineffective in the triggering of the dream, which can now only be triggered by important wishes—that is, with a greater capacity for instigation.

On the other hand, I observed an *increase in the frequency of frankly bizarre dreams* between Marco's first and second period—that is, between 4 to 5 years and 6 to 7 years of age, which is in line with the Freudian model of a positive relationship between the superego development and dream bizarreness.

The in-depth analysis of Marco's dream reports suggests that the appearance of censorship in dreams is a gradual process, both with respect to its *presence* and with respect to its *use*.

Sporadic dreams showing a primordial form of censorship activity (as the expression of the superego) were observed in Marco's first period (see for example the dreams of returning to school, #06, at 4 years and 8 months, and dream #25 about the timorous reporting of the fulfilment of an illegitimate wish [replacement of the father] at 5 years and 8 months). Other dream reports by Marco give direct evidence of a still non-continuous functioning of the censorship activity in the dream processes during the first period. For instance, in the "jumping dream", #3, that Marco had at 4 years and 7 months, he satisfied a wish denied by his parents openly without giving any sign of discomfort (e.g., guilt). This indicates that he did not feel the need to reject that wish or satisfy it in a disguised way. In any way, we see that in this dream, the forbidden desire "has escaped" to a very embryonic censorship.

On the other hand, in this period I also observed the first three really bizarre dreams that I suppose to be the result of defensive distortions of the dream and the oedipal dreams in which I plausibly assume the presence of defensive symbolism (i.e., censorship activity).

In the first period, we can say that the influence of the superego *begins* to be seen in the dream.

In the second period, we note the superego's influence on dreaming more clearly.

The evident presence of an allusive and symbolic (i.e., defensive distortion) fulfilment of *disapproved wishes* in dreams appear respectively at 6 years and 1 month (dream of karate competition, #39) and at 6 years and 3 months (bathtub dream, #44). In dream #47, the tooth dream (even more clearly than in the previous dream *of returning to school*), at 6 years and 4 months, a conflict of a moral/aesthetic nature (i.e., a wish that goes against the child's ego ideal) originates dream distortion that produces a bizarre aspect. In the second period, we also find in some dreams new dream-work operations which are used for defensive distortion.

A fact that is also consistent with the superego model is the disappearance of oedipal dreams in the second period. This is another indirect proof of the child's successful identification with his father and the interiorization of his rules and more generally of parental rules (progressive establishment of the superego) and of the child's progress in psychological maturity.

Here we note how the dream itself, through the analysis of its underlying wishes (simple/disapproved/inadmissible) and of the way in which they are satisfied (direct/indirect), gives us indications on the development of the ego and the interiorization process of parental and social norms (the superego's agency within the ego). Furthermore, by observation on how dreams deal with disapproved and inadmissible wishes, we may have clear indications on the different developments of the superego's function. This opens up the possibility of directly using the dream reports (also without interpretation) to evaluate some aspects of personality development in the clinical setting.[8]

In brief, in Marco's dream reports from the first to the second period, we find the following changes, in line with his ego and superego development and their supposed influences on dreaming (i.e., the Freudian dream theory and personality development):

- a clear decrease in the frequency of *direct* wish-fulfilment dreams (i.e., decline of infantile model of dream production);
- a lower *percentage proportion* in wish-fulfilment dreams of simple and ordinary wishes;
- a greater *percentage proportion* in wish-fulfilment dreams of the presence of repressed wishes—that is, forbidden and disapproved by the parents and wishes less admissible to the conscience, requiring some defensive distortion for their fulfilment, which results in bizarre aspects in the dreams (see Chapter 12, Figure 12.1);
- a greater frequency of frankly bizarre dreams, the content of which is not directly comprehensible in relation to daytime experiences;
- a clear presence of dream distortion and bizarreness of defensive/conflictual nature (i.e., due to the presence of disapproved and inadmissible wishes);
- a clearer need to introduce the concept of latent dream content in order to arrive at the true meaning of the dream;
- the consolidation of certain dream-work operations and the appearance of new ones, now employed also for the purposes of dream censorship activity

We will see in the next part of book how further changes in dreaming are consistent with the previous conclusions.

Notes

1   The understanding of this second Freudian explanatory model and its application to the concept of dream bizarreness was also favoured by the *personal communications* of S. Boag on the subject (2016) and collaboration on several aspects of the Freudian theory of dream (Colace & Boag, 2015a, 2015b). On dream bizarreness in relation to the Freudian model, see Colace, 2006a; Boag, 2006a, 2006b, 2017a, 2017b.
2   In my previous studies, I focused almost exclusively on this model, which has good margins of empirical controllability.
3   The effect of superegoic functions on dream distortion is affirmed elsewhere with regard to dreams in general (1916–17, p. 143).

4   The influence of education on dream forms was pointed out by Hug-Helmutth (pp. 148–149), who in his book states the following: "The child's dream expresses without disguise, and with appealing frankness, the wishes and longings which the day has left without fulfilment, and throws but the barest of cloaks over imagined experiences that reflect the sexual erotic tendencies which play so large a part in children's lives. The degree of complication introduced into the dream of this period accurately corresponds to the amount and effect of training which the child has received, with reference to the socially permissible and the socially forbidden. Even thus early the hidden forces at work within the mind begin their task of distorting the dream-desires, as they first frame themselves, so that the dream as it finally comes clearly to the dreamer's cognizance, may be in such a guise as to be acceptable to the rigid censorship of his own (half sleeping) consciousness, and still more to be able to withstand the criticism of his parents, to whom the child trustingly discloses the dream-experiences of the night. And more inclined those censors are to adopt a hostile attitude toward offensive-seeming dreams which express the child's interests in an all too undisguised (lit. = unveiled) fashion; or, again, the more intensive the efforts at repression which the child finds himself forced to make during his daily play, so much the stronger are the primary, wish-bearing thoughts with which the dream is obliged to deal, and so much the more concealing and distorting are the means taken to protect the wishes which, after all, the dreamer longs unconsciously to fulfil. The materials which the child finds in fairy-tales and weaves into his world of dreams serve simply to provide an outlet for the real wishes of the day, these are desires which he would fain transform into actual happenings, if this were permissible, without invoking this indirect mode of illustration".

5   A correlation between the raw scores of comprehension subtest-WPPSI and a measure of distortion in REM dreams was also found in Foulkes's classical study on children's dreams (Foulkes, 1982).

6   Other cognitive abilities seem influential on the possibility of producing dream bizarreness. In particular, the cognitive abilities involved in dream bizarreness seem to be those that concern its *process of production* (discrimination, symbolization, categorization, visuospatial ability) and its *expression/narration* (linguistic skills, verbal ability) (Colace, 2010). A recent study found that several correlations between cognitive skills and dream bizarreness are confounded by the age factor and proposed that such correlations are performed with age control (Sándor, Szakadát, & Bódizs, 2016). Probably the indications of Sandor et al. have a sense especially for those cognitive skills that are closely linked with neurocognitive development, whose course is closely connected with increasing age.

7   Some authors have suggested the existence of precursors of the superego (Ferenczi, 1925; Klein, 1932; Spitz, 1958) that are evident in the earlier manifestations of guilt and shame (see, for review, Frank, 1999; Laplanche & Pontalis, 1967).

8   The clinical implications of the study of children's dreams are many and deserve a separate volume.

References

Boag, S. (2006a). Freudian dream theory, dream bizarreness, and the disguise—Censor controversy. *Neuropsychoanalysis, 8* (1), 5–17.

Boag, S. (2006b). Freudian dream theory, dream bizarreness, and the disguise—Censor controversy. Response to commentaries. *Neuro-psychoanalysis, 8* (1), 59–68.

Boag, S. (2017a). On dreams and motivation: Comparison of Freud's and Hobson's views. *Frontiers in Psychology* (6 January) | https://doi.org/10.3389/fpsyg.2016.02001.

Boag, S. (2017b). *Metapsychology and the Foundations of Psychoanalysis.* New York: Routledge.

Colace, C. (1997). *I sogni dei bambini nella teoria psicodinamica: un contributo teorico e sperimentale* [*Children's Dreams in Psychodynamic Theory: A Theorical and Experimental Contribution*]. Unpublished Ph.D. Dissertation. Department of Psychology. University of Bologna, Italy.

Colace, C. (2006). Commentary on "Freudian dream theory, dream bizarreness, and the disguise-censor controversy (S. Boag)". *Neuro-Psychoanalysis, 8* (1), 24–27.

Colace, C. (2009). The study of bizarreness in young children's dreams: A way to test the disguise-censorship model. Poster presentation, 2009 International Congress of Neuropsychoanalysis, 26–29 June, Paris.

Colace, C. (2010). *Children's Dreams: From Freud's Observations to Modern Dream Research.* New York: Routledge.

Colace, C. (2012). Dream bizarreness and the controversy between the neurobiological approach and the disguise censorship model: The contribution of children's dreams. *Neuropsychoanalysis, 14* (2), 165–174.

Colace, C., & Boag, S. (2015a). Persisting myths surrounding Sigmund Freud's dream theory: A reply to Hobson's critique to scientific status of psychoanalysis. *Contemporary Psychoanalysis, 51* (1), 107–125.

Colace, C., & Boag, S. (2015b). The empirical study of infantile wish-fulfilment dreams. A reply to response of Allan J. Hobson. *Contemporary Psychoanalysis, 51* (1), 132–134.

Colace, C., & Violani, C. (1993). La bizzarria del sogno infantile come correlato della capacità di provare sensi di colpa. *Psichiatria dell'infanzia e dell'adolescenza, 60* (4–5), 367–376.

Colace, C., Violani, C., & Solano, L. (1993). La deformazione-bizzarria onirica nella teoria freudiana del sogno: indicazioni teoriche e verifica di due ipotesi di ricerca in un campione di 50 sogni di bambini. *Archivio di Psicologia, Neurologia e Psichiatria, 54* (3), 380–401.

Ferenczi, S. (1925). Psychoanalysis of sexual habits, J. L. Sottie (Trans.). In: J. Rickman (Ed.), *Further Contribution to the Theory and Technique of Psycho-Analysis* (pp. 259–297). London: Maresfield (1980).

Foulkes, D. (1982). *Children's Dreams, Longitudinal Studies.* New York: Wiley-Interscience Publication.

Frank, G. (1999). Freud's concept of the superego. Review and assessment. *Psychoanalytic Psychology, 16* (3), 448–463.

Freud, S. (1900). *The Interpretation of Dreams.* S.E., 4–5. London: Hogarth Press.

Freud, S. (1901). *On Dreams.* S.E. London and New York: Norton & Company, Inc.

Freud, S. (1910). *Five Lectures on Psycho-Analysis. Standard Edition, 11*, 3–55. London: Hogarth Press.

Freud, S. (1916–17). *Introductory Lectures on Psycho-Analysis. Standard Edition, 15* (16). London: Hogarth Press.

Freud, S. (1925). *An Autobiographical Study.* S.E., 20. pp. 3–70. London: Hogarth Press.

Klein, M. (1932). *The Psychoanalysis of Children.* London: Hogarth.

Laplanche, J., & Pontalis, J. B. (1967). *Vocabulaire de la psychanalyse.* Paris: Presses Universitaires de France.

Sándor, P., Szakadát, S., & Bódizs, R. (2016). The development of cognitive and emotional processing as reflected in children's dreams: Active self in an eventful dream signals better neuropsychological skills. *Dreaming, 26* (1), 58–78.

Spitz, R. (1958). On the genesis of superego components. *Psychoanalytic Study of the Child, XIII*, 375–404.

Part IV

Dreaming in middle childhood (ages 8 to 10)

Chapter 12

Changes in dream repertoire and developments in wish-fulfilment dreams at ages 8–10

In my previous studies, I focused on dreams from the age of 3 to the age of 8 and particularly on the most important changes that occur at around the ages of 5 and 6. This allowed me to find empirical confirmation to several observations by Freud, in particular about the role of simple wishes in triggering infantile dreams and the development of dream bizarreness (Colace, 2010, 2012, 2013).

In my study on Marco's dream reports, I tried to expand such observations and analyses to include the dreams between 8 and 10 years of age. There was no guarantee of success. In fact, I did not know if, and to what extent, the manifest content of dreams could still provide information about dreaming as it had happened for the dreams from the first period and partially for those from the second period. The basic question was, up to what age could the infantile module (that starts changing already at about 6–7) be extended?

Through the systematic study of the dreams between the ages of 8 and 10 in the perspective of the Freudian dream theory, I expected to be able to observe those changes (in content and form) that occur between the *late forms of infantile dreams and the stages preceding adult dreams as we know them*.[1]

Marco's dream repertoire from the third period

Between 8 and 10 years of age, Marco continued to have various wish-fulfilment dreams. What is striking about these dreams, however, is the *differences in the types of wishes* underlying the dreams. Indeed, several of these dreams are disguised (though still understandable) or distorted, or there is manifest timorous fulfilment of *disapproved* or *inadmissible* wishes. These wishes represent 54% of wish-fulfilment dreams. In part, such a difference had already appeared in the previous age range (6–7 years; see Figure 12.1).

The percentage of bad dreams in this period decreases, while that of *frankly bizarre dreams* remains stable compared to the previous period (6–7 years; see Table 12.1). However, the dream repertoire is in general more complex and bizarre due to the presence of several distorted wish-fulfilment dreams (see Table 12.1).

DOI: 10.4324/9781003184874-17

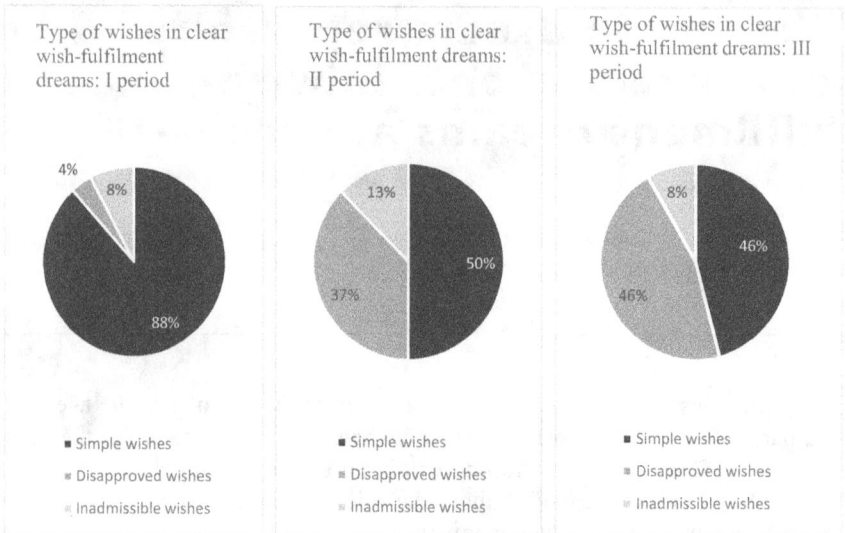

Figure 12.1 Types of wishes in clear wish-fulfilment dreams in the three observation periods

Table 12.1 Dream repertoire: types of dream reports by Marco between the ages of 8 and 10 years, 4 months

Bad dream and nightmares	20 (36%)
Bizarre dreams	20 (36%)*
Wish-fulfilment dreams	24 (43%)

*Bizarre dreams also include 8 bad dreams with several elements scarcely compatible and plausible compared to Marco's everyday experiences and/or less clearly associated with his everyday experiences.

Types of wishes underlying dreams and the forms of satisfaction in dream

Out of the 56 dream reports collected in this period, 24 (43%) contain the fulfilment of a wish in a fairly understandable way. However, by analyzing these dreams in detail, we observe that only 11 out of 24 (46%) concern the *clear* (undistorted) *fulfilment* of *simple daytime wishes*. These eleven dreams should be considered the only true residues of the early infantile dreaming module (see Table 12.2).

In the remaining part of wish-fulfilment dreams (*n* 13), *disapproved wishes* are predominant (*n* 11). These are wishes (known, conscious or preconscious) that the child may have tried to repudiate and suppress (often consciously) because they were disapproved by his parents. Due to parental opposition, the

Table 12.2 Examples of wishes in Marco's dream reports at the ages of 8–10

Simple wishes
I wish I were in the *Minecraft* PlayStation game environment.
I wish we went on the snow, like last year.
I wish I were fighting with my little friend and winning.
I wish I could remove a nagging stimulus and go on sleeping.

Disapproved wishes
I wish I owned a hoverboard.
I wish I could go to the beach later (when my friends are there).
I wish I had the PlayStation.
I wish I had the new version of Nintendo (Nintendo DS).

child must have learned to repress the fulfilment of these wishes, and yet they psychically survive in a latent state. As for the others, in one case, the dream was based on a *morally inadmissible wish* (i.e., in contrast with rules and moral/ethical principles, dream #5) and, in another one, on an explicit sexual wish (dream #10).[2]

In 9 of these latter dreams, the satisfaction of the disapproved wish, albeit identifiable, appears slightly disguised with some aspect of bizarreness. Thus, in some of these dreams, we may notice new forms of transformation that might be understood as a further development in the repertoire of dream-work operations.

In other 4 dreams, the satisfaction of a disapproved wish remains quite evident (i.e., undisguised), but with the presence—while reporting the dream—of unpleasant emotions such as fear and anxiety because of possibly disappointing the parents. In one of these (dream #10), there also was a sense of shame for the direct fulfilment of a sexual wish.

In all dreams, the fulfilment of wishes remains quite understandable, even if not as directly and clearly as in the dreams from the first period.

Infantile wish-fulfilment dreams as residues from the first period

Simple daytime wishes in dream

In the following dream report are some examples of wish-fulfilment dreams at the basis of which there are simple wishes. These dream reports are similar to the early forms of infantile dreams. See for instance the following dreams, where such similarity is evident:

M. 17(II)–8; 7.[3] *I dreamed of a* Minecraft *video game. I was walking in the game environment, then I don't remember well.*

In this dream Marco satisfies his wish to play his favourite video game, entering the very environment of the game. The dream report is very brief. Its content is centred on a video game in which Marco ends up superimposing fictional elements with elements of reality, as already observed in other children's dreams when the child is overexposed to watching TV (Colace, 2013; Colace, Dichiacchio, & Violani, 2006a, 2006b; see also: Stephan, Schredl, Henley-Einion, & Blagrove, 2012).

> M. 46(II)–9;9. *Dad, I dreamed that I was playing with* Disney Infinity, *and I had so much fun. I had many puppets* (characters)*. It was a beautiful dream. I was at home, and I had so much fun.*

Marco likes *Disney Infinity* a lot and he wanted me to buy it for him. In fact, a few days later, I bought it for him. This dream therefore appears as a classic *anticipation dream*. Considering that Marco was almost 10 when he reported this dream, we should consider this dream a true residue of infantile dreaming! However, it also possible to consider simple dreams like these as dream forms that survive, although as a minority, in the wish-fulfilment dream repertoire.

Frustrated primary needs in dreams

Among the wish-fulfilment dreams from this period there are also dreams such as the following one, concerning frustrated primary/vital needs.

> M. 35(II)–9;3. *I dreamed that you, Dad, came to my bed and cuddled me.*

Unfortunately, there had been a quarrel on the day before his dream. I had slept in a room by myself. My wife and Marco had slept in another bed. Marco had missed me. The dream directly satisfies Marco's need to have his father close to him. This is a classical infantile *compensation dream*. Here, too, a plain wish-fulfilment dream is based on a strong wish, in this case caused by the deprivation of paternal affection.

Fulfilment of the wish to cancel an annoying stimulus in sleep and continue sleeping through bizarre/comical representations

In the following dream, the wish to continue sleeping by removing an annoying stimulus coming from the recent state of wakefulness and that is protracted in sleep is fulfilled through the dreamlike staging of a *pleasant comical situation*. We have already observed this dream-work operation other times. In this dream it is at service of *the fulfilment of wish to continue sleep*, while in other cases, it is at service of dream censorship (see the following example, dream #10[II]). In this case, therefore, the bizarre aspect of the dream is to be attributed to dream distortion that is not of defensive origin.

M. 40(II)–9;4. *I was sleeping, and you suddenly came in front of the bed and started doing this: "What a taste, Santal! What a taste, Santal!"* (Marco laughed. It is a musical tune from an iced tea commercial, which Marco hummed.) *I was staring at you in the dream* (he stared at me)*, and I said to myself, "What the heck is he doing?"* (Marco laughed. Amused.) *You were near the bed* (Marco's bed).

Marco was the first to notice the bizarreness of his dream. He saw his father in front of him singing the tune from a commercial that Marco happened to see every day on TV, and he said, "It's annoying because they play it all the time". The dream was probably pleasant since Marco laughs, although he does not particularly like that tune. Here, too, we might have a dream that transforms an "annoying" stimulus into something pleasant and/or amusing. In his sleep, when the child is struck by the annoying and nagging stimulus, he wishes to put an end to it and *continue sleeping*, and the dream allows this by transforming that stimulus into something pleasant, preventing the child from waking up. We already know the mechanism through which this can take place, the "caricature effect". The dreamer makes fun of the actually annoying tune heard on TV by making his father sing it. The "comical/caricatural representation" is a type of dream-work operation that we have already observed other times. It may be neutral, as in this case—that is, not serve the purpose of censorship but rather the purpose of satisfying a wish to sleep (see Chapter 3, dream #32). This dream, and others like this, allow us to see clearly and directly the function of dreams as the "guardian of sleep". We know that in all dreams, the wish to continue sleeping plays an important role (Freud, 1900, p. 571), but in dreams of this kind, it appears as the main and only wish underlying the dream. The tune that bothers the child would surely have ended up waking him: through the comic processing of that stimulus, the dream allows him to go on sleeping. It should be noted that we are faced with a psychic stimulus that seems disturbing, like other physiological stimuli (e.g., thirst or the urge to urinate). Here, too, as we have seen with other wish-fulfilment dreams from this period (see dream #35[II], mentioned previously), there is a plain but *very strong wish* (i.e., to continue sleeping), which is able, alone, to trigger the dream.

Changes in wish-fulfilment dreams

In the dreams from this period that satisfy "disapproved" or (more rarely) "morally inadmissible" wishes, the dream distortion and the influence of censorship are as such that they still allow us to understand the latent contents of the dream and perceive the action of dream-work operations. This offers an extraordinary opportunity to observe how the dream acts on psychic material that is known to us, given our direct knowledge of the child. This is a more systematic and

objective condition than the observation of dream-work action on the unconscious latent dream material, which we know about via the interpretation of
adult dreams.

I am describing as follows, in *chronological order*, the various cases of wish-
fulfilment dreams engendered by different types of wishes, which is the reason
why major changes occur in the infantile module of dreaming.

Direct fulfilment of a disapproved wish (consciously rejected) with presence of fear

In the following dream, the fulfilment of the disapproved wish takes place directly
but with an *early form of fear of breaking the rules*.

> M. 2(II)–8;27. *I dreamed that I was at school with my Nintendo 3DS and I was
> playing a game . . . I said its name in the dream, but now I don't remember
> exactly which one it was. Next to me there were S, B. and C* (school friends). *It
> was a very nice dream.*

Marco owned the basic Nintendo DS console. Then he had been impressed
with the Nintendo 3DS (nicer and bigger) seen at a friend's home; he said
it was very cool. Marco had expressed his desire to have the new Nintendo
model years later (*long-time wish*), but it had never appeared in his dreams, and
although he asked for the 3DS several times, I never bought it for him. After
Marco finished reporting his dream, I asked him (already knowing the answer)
if he liked it; he replied *with a timorous and sad tone*, "I would have liked to
have the Nintendo 2DS or 3DS, but I never asked for it [consciously rejected
wish] because I already have the basic Nintendo and you, Dad, said no". This
form of *timorous verbalization* of the dream had already been observed in one
dream at 5 years and 8 months (see Chapter 8, dream #25). It should be noted
that we parents did not deny the fulfilment of the wish for contingent reasons,
such as the impossibility of buying that gaming console at the given time, but
rather for an in-principle prohibition concerning our will to convey the concept
of "appreciating what the child has at his disposal without asking for something else all the time". This means that this wish is in a state of repression or
at least that the child is trying to suppress it. This parental rule, interiorized
by the child, acts as a form of dream censorship where the open fulfilment of
the denied wish brings anxiety and fear, fear that is not expressed in the dream
setting (or at least there is no trace of it) but while reporting his dream to the
father. Later, however, it may be part of the dream experience—that is, it will
be interiorized, when the dream fulfills, in an undisguised way, a repressed
wish. This is also the case of "the authorization to proceed" that from external
(explicit request to the parents) may become internal—that is, the "authorizing parent" (the parents as dream characters who give permission, see dream
#04[II], as follows).

Fulfilment of two disapproved wishes in the same dream

In the following dream, *two* non-legitimate disapproved wishes contrary to parental dispositions are satisfied simultaneously. These are latent repressed wishes that appear to the dream in an open, still understandable (undisguised) way but that show a certain degree of implausibility with respect to the waking experience.

> M. 4(II)–8;3. *Mom went to the seaside and told me that I was supposed to stay at home with my grandfather and grandmother. And then, grandpa and I went to Game Stop* (a videogame store in Rome), *and he bought me* Dead Rising 3. *I was happy. It was a nice dream.*

A few days earlier, Marco had repeatedly expressed his wish to go to our holiday home at the seaside with his grandparents, meaning later than with us parents, because at the time we usually go there, none of his playmates would have arrived yet. *Dead Rising* is a PlayStation game that Marco had been asking for a long time. The two wishes in the dream are *satisfied in an open but implausible way compared to reality.* It is surprising that his mother would tell Marco to stay at home (exactly the opposite of what happens in reality); it is surprising that, straight in mid-August, Marco returned to Rome to go to the store to buy the video game. The daytime experiences can explain this bizarreness. Marco's wish to stay at home instead of going to the seaside, so he can play with the PlayStation, is a wish that his parents are definitely not pleased about. Marco knows this, and even in his hallucinatory satisfaction, he dares not satisfy his wish without his *mother's direct permission that is made to appear in the dream.* This dream-work operation, denominated as "*authorizing parent*", is the interiorization of something that in other previous dreams had taken place as an explicit request for approval to fulfil the wish asked to the parents during the state of wakefulness while the dream was being reported—that is, "*authorization to proceed*" (see dream #39 in Chapter 8). The "authorizing parent" is also present in the PlayStation dreams (#49 and #50, as follows). This means that, by staying at home, Marco can go with his grandfather to buy the video game, and this is the only way to get it because he knows that in reality, his parents would never buy it for him while his grandfather would. *With these two "tricks", the dream circumvents dream censorship to satisfy the two forbidden wishes.* The dream does everything to achieve the fulfilment of the wishes, pursues the goal in different ways and achieves it. This is a dream that gives evidence of a sort of cooperation between two wishes, where one serves the other. One wish alone would not have been enough to trigger the dream that therefore would not have found its hallucinatory fulfilment. In my opinion, this type of mechanism allows the finalized nature of dreaming to be understood as a significant psychic act, not at all random and/or secondary. We have seen this alliance also between the overdetermined dreams from the first period, but in that circumstance, the wishes were simple wishes. On the other hand, the same mechanism is known in adult dreams, where simple daytime wishes may be joined by unconscious wishes in instigating dreams.

Fulfilment (with bizarre aspects) of a wish somewhat in conflict with "moral" principles

The wishes that we have called "disapproved" are those that are against parental dispositions, based on various principles—for example, refusing to buy something because it is considered harmful for the child's health (e.g., the hoverboard, too many sweets, too much playing with videogames) or simply common rules of life, not necessarily on a strictly moral level.

In the following dream report, Marco expresses a "morally" inappropriate wish (betray his mother's love for him).

> M. 5(II)–8;4. *I was on vacation in France* (at a hotel that is not the one we actually stayed in), *and they were doing shows at the hotel. (I was alone. Mom and Dad weren't there.) Then, when I got back, I went to dinner with my class-mates. Then when we went for a walk, C. put her hand into mine* (while he says this, he lowers his voice and appears a little timorous, embarrassed), *and we walked hand in hand, so we were at the beach, by night (not at the Circeo, it was another beach) and it was night, me and C. hand in hand* (C. is Marco's little girlfriend). *You were in the dinghy with N. and G.* (Marco's friends), *and that's it. You had your dresses on. It was a very strange dream* (he laughs), *and so in the middle of the sea, there were plenty of jellyfishes, lots of them. Then there was a gypsy woman next to us with an ugly face, and she kidnapped us (me and C.). However, I managed to break free, and yet I did not have the courage to run away, because then I was afraid that she would kidnap me again. And then C. broke free by herself and we were coming to you, swimming, dressed. I was afraid because the water was VERY deep, and there were all the jellyfishes, and I was so scared, you see! And then when we got on the dinghy, the dream ended.*

Marco showed some resistance in reporting the dream to his mother but agreed to tell it to his father privately. Just before reporting his dream, Marco seemed a little ashamed and asked me to promise that I would not tell the dream to anyone, especially his mother. I asked Marco why he did not want to tell this dream at first, and he replied, "Because *I was ashamed to tell it to you*" (in a low tone). "Because you were hand in hand with C.?" "Yes. It is the most beautiful dream of my life [said enthusiastically], because I was hand in hand with C [his girlfriend]" (on resistance in reporting dreams with sexual themes, see also dream #10, as follows).

Marco was recently turned down by a young girl he had a crush on, during the summer holidays at the beach. Yet the dream satisfies a *long-time repressed wish* of Marco regarding his girlfriend of all time (C.), by whom he was turned down several times (*wish A*). Then there is also a reference to a recent vacation in France and the presence of the (unresolved) wish (*wish B*), actually expressed on that occasion as going to another hotel because he did not like the one where we were staying (it was actually a poor hotel). In the dream, the fulfilment of the second wish occurs by transposing the situation of the new hotel into another context, a context for the use of the first long-time wish. In fact, in the dream, at least initially, Marco is on holiday by himself, without his parents but with his classmates.

In this dream, the daytime references, although direct, are processed in the dream in a complex way. They appear to be sporadic elements that act as "detonators" of other motivational drives, fortunately identifiable and understandable thanks to the direct knowledge of the child and of his daytime experiences. So, having been turned down by the girl he had a crush on (within the beach holiday setting) becomes the trigger for satisfying his wish to walk hand in hand with his long-time girlfriend (C.). The disappointment about the hotel in France that he disliked becomes the trigger for the wish to go to a different, nicer hotel with evening shows and, to top it off, together with all his schoolmates! With respect to the theme of engagement, curiously enough, we observe that the dream acts as compensation, but unlike in early infantile compensation dreams, it changes the object of the wish, inserting another that is similar thematically but even more daring in its realization. The non-fulfilment of a daytime wish (getting to know a girl who actually turned him down) activates a *repressed long-time wish* (thematically linked to this one), which then finds fulfilment in the dream. In this way, the dream can act by allowing the fulfilment of a repressed wish and the discharge of unresolved past affective situations.

The dream presents various bizarre aspects (wearing dresses while in the water, the presence of a gypsy) and considerable complexity, so much so that Marco himself said that it was a strange dream. However, some elements in dream seem explicable. The presence of the gypsy, whom Marco had actually seen in reality, seems, on the one hand, a way to represent plastically Marco's anxiety about going hand in hand with his girlfriend and thus "betraying" somehow his exclusive love for his mother (the reason for repression); on the other hand, it gives the dream that scary and adventurous tone that makes his going out with his girlfriend more compelling (in the end, they manage to free themselves).

This dream was activated, but *only indirectly*, by recent unsatisfied daytime wishes (meeting the young girl at the beach, changing hotels). These wishes act as activators of another, much stronger wish (i.e., the real psychic substance of the dream), the only one capable of *directly* instigating the dream (i.e., walking hand in hand with his long-time girlfriend). The dream builds a scenario where: (a) a long-time wish is satisfied; (b) the hotel changes (functional to a school trip in which Marco can satisfy his past wish); and (c) affective discharge is allowed (thematically similar to the affective state of a past wish or the displeasure of being turned down by the girl in the recent daytime experience).

Disguised fulfilment of wishes against the rules, supported by the fulfilment of a sexual wish through comic/grotesque representation

A bizarre dream that is seemingly inspired by an explicitly sexual wish is the one subsequently mentioned, which Marco asked to report *only to the father*:

> M. 10(II)–8;4. *I had a ridiculous dream last night.* (Then he said that he wanted to tell it only to me). *We were in the Oviesse* (a department store)*, and we were waiting in front of the changing rooms. They were all occupied, and then that red-haired actress came and asked if there was a changing room available. You, Dad, told her that there was not, and she undressed and changed her clothes right there in front of us!* (Marco said that she was laughing in the dream.) *She is the Tuscan comic actress with big breasts who stars in Leonardo Pieraccioni's film* Una moglie Bellissima.

Oviesse is a department store we go to often. The day before the dream, we had not gone there, but Marco probably felt that he would soon have to go there to buy some overalls, and he usually dislikes going shopping, but his parents expected him to come. What takes place in this dream is a *comic/grotesque representation* that allows the fulfilment of two desires—the first is "to avoid going to the store" and the second, of a sexual nature, "to see the woman with big breasts". The dream stages a pleasant and improbable situation that converts a disliked place (the store) into a pleasant one. This transformation can take place thanks to the fact that the first disapproved desire (not to go to the store) is overcome thanks to its alliance with another (repressed) sexual wish. Yet the latter wish, too, in order to be satisfied, must undergo some partial transformation, assuming a grotesque tone. Furthermore, the fulfilment of this second wish causes *some resistance in reporting the dream*— that is, he is ashamed (Marco will only tell it to his father!). The fulfilment of this second wish establishes the condition (meeting the object of desire) through which one "accepts" to go to the store. It is as if the desire not to go to the store were also partially satisfied: "I'm going there, but only because I have a valid reason for it".

This dream-work mechanism—*accepting to do an unwelcome thing as long as it is mitigated by another pleasant one*—is the same observed in the dream of the grandfather who replaces the math teacher (see dream #21 as follows) and in the dream of returning to kindergarten (see Chapter 8, #52), where Marco accepts to be ordered to do something as long as it is his kindergarten teacher (his favourite teacher) who gives the order.

Disguised fulfilment of wishes against the rules, supported by the fulfilment of a simple daytime wish

Similarly to the case described previously, the dream that follows a disapproved wish finds fulfilment through the fulfilment of another wish. However, unlike in the previous dream, here the wish that allies with the disapproved wish is *simple* (although very strong on a motivational level).

M. 21(II)–8;10. *Grandpa Salvatore was my substitute teacher, then another teacher was to arrive so Grandpa had to leave because his lesson was over, and I started crying because I wanted to stay with my grandfather.*

"But did you know that he was your grandfather or did you think he was a real teacher?" "No, I knew he was grandpa. In fact I hugged him." "Was it a good or bad dream?" "A very nice one."

"What kind of teacher was he?" "I think he was a math teacher. The school was my usual one. My friends were there, but I don't remember who in particular. We had to be divided (they had to take us to another class)."

In this dream, Marco seems to solve his school anxiety by making his beloved grandfather become his math teacher (math being the subject that worries him most). It is a *person replacement* with the purpose of relieving anxiety. A character appears in the dream, the grandfather, who "understands and resolves" and who takes "the place of" and acts "in place of". The same mechanism had been observed in a previous dream Marco had (i.e., the dream of returning to kindergarten, #52) where his beloved kindergarten teacher replaced the less permissive elementary school teacher, which made Marco's compliance with the command to sit down more bearable. *It is unconscious dream-work operation.* On the previous day, Marco and I had gone to his grandfather's house, but he was unexpectedly not at home. Marco was very disappointed with this because he had hoped to meet him. After reporting his dream, Marco cried, recalling the experience of the day before. *His tears, however, appeared disproportionate compared to what happened*; in fact, Marco had seen his grandfather just a few days earlier. It was as if Marco was crying for other reasons: in fact, *his crying was actually related to not wanting to go back to school on Monday.* We should consider the fact that the dream was told on a Sunday morning. Marco felt discomfort about going back to school on Mondays and *was often reprimanded by his parents for his constant complaining* (i.e., the motive for which the wish is subject to repression). Marco tried to "solve" this problem by making his grandfather a substitute teacher. Some dreams like this are evidence of person replacement *(desplacement)* dream-work operation. To Marco's eyes, his grandfather is the one who solves problems, the one who in the end makes him happy in reality (more than his parents, experienced as less permissive). The latent idea of the dream is, "If Grandpa is my teacher, it will be easier for me to go back to school tomorrow". My impression that the crying was not disproportionate was correct. In fact, it was not related to his grandfather's absence but rather to having to go to back to school. The grandfather represents in a plastic way (consideration for representability) the need to be reassured. But in order to understand this dream, in addition to knowing Marco's daytime experiences, I had to resort to interpretation. Although Marco is aware in his dream that it is really his grandfather who is acting as teacher, we are faced here with an unconscious disguise—that is, automatic substitution/replacement of someone—which appeared clear to me only thanks to my knowledge of the child. Furthermore, in this dream, it is quite evident that we arrived at a meaning and a real content of the dream that do not coincide at all with its manifest content; therefore, we should resort to the concept of *latent content*. In this dream, an alliance of two wishes in instigating it can be detected. In particular, in this dream, an *unresolved simple daytime wish* ("I wish I could see Grandfather again!") gives way to the *unconscious repressed wish* ("I wish I could overcome my anxiety about school!" or "I wish I didn't have to go to school tomorrow!"); the real *latent motivational force of the dream* is settled through a bizarre compromise: "Okay, I accept going to school, but as long Grandfather is there as my teacher. In this way both wishes are fulfilled. It is quite likely that the *simple daytime wish* alone would not have been able to trigger the dream without allying itself with the *repressed wish*, far more powerful in terms of dream-instigating ability.

Repressed (long-time) wish at the basis of a serial dreams

In the following dreams, the child's deep-rooted (long-time) wishes appear. These wishes are so strong that they give rise to *serial dreams*—that is, several dreams united by the fact that they deal with the same wish. These are hardly achievable wishes, with high level of interest. For example, in the following dream we are faced with Marco's long-time wish to have a little brother or sister, for which Marco's parents had repeatedly said that it would have been hard to realize. It is a wish that is somehow hindered by the parents because it is repeated with insistence.

> M. 24(II)–8;11. *I dreamed that I had a little sister. I held her in my arms and hugged her and kissed her. It was a beautiful dream. But then I woke up and realized it wasn't true and I'm sad* (Marco was sad while telling his dream).

The wish to have a brother or sister was expressed several times in real life. With Marco's great regret and disappointment (and that of his parents too!), this wish could not be satisfied due to objective impossibilities, and the reasons were explained to Marco. He often sadly says that he is unfortunate for not being able to have a little brother or sister. *Marco sometimes even got scolded for his insistent requests.* This wish has the power to trigger dreams as a "long-time wish" and, at the same time, probably because it is *a wish that is repressed or subject to repression attempts.* The child had to learn to reject it as impossible. Serial wish-fulfilment dreams like this one testify that the drives of certain strong wishes are only seemingly exhausted and are ready to get reactivated at any moment (see dream #47[II] at 9 years, 11 months, as follows).

In another dream from the same period, Marco had expressed *the same wish* in direct form, accompanied by anguish:

M. 13(II)–8;6. *You* (Dad) *were in the car and you were driving, and Mom was sitting in the back with me. And you had my little brother by your side, and then you gave it to Mom. My little brother wanted Mom, and then Mom gave it to me. I held him in my arms, gave him caresses and then gave him kisses, and then it ended like this (sad).* Was it a beautiful dream? *Yes.* And then he adds sadly, *I can't have a little brother!*

Testimonies of long-time wishes like this that reappear one or more years later were also found in a previous study (Colace, 2010).[4]

As we have seen, *simple wishes* can trigger serial dreams about the same desire already in the first period. So it is not surprising that *repressed wishes* (far more powerful than simple ones) can also trigger this type of dream. When a wish gives life to serial dreams it means that we are faced with a very strong wish, which does not exhaust its wishful impulse through hallucinatory fulfilment in a single dream. *The seriality of these dreams testifies the strength of the wishes that have instigated them.* Serial dreams now refer to wishes that have become "historical" ' and are *deeply rooted* in the child, and over time, they have increased their motivational demands instead of fading.

In the following example, we observe serial dreams based on unresolved wishes that are strong because they are opposed by the parents and subject to repression. When I use the term "repressed", I mean a wish that the child has tried to repress at least once or knows he must do so because the wish cannot be satisfied (in real life).

M. 49(II)–10;4, *I dreamed you were giving me back the PlayStation.*

Marco had been punished, and both his PlayStation and his smartphone had been taken away. The next day, he reported another dream on the same theme:

M. 50(II)–10;4. *I dreamed that you gave me back the PlayStation, and in addition, you gave me a new game.*

In this case, there is a further element which acts for dream instigation: in addition to the strength of the wish to have the PlayStation back, *there is a second wish* that needs to be repressed as it is contrary to his parents' will (i.e., *to have a new game*), which makes the dream even more overdetermined on the motivational level. It should be noted that in both dreams, the disapproved wishes are satisfied in an open way and without anguish. However, in both dreams, there is some distortion of what happened in reality: the wish denied in the daytime becomes "authorized" in the dream (by the father himself). This gives the dream a strange and implausible aspect compared to the waking experience. There is therefore a distortion—that is, a dream-work operation defined as "authorizing parent", and the full meaning of the dream is understood only thanks to the direct knowledge of the child and of his waking experiences.

The following is example of a serial dream, an expression of a deeply rooted long-time wish like the ones reported previously. I take this one as an example because it shows again, very clearly, the dream mechanism of the "authorizing parent".

> Marco 33(II)–9;m. *You had bought me a hoverboard and I went out riding it* every day. *It was a very nice dream.*

Again, this is an extremely strong wish. The (disapproved) wish of owning a hoverboard may have been consciously repressed at least once, then it was probably repeated automatically without him having clear awareness of it. This long-time wish had been *actualized* (see Chapter 5) two days before since Marco had used the hoverboard of a friend. In this dream, we also observe the *exaggeration* (every day!) that is typical of infantile dreams.[5]

In this dream, Marco represents his father in the dream scenario, who (finally!) buys him the hoverboard. In reality, I am against buying this object because I think it's very dangerous, although Marco continues to hope that one day I will be convinced to buy one. In this dream, not only does the father give permission, but he himself buys the hoverboard, producing the total overturning of parental will compared to reality. Through this transformation, therefore, what is forbidden becomes authorized by the same person. The parent himself is a *permissive dream censor* who opens the doors of censorship to the satisfaction of the wish.[6] In this way, the wish becomes magically legitimate and can be directly satisfied. The dream, as a whole, takes an implausible aspect compared to reality.

I am reporting as follows the first dream of the "hoverboard" series that Marco had about a month earlier:

> M. 27(II)–9;1. *I dreamed that a gentleman* (whom I did not know) *had bought me a hoverboard with all the accessories. This gentleman was the owner* (the "fat and bald" one) *of the restaurant where we had gone for dinner the night before. It was a beautiful dream.*

This is a dream where the fulfilment of wish appears together with other bizarre aspects. Marco's wish to own the hoverboard, reaffirmed in the state of wakefulness on the occasion of his upcoming birthday, is completely fulfilled by a man he had seen the night before at a restaurant. The bizarre element of the dream—that is, the character from the restaurant—requires a principle of interpretation because it is behind the nature of the associations that Marco would make with respect to this character that could be described even better in the dream. Note the variation in the "authorizing parent" theme with respect to the other dream.

In this dream, Marco dares not receive approval from his father: an unknown adult character appears. And yet, the concept of authorization requires someone to embody it for the *consideration of representability*. In this dream, we also note the reappearance of the mechanism of *exaggeration* already observed in Marco's infantile dreams: Marco is not content with obtaining the hoverboard but also gets all the related accessories.

Fulfilment of a forbidden repressed wish in moderate form

In the following dream we observe the satisfaction *in moderate form* of a disapproved wish.

> Marco 32(II)–9;1. *I went shopping with my friends and bought pudding. Mom was there too. I asked you if I could buy a giant box of pudding, and then I asked you for a box of three and you said yes.* (Marco says that this dream was very nice because his mother bought him pudding.)

In the immediately preceding days, his mother hadn't bought him any more pudding because he had been eating too much of it, and Marco was very sorry about this. In his dream, Marco satisfies a forbidden suppressed wish. In order for this to happen in the dream, the mother appears to approve (the "authorizing parent" dream-work operation), making legitimate a wish otherwise denied. *The dream loses some plausibility with respect to the daytime experience, even if it maintains a direct and understandable reference to it*. The wish to have pudding is a wish inherent to basic needs (hunger), which are also at the basis of certain *infantile dreams of adults*. It is therefore a wish with a very strong dream-triggering force. An interesting aspect of this dream is the shift from an exaggeration (a giant box of pudding), a typical feature of certain infantile dreams, to an *accepted and unexpected (bizarre, implausible) moderation* regarding the *quantity* of the desired food (a box of three pieces of pudding). As we have observed, exaggeration is present in infantile dreams from the first period (although we continue to have some evidence even in this period, as mentioned previously) and is plausibly an expression of the *primary process* (Freud, 1900). Vice versa, *moderation is presumably the sign of the activity of rational thought (secondary process)*, which in this case also serves as dream censorship (the numerical definition of quantity is also an expression of thought). Here the mechanism that allows the resolution of the conflict is a sort of "be content with what you have". Incidentally, here we have another example of how, by examining the dreams at this stage of development (4–8 years), we may have indications not only on the development of the ego and superego but also on the evolution of the general modes of mental functioning (i.e., primary vs. secondary processes). We are close to the thoughts of David Foulkes when he affirmed that, from a cognitive point of view, the dream offers a way to investigate the mental functioning of the child (Foulkes, 1982, 1999). However, when we talk about mental functioning, we must consider, beyond the cognitive aspects, also the unconscious dynamic aspects of mental functioning, which the dream allows us to observe in this age period even without resorting to classic dream interpretation.

Fulfilment of disapproved wish with a symbolic allusive satisfaction

In the following dream, we can recognize the mechanism of *displacement*. Marco fulfils his repressed desire that his parents give him a little brother or sister by limiting himself to an allusion.

> M. 47(II)–9;11. *I had dreamed that the turtles had had hatchlings. One was very tiny, and another one was the same size as them. We had a big fish tank (a separate tank) that was next to that of the turtles, and the fishes wanted to eat them all. Then a fish jumped as it wanted to eat the turtles, and I caught it and tried to kill it. I caught it even though it bit me. It was a beautiful dream because my turtles had hatchlings.*

The day before, Marco said that he had seen the turtles and that he wished they had hatchlings because he thought they were beautiful. The desire makes a direct allusion to his repressed long-time wish "that his parents may soon give him a little brother or sister" (see the previously mentioned dreams #24[II] and #13[II]). In this dream, the use of the dream-work mechanism of displacement is evident: if I cannot directly express the wish that my parents have another child (so that I can have a brother), I can allude to it by transposing this wish to the turtles.

Changes in the modi operandi of wish-fulfilment dreams

We have observed that wish-fulfilment dreams are broken down into at least 4 types: *compensation, continuation, anticipation, mixed.* While we did not notice any material difference in the distribution of these various types in the first period and we saw *continuation dreams* almost disappear in the second, in the wish-fulfilment dreams of this period, we may confirm the scarce presence of *continuation dreams* (13%) but also the *disappearance of anticipation dreams* (4%), while *compensation dreams* prevail (83%).

We have defined as continuation dreams those dreams that refer to an experience in which the wish object of the dream itself finds *partial* satisfaction during the daytime; hence, the dream continues and/or repeats a pleasant experience that in any case had started to be fulfilled already in the waking experience. In other words, we are faced with a waking experience of partial dissatisfaction. Probably the wish object of this experience has less motivational force compared to the totally unfulfilled wishes that are at the basis of *compensation* and *anticipation* dreams. The latter, in fact, relate to a daytime experience of the non-satisfaction of a wish, an experience that is unpleasant. This suggests that *at the basis of the wish-fulfilment dreams from this period, there are mostly wishes that in the daytime have remained totally unsatisfied* and are therefore stronger in terms of motivational force. Indeed, we are faced with the fact that most of them are repressed wishes which cannot be satisfied in the reality of the daytime experience. However, we can also assume that the wishes at the basis of *compensation dreams are stronger in their ability to trigger dreams than those at the basis of anticipation dreams.* Probably in this latter case, the older child learns to desist from the hallucinatory fulfilment of a desire whose gratification will come true in reality, and he has only to wait for it. If this interpretation is correct, the scarce presence of anticipation dreams is in line with Freud's claim that older children and adults try to postpone the fulfilment of the wish through the progressive domain of thought over the simpler wishful impulses, finding gratification by changing the external reality rather than in the dream experience (see previous chapter).

Now we fully understand the difference and the usefulness of distinguishing wish-fulfilment dreams into compensation, continuation and anticipation dreams. These categories of dreams give us direct information about the strength of the wishes that instigated them.

The strength of wishes and the triggering of dreams

The common element in the wish-fulfilment dreams from this period is the *greater strength of the underlying wishes.* Indeed, several of these are strong *repressed wishes*, and the simple wishes are frequently those that were *fully unsatisfied* in the daytime experience.

Certain hints of this trend were also noticed in the wish-fulfilment dreams from the second period, but the change becomes even clearer here.

We know that Freud "classified" wishes according to their "capacity for instigating dreams" (Freud, 1900, p. 552). In order to start a dream, a certain minimum wishful request, or motive force, is necessary (Freud, 1900, pp. 560–561). In adults, only unconscious wishes have the highest degree of ability to trigger dreams. In Chapter 8, we suggested that by studying dreams in the developmental age, we may access a *range of wishes* with different levels of this dream-triggering ability.

The ability of a wish to trigger dreams probably resides in its greater strength, intended as the ability to arouse interest in the subject and to activate a motivated and finalized psychic process with a specific task and meaning. In older children and in adults, the wish must be a stronger one compared to those of younger children. At the basis of infantile dreams, there are very simple and common wishes capable of triggering dreams; in older children, there are stronger wishes that are repressed or subject to repression; and in adults, there are strong and unconsciously repressed wishes. We have also repeatedly observed in Marco's dreams that the *dreaming process* and *dream work* tends to be an opportunistic way *to seek allies* (other wishes) in order to trigger the dream as well as in order to find *mutual support* to find gratification.

Daytime sources

Dreams about simple daytime wishes

Direct vs. vague connection

In simple wish-fulfilment dreams, the connection to daytime experiences often remains direct and understandable (8/11). Only in three dreams is there a vague/uncertain connection.

Affective states

In these dreams, the affective states related to excitement/contentment prevail (not sufficiently elaborated in wakefulness), and impatience and disappointment scarcely appear.

Time distance

Most of these dreams have a direct reference to the *previous day* (6/11); however, for others the temporal distance of the diurnal residues is more uncertain (5/11).

Dream with disapproved or inadmissible wish

Direct vs. vague connection

In dreams relating to the fulfilment of disapproved or inadmissible desires, despite the action of deformation, the comprehensibility of the dream remains quite good, and also thanks to the direct knowledge of the child's wishes, the connection with the waking experiences remains fairly direct and clear. Only in two of these dreams is the understanding of the dream reached through an "interpretation", and for another dream, the connection remains uncertain and the meaning hard to understand.

Affective states

Unlike in dreams relating to the fulfilment of simple wishes, we observe that in these dreams, the affective states of wakefulness associated with wishes are all oriented towards the negative pole—for example, *disappointment, regret, sadness.*

Time distance

The connection with daytime experiences remains, in many cases, clearly the *previous day* (7/13); in two dreams, it seems to go back to a couple of days, and in another to a week. In the other three dreams, the temporal distance is uncertain.

Notes

1   Freud focused on the earliest forms of direct wish fulfilment and the early appearance of disguised dreams in young children until about 8 years of age—that is, his son Martin at the age of 8 and of his daughter Mathilde at the age of 8 years and 6 months (Freud, 1900, 1901; see Colace, 2010, pp. 13–14 for details).
2   It is important to note that also in this period, as in the previous ones, among the repressed desires (still recognizable in the dream), those forbidden for unethical and/or moral reasons are prevalent. The forbidden desires, unacceptable on the ethical/moral level, have been difficult to identify in the various periods. I believe the reason for this is that these kinds of desires are more effectively subjected to the work of distortion defense and are likely to underlie those dreams that we have not been able to understand.
3   The number in parentheses indicates that the dream belongs to the second collection.
4   Evidence of very strong wishes (with a strong motivational drive) that are repeated years later in dreams are also derived from certain types of infantile dreams in adults (see Chapter 16).
5   We have seen previously that exaggeration is also in the service of the effective gratification of wish.
6   As Boag (2006) pointed out, Laplanche and Pontalis (1973) suggest that a *permissive aspect* is present in the Freudian concept of dream censorship. Indeed, the term "censoring agency" "implies an authority judging what is or is not permissible" (Laplanche & Pontalis, 1973, p. 16). That is, Freud's analogy of "watchman" (Freud, 1916–17, p. 295), as underlined by Boag, implies the function of "allowing or prohibiting" Boag (2006, p. 7).

References

Boag, S. (2006). Freudian dream theory, dream bizarreness, and the disguise—Censor controversy. *Neuropsychoanalysis, 8* (1), 5–17.

Colace, C. (2010). *Children's Dreams: From Freud's Observations to Modern Dream Research*. New York: Routledge.

Colace, C. (2012). Dream bizarreness and the controversy between the neurobiological approach and the disguise censorship model: The contribution of children's dreams. *Neuropsychoanalysis, 14* (2), 165–174.

Colace, C. (2013). Are wish-fulfilment dreams of children the royal road for looking at the functions of dreams? *Neuropsychoanalysis, 15* (2), 161–175.

Colace, C., Dichiacchio, C., & Violani, C. (2006a). Effects of television viewing on sleep habits and dream contents in children at ages 3–8. *Sleep, 29* (1035), A354–A355.

Colace, C., Dichiacchio, C., & Violani, C. (2006b). Effetti della televisione della TV sul sonno e sognare nei bambini dai 3 agli 8 anni di età. *Psichiatria dell'Infanzia e dell'adolescenza, 73*, 31–40.

Foulkes, D. (1982). *Children's Dreams, Longitudinal Studies*. New York: Wiley-Interscience Publication.

Foulkes, D. (1999). *Children's Dreaming and the Development of Consciousness*. Cambridge and London: Harvard University Press.

Freud, S. (1900). *The Interpretation of Dreams*. S.E., 4–5. London: Hogarth Press.

Freud, S. (1901). *On Dreams*. S.E., 5. London and New York: Norton & Company, Inc.

Freud, S. (1916–1917). *Introductory Lectures on Psycho-Analysis*. S.E., 15/16. London: Hogarth Press.

Laplanche, J., & Pontalis, J.-B. (1973). *The Language of Psychoanalysis*. London: Karnac.

Stephan, J., Schredl, M., Henley-Einion, J., & Blagrove, M. (2012). TV viewing and dreaming in children: The UK library study. *International Journal of Dream Research, 5* (2), 130–133.

Chapter 13

Dream distortion and new dream-work operations

Introduction

In the previous chapter, we analyzed dreams in which an indirect but still recognizable satisfaction of the repressed wishes occurs. These dreams allow a close analysis of *dream-work operations* as well as the action of *dream censorship*, which determines the defensive distortion of the dream and its bizarreness. In this chapter, I return to these dreams by attempting an in-depth and systematic description dream-work operations and dream distortion.

Several examples of *frankly bizarre dreams* from this period allow us the observation on a phenomenological level a variety of bizarreness that I report here a in systematic way.

Dream-work operations and dream-censorship activity

The direct knowledge of the child and of his waking experiences allowed for reasonably certain knowledge of the (repressed) desires underlying his dreams, even when they do not appear directly in their manifest content, and hence to observe how dream-work operations have acted. There is a material difference compared to adult dreams, because in the latter, we come to understand how dream-work operations have affected the latent material of the dream only after identifying such material indirectly, through the patient's free associations. In a nutshell, I would say that in children's dreams, the observation of the material starts *from the bottom*, *a priori*, of which the researcher has *certain and direct knowledge*, while in adult dreams, the researcher makes *a posteriori* observations of material identified through reconstruction. I am presenting as follows a systematic description of the dream-work operations that emerged clearly in Marco's dreams.

In the dreams from this period, there is still *exaggeration*, an operation that once again seems to be at the service of a better and more complete fulfilment of the wish. For example, in the hoverboard dream (#27[II]), Marco is not content with obtaining the hoverboard (that he would love but that his parents won't buy); he also gets all the related accessories. In the dream about the "holiday in France"

DOI: 10.4324/9781003184874-18

(dream #05[II]), this same operation gives a more adventurous and reckless tone to the entire dream, with "very deep water" and "so much fear" serving the desire, making the actions of the dream protagonist who saves his loved ones even more heroic and fulfilling.

That same dream (dream #05[II]) also shows *considerations of representability*. We see that the presence of the gypsy, apparently completely out of context with respect to the dream, lends itself well to represent Marco's emotions (i.e., fear, emotional arousal) while going hand in hand with his girlfriend and gives the dream a scary and adventurous tone that makes his going out with his girlfriend more compelling (in the end, they manage to free themselves).

In other dreams, the *strategic alliance between desires* serves the purpose of *bypassing dream censorship*. A disapproved wish may find undisturbed fulfilment by relying on the fulfilment of a simple desire that dominates the dream, apparently becoming its central theme and thus misleading about the true (latent) meaning of the dream. So in the dream where the grandfather replaces the math teacher (dream #21[II]), what might seem to be the fulfilment of a simple desire ("seeing Grandpa again") hides another repressed desire, much more powerful in terms of dream triggering and yet that cannot be expressed openly ("not wanting to go to school"). By the same mechanism, in the dream of the clothing store (#10[II]) Marco satisfies a repressed desire (not wanting to go to the store as his parents would like him to do), this time relying on an explicit, rewarding sexual desire (although expressed in a comic and grotesque representation) in the dream that can be confessed only to his father. In the former case, there is an improbable *character substitution* (the grandfather takes the place of the maths teacher), and yet the repressed desire manages to find its way and survive the censorship action through the evidently *disproportionate crying* that is unconsciously linked to the other desire—that is, not wanting to go back to school (which is obviously impossible in reality) and therefore inadequate and unusual compared to the manifest desire expressed by the dream (*affective displacement*). In this case, we may assume that the manifestation of affection with desperate tears tied to the repressed desire (not wanting to go back to school), detached from the representation and was transferred to another—permitted—plain desire (crying for not wanting to leave Grandfather).[1]

In the latter case (#10[II]), the dream turns into a pleasant place that the child usually hates by allowing the satisfaction of a sexual desire of the child—that is, watching the striptease of an actress he likes (the dream stages a comic and surreal representation). This operation is at the service of censorship that demanded the indirect satisfaction of repressed desires.

We can also speak of *displacement* in the turtle dream (#47[II]) where Marco's (repressed) desire that his parents have a child (and therefore to have a little brother and/or sister) is realized by transferring such desire to his turtles.

Another example where the *alliance between different desires* helps in circumventing dream censorship appears in dream #4(II) (the beach dream). Here, the fulfilment of a repressed desire—to stay home and go to the beach only afterwards, when all the friends are there—allow the fulfilment of a second (denied) desire, to buy more PlayStation games. By staying at home without his parents, Marco succeeds in obtaining those games from his more permissive grandfather.

Dream-work operations are generally focused on *opportunism* and *compromise*. Their duty is to try and fulfil wishes, a task to pursue by all means. The dream does everything to achieve wish fulfilment: it pursues such goals in various ways and achieves it. This dream gives evidence of a sort of cooperation between two wishes, where one serves the other. The same cooperation between desires is the only condition that permits the instigation of the dream, and it is another reason why it is sought. One wish alone would not have been enough to trigger the dream that therefore would not have found its hallucinatory fulfilment. In my opinion, this mechanism allows the nature of dreaming to be understood as a meaningful psychic act, not at all random and/or secondary.

The most repressed desires are ready to make their way as soon as the opportunity presents itself. The child (dream #4-II) is permitted to stay at home directly by his parents, and since they are seaside, he seizes the opportunity to have Grandpa buy him the video games that his parents won't buy. In this way, he satisfies two repressed wishes in a completely legitimate way—a true psychic performance that comes at the expense of the *apparent nonsense* of the dream.

The dream-work operations of displacement and alliance between wishes often give dreams a bizarre aspect. In dreams like these (#10, #21, #4), the need to resort to the concept of *latent dream content* is quite evident. Such latent content is understood thanks to the direct knowledge of the child's "hidden" wishes and of the child himself. We can see, however, that the child would have confessed these wishes if questioned more insistently, without resorting to free associations. In other words, we are faced with repressed wishes that can be detected in some way and that for this reason are *not exactly unconscious*, or at least not in the sense by which we intend this term for the unconscious desires at the basis of adult dreams.

I also find particularly interesting the dream-work operation of the "*authorizing parent*" in the attempted satisfaction of wishes that the child knows he is expected to repress (see for example in Chapter 12 dreams #4[II], #32[II], #49[II] and #50[II]). This is the "authorization to proceed", in a fulfilment of a disapproved wish (see Chapter 8, dream #39) that from external (explicit request to the parents) becomes internal (the parent appears as a dream character who gives permission). Parental permission is hence incorporated directly into the dream plot. The concept of the authorization to proceed is *represented plastically* through the direct appearance of the forbidding parent in the dream (i.e., considerations of representability). In hindsight, it is a rudimentary version of the action of moral conscience, where an "internal voice" in this case authorizes instead of prohibits, and for which everything becomes possible. A permissive positive aspect of dream-censorship activity is embodied by the parent himself, who becomes a dream character and opens the doors of censorship to the satisfaction of the wish. We note that when the mechanism of the "authorization to proceed" moves from being external to internal, the dream becomes bizarre and unlikely.

In particular, we have seen this operation at work in the case of the beach dream (#4[II]), where the mother implausibly (i.e., contrary to what happens in reality) allows Marco to stay at home and go to the beach later. But the "authorizing parent" also appears in the PlayStation dreams (#49 and #50[II]), where the father's permission to use the PlayStation and buy new games is completely implausible (it is quite the contrary in reality). The hoverboard dream (#33[II]) is even more improbable. In this dream, Marco represents his father in the dream scenario who (at last!) buys him the hoverboard. I am actually against buying this object because I think it's very dangerous, although Marco continues to hope that one day I will be convinced into buying one. We note that the "authorizing parent" mechanism avails itself of the cooperation of an operation other than the "consideration of representability", which here serves the purpose of censorship.

A form of (external) self-censorship upon awakening, at the end of the verbal report of dream, has been observed in the "little brother dream" (#13 from the second). Here Marco satisfies directly in his dream his desire (which he knows that he must repress) to have a little brother, and then while telling his dream, he shows that he is critically aware that his wish will never come true by sadly exclaiming "I can't have a little brother!" Here Marco verbalizes a known answer to an internal question that sounds like an authorization not to proceed. The same sad awareness was expressed later, upon awakening from his dream, when he realized that his desire to have a little sister, although fulfilled in his dream, did not correspond to reality (dream #24[II]).

Through these examples, we can establish with certainty that, in these cases, the generation of dream bizarreness is by no means accidental. We understand from Marco's dreams, which show clear operations of latent content distortion, that behind many elements of dream bizarreness, there is always a mechanism that produced them to serve different needs, be they merely of a visual representative nature (transformations of thoughts in a visive form) or, mostly in the third period, of defensive nature (i.e., defensive dream-work activity or censorship activity).

Other times, dream-work operations can help in realizing the wish to continue to sleep, eliminating an annoying stimulus. For example, in the tea commercial dream (#40[II]) Marco transforms an annoying stimulus (a nagging advertising jingle) into something pleasant and/or amusing (his father singing it). This produces a bizarre/caricature effect. We have seen this caricature-like transformation of an annoying/unpleasant stimulus also in dreams from previous periods.

A dream-work operation not observed previously and that nevertheless fits well with the Freudian theories concerning the relationships between the development of the ego, the evolution of psychic functioning (i.e., primary process vs. secondary process) and the development of the dream function is that of *moderation*, like in the pudding dream (#32[II]) that Marco had at 9 years and 1 month. Here Marco satisfied a denied wish but reached a compromise in it, agreeing to use moderation (a decrease in quantity: from a giant-size pack to a three-piece pack). At other times, the prohibition to eat pudding in the evening before the dream would have given rise to the opposite: an exaggerated representation, as it happened in other dreams (see dream #08, p. 28).

If we want the same definition of quantity in numbers (i.e., the three-piece pack) rather than a qualifying adjective, it is an expression of a *rationalization* and of a *measure in the wish satisfaction*.

We therefore consider moderation as another operation at the service of censorship: a sort of compromise between achieving the goal and showing thought development.

The subsequent table (Table 13.1) lists the main dream-work operations observed in the dreams from this period. These are in addition to those dream-work operations observed in the previous periods that continued to appear also in the dreams from this period.

Table 13.1 New dream-work operations

Dream-work operation	Description
Affective displacement	A forbidden feeling or desire is shifted to a surrogate character or situation.
Moderation	The child in the dream limits (implausibly) the fulfilment of his wish. It may be viewed as a form of rationalization
Comic/grotesque representation	An explicit, rewarding sexual desire is expressed in the form of a comic, grotesque representation.
(Unconscious) substitution of a person	A character is unconsciously replaced by another because it is functional to the fulfilment of a wish.
Strategic alliance between wishes	An alliance between wishes helps in circumventing dream censorship and allows the fulfilment of a forbidden wish.
Finding a compromise	The child accepts to do an unwelcome thing as long as it is mitigated by another pleasant one.
Rationalization and limitation in the wish satisfaction	The child implements (in the dream) limitations in the satisfaction of desire.
Authorizing parent—that is, interiorized "parental authorization to proceed"	Facing the fulfilment of a wish forbidden by the parents, one way of satisfying it directly without having to feel anxious and without true deformation is by "changing" parental rules in the dream, in the sense that the denied wish becomes legitimate and is authorized directly by the parent.
Parent's authorizing act	This is similar to the "parental authorization to proceed" mechanism but even stronger. The parent performs the action that leads to the satisfaction of the desire that he/she himself denied (in reality).

Table 13.1 (Continued)

Dream-work operation	Description
Self-censorship upon awakening (external)	There is awareness (expressed verbally) that the wish fulfilled in a dream cannot actually be realized.
Resistance, reluctance in reporting the dream	Marco shows resistance in reporting the dream because of its contents, which he is ashamed of.
Request for reassurance so that the dream report remains a secret with the father	While telling the dream, the child seeks approval of its content, trusting that it will remain secret, with reference to the explicit satisfaction of a sexual desire. A first example of this dream-work operation has been viewed in a dream from the first period (i.e., the timorous verbalization of dream).

Resistance to dream reporting

In some wish-fulfilment dreams from this period, it was observed that dream censorship can be expressed, rather than through distorted dream actions, through an evident *resistance in reporting the dream verbally*. In some dreams in which repressed desires are openly satisfied, we observe forms of resistance in the dream report that manifest themselves in a timorous, fearful, unwilling, selective reporting (to one of the parents) or by showing embarrassment and/or shame. Such resistance have also been noted in some dreams from the previous periods and should be considered as an extension and action of dream censorship, as it occurs only and exclusively when we face an excessively self-evident fulfilment of a forbidden desire, disapproved by the parents, morally inappropriate, overtly sexual, etc.

In the already mentioned "Nintendo dream" (dream #02[II]) I observed a sort of *liberating confession* of the repressed desire in Marco's timorous reporting of the dream.[2] Such confession was probably made easier by the fact that the child was likely to receive some "permissive feedback" from the listener of his dream report. In the case of dream #02(II), the fulfilled wish broke the rule that "the child should be content with what he has". This parental norm, interiorized by the child, acted as a very early form of dream censorship where the fulfilment of the wish brings anxiety and fear, which are not expressed in the dream setting (or at least there is no trace of it) while reporting the dream to the father.

In another case (dream #05[II]), before telling his dream, Marco wanted to be guaranteed and reassured that the dream was not going to be revealed to his mother. Marco's *hesitation and uncertainty* are another clear expression of his resistance to refer to the forbidden contents of the dream. Marco confirmed that he did not want to tell the dream because he felt ashamed.

Another example of resistance is found in the clothing store dream (#10[II]), in which Marco openly satisfied a sexual desire (seeing a woman's naked breasts).

In this case, too, Marco asked to tell the dream to his father alone, hiding it from his mother. His resistance was caused by the detection of a sexual desire, the object of which was not the mother. Again, this is a form of censorship that takes place not so much within the dream but rather in its reporting.

Resistance in verbal dream reporting must be understood as the actual failure of dream censorship that was unable to disguise the forbidden desire at the basis of the dream. Other times it is the expression of a more permissive form of censorship, as if to say "I accept to satisfy my desire but reserve some difficulties in telling the dream" (i.e., a kind of compromise).

We may assume that, as the child grows, his fear/anxiety for the undisguised fulfilment of a denied wish appears first in his verbal reporting of the dream and then will be part of his dream experience—that is, it will be interiorized, as we observed for the mechanism of the "authorization to proceed", which from external (explicit request to the parents) becomes internal (i.e., "authorizing parent"). I believe that these latter changes are a tangible sign of a more stable and structured dream censorship in the child.

Old and new forms of bizarreness

In this period, although the presence of frankly bizarre dreams remains substantially stable compared to the previous period (6–7 years), I found that the level of bizarreness in dreaming increases also in wish-fulfilment dreams, since more than half of these stage distorted satisfaction of wishes that are (or should be) repressed (see Figure 13.1).

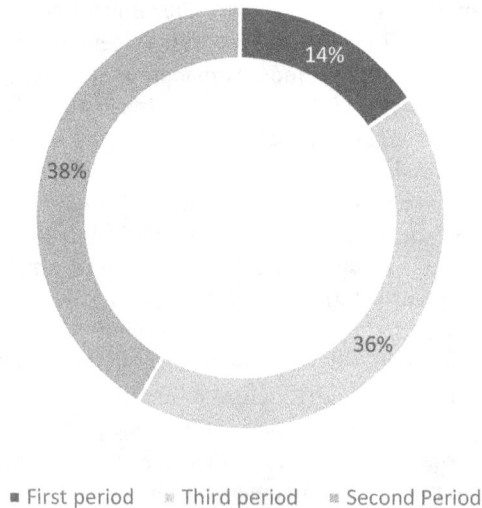

Percentages shown: 14%, 38%, 36%

■ First period   ▨ Third period   ▨ Second Period

Figure 13.1 Percentage of frankly bizarre dreams in dreaming repertoire from the first, second and third periods

Furthermore, I noticed that *in every single frankly bizarre dream, there is a quantitative and qualitative increase in the bizarreness and complexity of the plot and scenario.* Indeed, Marco's dream reports show an increase in the number and variety of bizarre elements (e.g., intrinsically bizarre characters, bizarre actions, incongruous and improbable overlapping of places, etc.).

On a qualitative level, the incongruity of certain dream characters and actions becomes even greater, compared to similar bizarre elements from previous dreams. Frankly bizarre dreams now become even more obscure in meaning. It is important to note that Marco also no longer defines dreams as simply "nice" or "bad". He starts using new terms, such as "ridiculous", "strange", "boring" and "annoying", which is further evidence of the increased complexity and differentiation of his dream scenarios and phenomenology.

The analysis of the dreams reported in the previous chapter, where there is an indirect but still recognizable satisfaction of repressed wishes, allows a close analysis of the dream-work operations and of the factors that engender dream distortion/bizarreness. However, while the dreams classified as frankly bizarre do not allow us to perform this analysis, they are useful for a phenomenological analysis of the various types of bizarreness (Colace, 2003; Colace et al., 1993; Resnick et al., 1994; Winget & Kramer, 1979; Rosen, 2018).

Some examples of dream bizarreness

Sudden space-time discontinuity

Dream length and complexity go hand in hand with the presence of various sudden space-time discontinuities in them.

A strange dream with notable sudden space-time discontinuities and numerous bizarre aspects is the following:

M 41(II)–9;5. *I dreamed that we were at the beach, and I saw this little girl who was afraid. Freddy Krueger* (from the film *A Nightmare on Elm Street*) *arrived. He made this gesture with his glove as if to kill her. He was five metres far, but it was as if he had touched her with his glove and she died. She was a character from the film (I didn't know her), then I saw Jason* (from the film *Friday the 13th*). *I was on the beach with N., G., R. and M.* (Marco's friends), *and so I took the ball. I wanted to throw it at him, but suddenly he started talking and said, "Guys, if you want to really learn football, you have to follow me". He was good at first, then all at once, he took a knife and wanted to kill us, like I was here. He wanted to kill me. I jumped back and saved myself. I went to my friends. I don't know why I was behind N., maybe because I wanted to save myself. I didn't want to be the first to be killed. We were like in some kind of prison, in huge rooms that you couldn't jump over and run and walk away.*

First we were at the beach, then in this prison. Then we were back at the beach. I was like in a carriage. The gate opened, and so there was a madman with a horse who wanted to kill us all. (In the dream, there were various scenes. Marco said he woke up four times and then the dream continued.)

"Was it a scary dream?" "Yes, but when I made that move against Jason (so that he couldn't kill me), it became a bit nice." (At the end, Marco said it was a nice dream.)

In this dream, the setting suddenly changes into another. Here, too, there is a complex overlapping of fictional scenes and characters with real ones.[3] *The diurnal reference appears merely as dream construction material rather than as a clear motivational instigator.* Some scenes might even not be considered "bizarre", as they are taken directly from the film and daytime fantasies based on it, but other aspects of the dream are frankly bizarre. The meaning of this dream remains obscure.

Bizarre space-time discontinuities in the dream scenarios also appear in the following very pleasant and adventurous dream:

M. 8(II)–8;4. *I dreamed that there was a hotel, that in this hotel there were so many people that then, as in the stadium, they did not know whom to give the rooms to. Then among the people who were there, there was a gentleman hand in hand with his daughter, but she was a robot. And then another gentleman next to him pointed a knife at him and said to him (to the one who was holding the child's hand), "Go and rob!" then the one with the child took his knife, then that gentleman held a rifle like that, and the other one kicked him. Everything exploded, but then there was a robot battle, and then it was all over. It was a very nice dream.*

Marco defined this one as a very nice dream, although apparently it is not a wish-fulfilment dream. In this dream, some elements are taken from different daytime experiences and combined. There is a reference to a crowded hotel (true experience) from our recent summer holidays (the dream was told in early September). There are also elements taken from different situations, perhaps from Marco's video games.

From a phenomenological point of view, space-time overlaps may be one of the earliest forms of bizarreness. In fact, it is also a typical trait of *primary bizarreness*, where in an attempt to satisfy multiple wishes at the same time, the dreamer ends up forcing disparate elements together. However, in the dreams from the first period, the phenomenon was due to the need of the dream to satisfy several (known) desires together, which could give an explanation to its bizarreness, and in any way, the space-time overlaps did not hide the full wish-fulfilment nature of the dream.

Bizarre environments

In the following dream report, we observe a *bizarre environment* caused by the *incongruous overlapping of places:* a mix between a hospital and a playground.

> M. 3(II)–8;2. *I was in the hospital. Basically this hospital was a playground. You had to slide down a slide, then there was a button that you had to push like this, and if you pushed well you would win a lot of coins. I did this and I got two coins. Then I talked to N. . . . and then it was over.* Marco said it was a mix between a hospital and a playground.

There are no clear daytime connections to this dream. Marco could not understand its meaning.

There are also bizarre environments in the following dream:

> M. 1(II)–8;0 months *I had a dream that there was a Trony Store* (an appliance store), *but it was in front of the school. There was snow and we were in snowsuits. There was you (Dad), Mom and Uncle C., Aunt B. and G.*

In this dream, an environment appears that superimposes two real places in a bizarre way, which in reality are located far away from each other: the Trony Store strangely appears in front of the school.

Strange happenings

> M. (II)26–8;11. *I dreamed that the battery of the tablet was completely uncharged. Because I had recharged it up to 100 and instead it was completely uncharged.*

In this dream, something *strange* and unlikely happens compared to everyday reality since Marco never forgets to recharge his tablet.

Daytime sources of bizarre dreams

Several frankly bizarre dreams from this period are characterized by having obscure and/or *indirect references to daytime experiences.* This often prevents a precise temporal connotation of the diurnal sources of these dreams. The diurnal residues (characters, environments, situations) taken up in the dream do not explain its meaning. The connection with the diurnal elements becomes contorted and no longer self-explanatory. Sometimes, when one succeeds in finding the daytime references, these appear *only as ideas or elements that are then used out of context with respect to the construction of the dream plot,* which develops in a complex and imaginative way. These day residues appear as functional material for the construction of the dream, which uses them in order to stage the fulfilment of a wish that is independent from them and that has more latent origins. In this way, the diurnal residues are used in the dream outside their usual and original context and function. All this increases the complexity of the dream.

In some of these dreams, we might also assume the presence of simple wish fulfilment; however, this cannot be established clearly because there are several elements of bizarreness that make the meaning of the dream uncertain. See, for example, the complexity of the frankly bizarre dream in the following example, where there are various diurnal references that complicate the dream. Some dreams, like the following one but also like #8 (II) and #41 (II), are characterized by the fact that the *dream plot is very complex*, with different situations and characters. The dream, although inspired by a recent event (not always immediately identifiable), ends up going completely beyond it:

M. 37(II)–9;3m. *Basically, there was this sort of a mansion, and there was a war. We had to beat France. The war began in this mansion (with guns), all the people scattered, dead, me with the machine gun, then I took the axe. It was very cool. I was alone. I was with London, and on the other side there was France. I took the axe and I cut off the head of one of France, and then I took the machine gun, so basically one was doing Tarzan. I hit him with the axe! I slammed him away! I looked like Superman, then all of a sudden, music was heard* (Marco plays the tune), *and I started dancing, and I shot at times. When the war was over, I slept in a kind of bed, and your house was at two kilometres' distance, so to come to your place, I had to travel two kilometres. I lived on my own with a rich man.*

Marco about the day before (daytime source). *Yesterday, with F., we talked a lot about World War III, and I dreamed of war. F. said that when he was at the summer camp the children had heard that President Trump had thrown a bomb and that World War III had broken out and everyone had started crying (but it was not true—fake news).*

This is an adventurous and exciting dream inspired by a previous-day conversation about war. The dream, however, presents numerous characters with very different contexts in origin, sudden space-time discontinuity, strange and implausible actions and various elements of bizarreness.

Daytime sources used out of their original context

The following dream is probably one of the most bizarre ever told by Marco. It was reported at the age of 9 and expresses well the clear difference between the early infantile forms of dreaming and his first "adult" dream.

M. 34(II)–9;1. *We were at home, and then the three of us (myself, Mom and Dad) went to the restaurant with grandfather and grandmother. And then in the restaurant, tied near a stage, there was the killer doll from* Child's Play. *Mom told me not to touch her nor say anything to her or she would persecute us. Then everyone ran away. We, too, ran away with the car. Then when we got back to our house, we found a little girl on the sofa and her mom and dad. The little girl sang, and her parents applauded her (she was a normal child). So I went to get the bread knife. Then Grandfather and Grandmother arrived at our house and broke the door. I stayed with them. Mom and Dad went looking for a house (we had to move house), then I, with Grandfather, went to a dance school, and Grandfather started running into the mirrors but then he stopped and we started building a home. Then Grandma, Mom and Dad also arrived, and we lived happily and the dream ended.* Marco said that it was a bad dream and he was scared.

"Who were these parents and this child? Do you know them?" "No, I don't." "Was the restaurant a familiar one?" "No." "Isn't it strange that we went eating out in the afternoon?" "Yes, but then when we went to Sperlonga [a recent trip]. We also ate out in the afternoon with F. and F." "Yes, we went to eat fish in Sperlonga. It was late lunch time." Marco replied, "Yes, but it was almost afternoon!" "Was the dance hall familiar to you?" "No, but it looked like that of C. [a cousin who goes dancing]. Grandfather went through the mirrors running, but it was strange because when he went in and out of the mirrors, he was always wearing the same clothes."

"Did you watch "Child's Play" yesterday?" "No. But last night, it was midnight when I heard the sound of Grandmother's footsteps while she was going to bed. I thought of the killer doll walking towards us."

This is a bizarre and long dream that resembles adult dreams. This dream is included among bizarre dreams because bizarreness is what characterizes it most; however, it is also a clear *bad dream*. There are many daytime references taken here and there from real experiences but then used *out of context* and *out of their original meaning*. The meaning of the dream remains obscure. In this dream, we can also observe *characters who do unusual things* and *intrinsically bizarre characters*.

The following table (Table 13.2) lists the new forms of bizarreness observed in the frankly bizarre dreams from the third period, in addition to those already observed in dreams from the previous periods. In Table 13.3, I provide a concise list of the most important dream-work operations found in Marco's dream reports from 4 to 10 years of age.

Table 13.2 New forms of dream bizarreness (phenomenology)

Increased complexity in dream scenario and plot	The number of dream situations, characters, places and scenarios increases, and they are often put together in an incongruous way with respect to space and time. This aspect is accompanied by a greater length of the dream reports.
Environments and places out of their original context	In the dream, environments and places taken from reality appear outside their usual context.
Very incongruous and bizarre characters/actions	The characters and actions are very incongruous with respect to those that appeared in previous bizarre dreams.
Improbable and strange happenings	In the dream, there are some things that are very improbable and strange with respect to common life.
Incomprehensibility	Bizarre dreams often become totally incomprehensible. Even with respect to the child's experiences, the meaning is not clearly understood.
Lack of evident and explanatory links between waking experiences and dream content	There is no clear and direct connection between the child's daytime experiences and the dream contents that can be detected.
Overlapping of fictional elements with real characters	In the dream, fictional characters, actions and situations are mixed up with real characters and situations.
Incongruous affectivity in reporting the dream	An affective manifestation (crying) while reporting the dream appears disproportionate with respect to the dream contents.

Table 13.3 Dream-work operations in Marco's dream reports from 4 to 10 years of age

Transformation from optative formula into present time
Tendency to exaggerate
Forcing in cognitive synthesis
Condensation
Alliance between two or more simple wishes (triggering dream)
Primary form of displacement
Considerations of representability
Transformation of something negative into positive
Caricatural transformation of disturbing stimulus
Fearful verbalization (in dream reporting)
Authorization to proceed (external)
Allusive disguising
Unconscious symbolism
Direct dream-censorship activity

Table 13.3 (Continued)

Displacement (replacement of person)
Alliance between simple and repressed wishes (triggering dream)
Strategic alliance between wishes (circumventing dream censorship)
Affective displacement
Moderation
Comic/grotesque representation
(Unconscious) substitution of person
Finding a compromise
Rationalization and limitation in the wish satisfaction
Authorizing parent (in dream)
Parent's authorizing act (in dream)
Self-censorship upon awakening (external)
Resistance, reluctance in reporting the dream
Request for reassurance so that the dream report remains a secret with the
    father (external)

Notes

1 According to Freud (1900), the concept of displacement is also inherent in the considerations of representability, which presuppose the possibility that an abstract idea is represented by an element capable of representing it (however, in Freud's view, displacement is also at the basis of condensation).
2 In a previous dream, Marco apologized while reporting the dream for having fulfilled a forbidden wish in the dream (dream #25, Chapter 8).
3 The overlapping of fictional or TV characters with real characters and situations with an intense emotional involvement in the dream plot and scenarios is more frequent in children who watch TV for a long time (Colace, Dichiacchio, & Violani, 2006a, 2006b).

References

Colace, C. (2003). Dream bizarreness reconsidered. *Sleep and Hypnosis, 5* (3), 105–128.
Colace, C., Dichiacchio, C., & Violani, C° (2006°). Effects of television viewing on sleep habits and dream contents in children at ages 3–8. *Sleep, 29* (1035), A354–A355.
Colace, C., Dichiacchio, C., & Violani, C. (2006b). Effetti della televi sione della TV sul sonno e sognare nei bambini dai 3 agli 8 anni di età. *Psichiatria dell'Infanzia e dell'adolescenza, 73* (1), 31–40.
Colace, C., Doricchi, F., Di Loreto, E., & Violani, C. (1993). Developmental qualitative and quantitative aspects of bizarreness in dream reports of children. *Sleep Research, 22,* 57.
Freud, S. (1900). *The Interpretation of Dreams.* S.E., 4–5. London: Hogarth Press.
Resnick, J., Stickgold, R., Rittenhouse, C., & Hobson, J. A. (1994). Self-representation and bizarreness in children's dream reports collected in the home setting. *Consciousness and Cognition, 3,* 30–45.
Rosen, M. G. (2018). How bizarre? A pluralist approach to dream content. *Consciousness and Cognition, 62,* 148–162.
Winget, C., & Kramer, M. (1979). *Dimension of Dream.* Gainesville: Presses of Florida.

Chapter 14

Changes in bad dreams

Bad dreams (20 in number) account for about one-third of the dreams reported between 8 and 10 years of age, so there is a sharp decrease compared to the previous period in the proportion of this type of dreams with respect to the dream repertoire. In this chapter, I describe the most frequent themes and the different types of bad dreams.

Themes

The themes of bad dreams are different compared to the bad dreams from the second period (see Table 14.1). "End of the world"/"natural disaster", "getting lost" and "Marco doing bad things" themes appear. While scary characters continue to be present in various dreams, there are no more bad dreams referring to "disappearing parents" or "parents no longer there", "being abducted" and" being put in jail".

Types of bad dreams

Bad dreams of this periods fall into the *same categories* as the bad dreams previously described (see Chapter 10, Table 10.1). Thus, we continue to differentiate *bad*

Table 14.1 Examples of bad dream contents

Horror movie characters (i.e., zombie)
Threatening and unknown characters
Ugly people
Marco doing unusual and bad things
Scary characters, totally invented without any connection with reality
Loss of favourite things (e.g., toys)
End-of-the-world issues
Catastrophic natural events (e.g., earthquakes or storms)
Getting lost
Being killed
Death of the father
Dying (him and the parents)

DOI: 10.4324/9781003184874-19

dreams with awakening and those *without*, those that occur *caused by specific fear-some daytime stimuli or distressing situations*, those *about general or sometimes specific fears* but without any precise daytime reference and finally, the "false" bad dreams that persist (with a similar percentage compared to previous periods (i.e., about 30% of bad dreams)—that is, frightening dreams with aspects of adventure and daring challenges. These latter dreams are sometimes more complex and imaginative. Bad dreams with nocturnal awakening—that is, true nightmares decreasing sharply (about 20%) compared to previous period. Some bad dreams from this period (about 40%) are also characterized by strong bizarreness. I also observed *recurring bad dreams*. There is one bad dream that seems to be about an oedipal theme. Finally, *moderately bad dreams* are rare in this period compared to previous ones (see box 14.1). I report here some examples of types/themes of bad dreams.

Box 14.1   Main changes in bad dreams compared to the second period

Bad dreams decrease
Nightmares decrease
Bad dreams caused by specific scary stimuli increase
Recurring bad dreams appear
New themes: end of the world/natural disaster, getting lost, Marco doing
    bad things

Bad dream caused by specific frightening daytime stimuli

M. 23(II)–8;11. *I had a bad dream. I was lost in the museum, then the class found me.*

Marco had to go on a school trip to the museum that day. In the past few days and even the previous day, he was very happy and excited about this. The night before on the sofa, his mom had conveyed her anxieties to him by telling him, "Marco, be very careful tomorrow when you get off the bus. Stay close to the teacher, especially when you cross the street. Don't make me worry". In these cases, desire (to go to the field trip) is more likely to prevail, and that could have triggered a simple dream of anticipation, but the worries of the mother prevailed.

Bad dream about catastrophic events

Marco 9(II)–8;4. *I dreamed that the three of us were at home, lying on the sofa and kissing each other. Then suddenly we heard a bang. I started crying, and a bomb went off at my house and the building collapsed and we died.*

The recent images of an earthquake seen on TV certainly had an influence. The first part of the dream can also be interpreted as the fulfilment of a wish (after a long holiday period, Marco missed the family situation of the three of us sitting on the sofa at home, watching television). The dream may also have been influenced by the fact that the evening before, while we were eating on the balcony, we had seen thunder and lightning due to a summer storm in progress and had been frightened by a pigeon that had flown onto our balcony, seeking shelter from the rain.

Bad dream with ugly characters

Bad dreams with scary characters continue to be present in this period. See the following example:

> M 25 (II)–8;11. *There was an ugly person behind me. I was looking at the mirror, and behind me there was a person dressed in white with black eyes and a white face.*

Recurring bad dream

Recurring bad dreams were not observed in the previous period. The following dream proposes again the theme of the *killer doll* character, already present in some previous bad dreams. The same theme appeared in a more adventurous form (false bad dream) in the dream #19 (see p. 165) but also in another bad dream (#34, see p. 159). The dream was interrupted by awakening (with Marco rushing into his parents' bed) and refers to a scary daytime stimulus.

> M. 44(II)–9;8. *Marco: You remember yesterday, when we were scrolling on our phones the films that we wanted to rent? There was that film that I liked. There was the picture of the killer doll, so I got scared and dreamed of it at night. I dreamed I was with S. and L., and L. bumped into this doll and I got scared and woke up. In the dream, we were all in your room* (bedroom). *The doll moved by itself. My friends weren't scared. They looked at her. I, instead, was anxious.*

Traumatic dream following an earthquake

> M. 14(II)–8;6. *I was staying with friends at home, with you* (Dad). *But then you went out one day, and you were hanging out with some friends. Then the earthquake came. Then I couldn't see you anymore. You never came back home, so I started crying because I thought you were dead. But then you arrived.* Marco added that although the dream had a happy ending, he was afraid at the beginning and was very sad in the dream. Even while recalling the dream, he appeared sad.

The dream refers to an earthquake that was felt in Rome recently and was therefore based on a specific fearsome diurnal stimulus.

False bad dreams

The following is a typical "false" bad dream: an attempt to prove oneself brave while in the end of the dream, fear prevails.

The dream of the zombie house.

Marco 25(II)ter[1]–9. *It was a dream about Mirabilandia* (a theme park). *I dreamed that Mirabilandia was like a scary hotel, so we had to escape. It was like a haunted house. But then, when I woke up, I remembered that Mirabilandia was different and therefore it was not true. Because the true Mirabilandia is all outdoors. Instead I dreamed that it was in a closed place, that Mirabilandia was like a house. In the dream there were F. and Fr.* (friends). *Have you seen the zombie game? It looked like it. See the zombie house? They don't scare me.*

The following may seem like a bad dream, but in reality it is not:

M. 19(II)–8;8. *We were in class, all those in class III b, and then suddenly the* killer doll (i.e., *Child's Play*)[2] *arrived. Practically we were going crazy and practically she was going to kill us, almost everyone by now. Then she killed almost everyone, too, and she killed me* (he smiles).

This dream, with no additional questions and no knowledge of the child's daytime experiences, could be confused with a classic bad dream. The father asked, "But was it a scary dream?" Marco says, "*Absolutely no! I enjoyed myself*".

Bad dream about the death of the father

M. 42(II)–9;4. *I was at home, and you* (parents) *were at the mall, then when you were coming back, you had an accident, and then Mom, when she came home, said you were dead, and I started to cry.*

Marco tells this dream in a distressed way. To stay home alone is Marco's wish. It could be hypothesized that this desire triggered feelings of guilt (for having preferred to stay at home rather than going with the parents) and fear that some misfortune could happen to the parents. On the other hand, this dream could be also interpreted as an oedipal dream.

Bizarre bad dream

In this period, there were also examples of *particularly bizarre* bad dreams. In the following example, Marco makes an ugly and bizarre gesture:

M. 25bis (II)–8;11. *We were in a restaurant, and I spat into a little girl's dish. Then you* (Dad) *yelled at me. You were mad at me and took me away. In the dream, there were only me, you and the girl. And then the TV news talked about this thing that had happened. It was a bad dream. The little girl did not notice that I had spat into her dish. All they said on TV was that a boy had spat into a little girl's dish.*

(The girl in the dream is someone unknown to Marco.)

There are no specific daytime sources directly related to the dream content. However, two episodes happened on the previous day, in which Marco was scolded by an adult. Both of these episodes could have made Marco feel like a "bad" child. While we were checking out at the supermarket, the cashier had told Marco to watch out, because in order to help his mother, he had hit the eggs and risked breaking them. In addition, he had opened the bag by slamming it. The cashier had told him, "Don't come to this checkout again if you behave like this". In the afternoon, Uncle C. had told him (half-serious, half-joking), "Look, I might slap you too" because Marco and his schoolmates, engaged in a group school research, were making a big mess. It is a very bizarre dream, reminiscent of those of adults.

"Moderately bad" dreams

Marco 31(II)–9;1. *I was about to join karate competitions, but we were at school (my school), and then, I don't know why, the parents wanted to start the competitions right away and started to go crazy, kicking at the doors. We were in a room, and they were getting us ready. The teacher wasn't F., my real karate teacher. He was the one from the* Karate Kid *movie. The parents were screaming, "Kill! Kill!" I mean, the parents in the dream were screaming like the students in the bad guys' karate school do in the movie. This dream was bad because of the way that those parents behaved.*

In those days, Marco had been rewatching the entire *Karate Kid* film series (four films), and in a week's time, he was supposed to take his belt-passing exam. These are possibly pleasant wish-fulfilment themes, yet bizarre and unclear aspects prevail. The dream, despite being inspired by Marco's favourite things, was defined by Marco himself as a bad dream.

Marco reports the following unpleasant dream in a sad tone:

M. 12(II)–8;5. *I was in the shopping centre with my mother, and then some children made me fall the spacecraft –toy with the puppets (i.e., toys), then I couldn't find them. It was a bad and sad dream because I had lost the puppets.*

Daytime sources

About 50% of bad dreams are caused by specific frightening daytime stimuli that are clearly referred to the day preceding the dream (i.e., day residue). In these dreams, daytime experiences explain the meaning of the dream. Indeed, in these dreams, the frightening daytime stimuli are resumed and treated (see next chapter about the function of dreams). The other bad dreams are about general or specific bad themes (see Table 14.1), which apparently have no reference in the daytime experience. From this point of view, the latter dreams are hard to understand. In one dream (see dream #25[II]bis, mentioned previously) a specific daytime stimulus (i.e., referring to the day preceding the dream) triggers an ugly and bizarre gesture by Marco, which does not seem directly related to the daytime experience, but it seems thematically similar (i.e., feeling bad, doing something that is not good to do, to be scolded).

Notes

1 To indicate that this is the third dream from the same night.
2 The protagonist of the horror film *Child's Play* (2019, Lars Klevberg).

Reference

Klevberg, L. (2019). *Child's Play*. Movie, USA: Orion Pictures, KatzSmith Productions.

Part V

The meaning and function of infantile dreams

Chapter 15

The function of dreams

The affective-reestablishment (AR) hypothesis

The dream resolves perturbing affective states

Data collected from several systematic studies show that wishes fulfilled in infantile dreams were experienced by the children during the daytime life, where they were associated with an intense emotional state (cheerful, surprised/excited, displeased, nostalgic, regretful, impatient) that was not fully processed and elaborated psychologically and therefore resulted as somewhat "perturbing". Through the fulfilment of the wish, the dream resolves the associated affective state and, in turn, allows the child to obtain emotional discharge and "affective reestablishment". I call this process the hypothesis of the *affective-reestablishment (AR) function of dreams* (Colace, 2010, 2013, 2017, 2020a, 2020b, 2021) (see Figure 15.1).

Marco's dream reports, with the wealth of information about his daytime experiences, give way to increasing specification, confirmation and clarification of the AR hypothesis.

Marco's typical wish-fulfilment dreams that we have seen in numerous previous examples of dream reports refer to daytime experiences (mainly from the day before the dream), in which a strong wish of the child remained partially or totally unfulfilled and was accompanied by an intense affective state; a portion of it remained unelaborated because it was not processed or discharged psychologically due to the incomplete gratification of wish, thus perturbing the child's emotional state (see Chapter 5). For example, Marco's (unresolved) daytime wish that it was my birthday party is associated to an affective state of *impatience*, of which at least a part remained unelaborated in the form of a perturbing affective state (see dream #1). In another case, Marco's (unresolved) wish about jumping on the trampoline is accompanied by an affective state of *sorrow* and *disappointment* that remained in part unelaborated (see dream #03). In both these cases, the unfulfilled wish and the portion of unelaborated affective state represent a state of activation (emotional arousal) that persists at the time of going to sleep and during the sleep state. This is exactly the psychological situation underlying the dream experience, its triggering ground.[1]

The dream acts in a targeted way with respect to this psychological state: it enables a hallucinatory and vivid experience of wish fulfilment and gratification

DOI: 10.4324/9781003184874-21

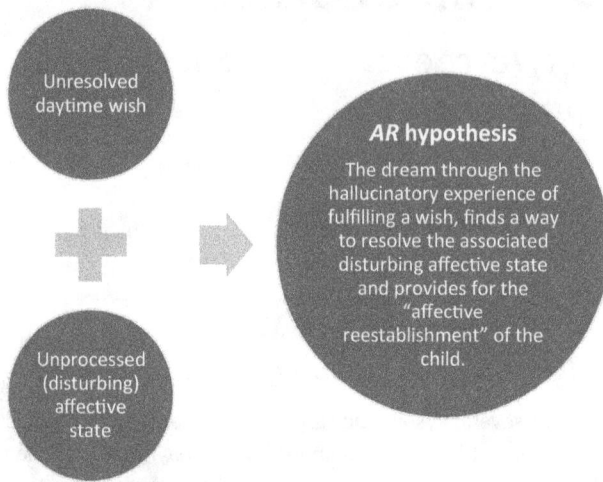

Figure 15.1 The affective-reestablishment (AR) hypothesis about dreams

(perceived as real), which enables in turn the full psychological elaboration and resolution of the affective state associated with the wish and the affective-reestablishment of the child. These dreams operate in a way that safeguards health and psychological functioning and lets the children continue the sleep.

The most important component of the AR hypothesis is the concept of the *resolution or alleviation of a disturbing affective state*. This restoring effect is to be regarded as the alleviation and/or reduction of the disturbing affective load and restoring of the emotional network system normally used for the management and regulation of emotions in the state of wakefulness. In the AR hypothesis, the concept of the reduction or regulation of a disturbing affective state is closely linked to wish fulfilment because *it is through the gratification of a wish that the dream exercises this function.*

Following are some examples of dreams to explain this function.[2]

Let us go back to the example of the dream about the Spider-Man stocking.

> M. 05–4;8. *I dreamed that the Befana brought me a Spider-Man stocking. She left it for me on the sofa.* (At the end of his dream report, Marco snapped, "I can't wait for the Befana to come!!")

On the evening before, we had spotted certain Befana stockings at the supermarket, and he had been particularly attracted by those with a Spider-Man theme. He had asked me to buy one for him, but I had replied, "No, Marco, the Befana is going to bring you one". This had left him a bit disappointed; he had hoped to have it right then. In this dream, the hallucinatory experience of wish fulfilment allows to treat psychologically the daytime *affective overload* of *delusion* and *impatience*. What happens in the dream is to enjoy having obtained the desired stocking and recovering from the affective perturbing state that is now discharged (Marco was smiling in his sleep).

The affective reestablishment function is evident also in the SpongeBob dream.

M. 09–5;2. *Last night I dreamed that you bought me the SpongeBob trolley.*

As we said previously, the dream refers to the failure to purchase the Sponge-Bob trolley on the day before that left Marco disappointed. The SpongeBob dream is an extraordinary example of an infantile dream. In this dream, Marco fulfils his wish to own the SpongeBob trolley. It is a very pleasant dream, as one can see from Marco's drawing of it. The dream experience, through the gratification of the daytime wish, enables the reduction (or mitigation) of the disturbing affective load—that is, the big disappointment for the missed purchase of the trolley—and presumably operates an affective-reestablishment in the child, resetting his general affective network system.[3]

Let us look at the function of the dream in the following dream:

M. 18–5;3. *I had the Nintendo with the game, I had won it with the fruit juice. It was a nice black toy. It had the Rabbids game, the one that was on the fruit juice.*

The dream is about the Rabbids game depicted in the cardboard wrap of a fruit juice brand, along with the picture of a portable Nintendo console and a card to join a prize draw and win it. In the dream, Marco fulfils his wish to have that game and win the Nintendo console (for details, see Chapter 6). This allows him to process and treat his affective state of disappointment. Once again, the dream, through the fulfilment of the wish, grants emotional re-establishment to the child.

The same AR function is evident in dreams of the indirect (i.e., symbolic) fulfilment of a disapproved wish. For example, in the "bathtub dream" (# 44), Marco fulfils his wish to drink by having a parent bring him some water at night, a wish denied by his parents. In that dream, his wish to drink is accomplished symbolically by bathing in the bathtub, which Marco usually fills up with water before taking a bath.

Thanks to the loss of reality testing, in the dream experience, at the time of its occurrence, the child experiences the alleviation and resolution of his current affective state, which allows him to continue sleeping more serenely and then prepares a full reset of his emotional regulatory system for the next daytime experience. The benefits of the *emotional regulation* of dreams can be *non-specific* because the uninterrupted sleep state (thanks to the dream's gratifying experience) has a restorative effect (this data can be seen subsequently), and *specific* because the dream's subjective experience relieves the specific emotional discomfort.

We should not forget that, as Freud affirmed, while we sleep, we believe in the dream. This is even more true in children because their dream imagery appears like real perceptions, as it is harder for children to tell fantasy from reality (see Freud, 1901, p. 66). This enhances the effect of discharging the disturbing affection as the experience of satisfaction is "real". From this point of view, an interesting aspect that deserves further investigation is the evaluation of the effects of these dreams of fulfilment in terms of real wish gratification and affective reestablishment during the post-sleep period.[4]

Affective-reestablishment and tendency to exaggeration

A clear characteristic of some of Marco's wish-fulfilment dreams is the *tendency to exaggerate*. This feature was already noted in previous systematic studies of young children's dreams (Colace, 2010). As we have already seen, Freud noticed in children's dreams a tendency towards exaggeration and described this as a typical characteristic of the infantile dream, and he put this characteristic in relation with the difficulty for young children to desist from the satisfaction of a wish:

> The appearance in dreams of things of great size and in great quantities and amounts, and of exaggeration generally, may be another childish characteristic. Children have no more ardent wish than to be big and grown-up and to get as much of things as grown-up people do. They are hard to satisfy, know no such word as "enough" and insist insatiably on a repetition of things which they have enjoyed or whose taste they liked. It is only the civilizing influence of education that teaches them moderation and how to be content or resigned. (Freud, 1900, p. 268, fn. 1)

Referring to the dreams of his children Anna and Robert, he spoke of them in these terms, in a letter to Fliess:

> At some point the "bigness" in children's dreams must indeed be considered; it is related to children's yearning to be big; to be able for once to eat a bowlful of salad like Papa: the child never has enough, not even of repetitions. Moderation is the hardest thing for the child, as for the neurotic. (Freud, 1985, letter dated 6 August 1899, p. 365)

The tendency to exaggerate is also present in some infantile dreams described by Piaget (1962) even if he does not speak directly of it, as seen in the following dream of a child at 5 years and 8 months: "All the guinea-pigs were dead and there were lots cats in the hen-house (where the piglets are)" (Piaget, 1962, pp. 177–178).

Marco's dreams suggest that *the tendency to exaggerate* could be one of the dream-work operations which also serve the purpose of *affective re-establishment*. Indeed, *repetition* or *exaggeration* in the fulfilment of a wish might be one way to exhaustively gratify the wish in the dream, enabling the complete discharge of the disturbing affective state. Moreover, from this point of view, I believe that the theme of repetition and exaggeration in the dream is consistent with the daytime experience of fulfilling a wish or of doing something pleasant. The very act of repeating is pleasant to a child. For example, when my son Marco, like other children, watches for an endless number of times a favourite film or cartoon, he enjoys it every time, even in the pleasure of anticipating the scenes and the characters' dialogues and in mastering an event that is a source of pleasure and an object of desire.

Here are some examples of dreams in which the tendency to exaggerate appears in the form of repetition and exaggeration.

In the following dream, Marco exaggerates the dimensions of the crab object of his adventurous games:

M. 49–6;5. *I dreamed that G. had a big crab on his shoulder, so he did what. When the crab made a fast move to bite him, its claw ended up in G.'s mouth and G. ate it and the crab died. The claw he ate! He swallowed it all, raw, and the crab died. Gulp! I had warned him, I had said, "Watch out, G.!" You know what kind of crab it was? It wasn't like the ordinary crabs with the head like this* (he gestures). *It was one of those crabs with big, big claws, one of those, but it was enormous.*

In the already reported dream of jumping (#03), Marco fulfilled the disapproved wish to go jumping by "double serving", so to speak:

M. 03–4;7. *I went to the playground, to the jumping trampoline. You* (Daddy) *and Mummy were telling me not to go. But I went there, I jumped a lot, I jumped high, sky-high!!*

Marco exaggerates, as follows, the dimensions of the scorpion replica he longs so much for, which in reality is of normal size, the same as the other insect replicas in his collection.

M. 53–6;6. *I dreamed of the giant scorpion in the insects' case. I dreamed of the black scorpion (now I have the small yellow one). It's the one that's to be released next Tuesday. I dreamed there were three baby crocodiles around it (in the case compartments around the one with the scorpion) and the scorpion was there in its compartment. They were not real crocodiles (they were replicas like the insects).*

See other examples of exaggeration in dream #8 (p. 28). Some example of the tendency to exaggerate also appear in some infantile dreams of III periods.

> Marco 33(II)–9;1m. *You had bought me a hoverboard, and I went out riding it every day. It was a very nice dream.*

I have described several forms of infantile dreams in adults (Colace, 2009, 2014, 2020c; Colace, Salotti, & Ferreira, 2015, 2019) in which exaggeration also appears. This might lead us to assume that the analogies between the dreams of children and the infantile dreams of adults are not only in the contents but also in the peculiarities of the formation process of the dream.

The circadian aspect of the AR function

Some authors pointed out that dreaming activity has several chronobiologic features (for review, see Nielsen, 2005). However, a comprehensive theory connecting chronobiology concepts and findings with dreaming processes is still missing. Marco's dream reports, together with the information about his daytime experiences, may provide a valuable contribution to the understanding of another possible aspect of the AR hypothesis. The observation that the dream reports refer *almost exclusively*, or even selectively, to experiences from the day preceding the dream suggests that *the affective-reestablisment function of dreams is somehow considered to be of circadian nature*. The oneiric repertoire of one night of sleep possibly *selects* the wishes and the related disturbing affective loads from the day that just ended, and this is thought to happen every night, with reference to the day immediately before. In other words, any repertoire of nocturnal dreams is thought to have the function of coping with the daily affective load, a process that is presumably repeated day after day. In this way, the dreams apparently also have the function of resetting the subject's psychological/emotional system and restoring its optimal condition, getting it ready for the following day (see Figure 15.2).

Recently, Sándor (2015), after studying the dreams of children aged 4–8 years, concluded:

> Our findings provide further support to various theories suggesting a role of dreaming in state-like emotional processing from one day to another and trait-like characteristics of emotional coping and attachment style.
>
> (p. 13)

As we will see, while this theory about the circadian nature of the dream function is rather daring, it is consistent with recent theories about sleep as regulator of diurnal emotional states (e.g., Van der Helm & Walker, 2009; see: Kahn, Sheppes, & Sadeh, 2013).

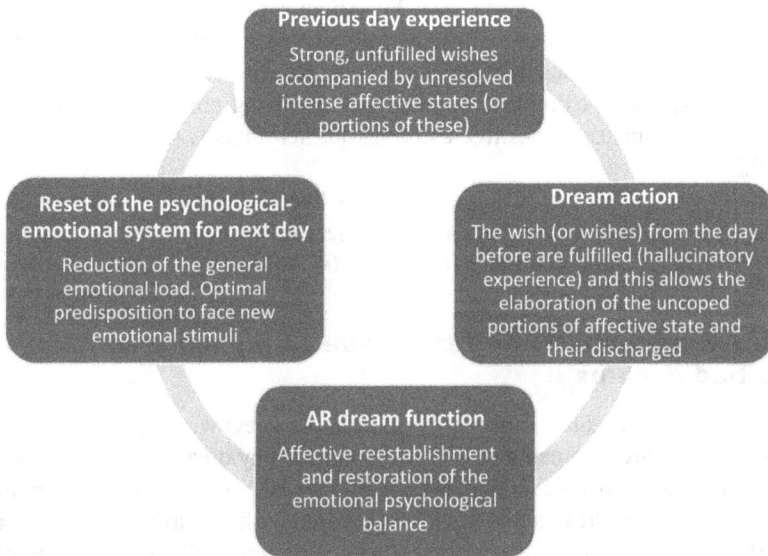

Figure 15.2 The circadian character of the AR function of dreams (from Colace, 2021)

AR hypothesis and emotions in dreams and in post-dreaming daytime

If the dream acts in order to fulfil a wish and process a disturbing affective state, it follows that the emotions in the dream and upon awakening tend to be positive and pleasant.

Most of Marco's wish-fulfilment dreams show a pleasant tone, and frequently this is explicitly expressed by Marco with expressions such as "The dream was beautiful" or "It was a funny dream".

A recent study reports that the predominant emotions in childhood dreams (self-rated by the children themselves) are pleasant ones (feeling calm, happy or good), and the general quality of the dream is rated as pleasant in most cases (Sándor et al., 2015; see also Sándor, 2015 [thesis]).

In several cases, children verbalize their emotions in dreams using expressions such as "I felt happy [in the dream]" or "I was happy while it happened" (Colace, 2010; Mari, Beretta, & Colace, 2018). Even in Foulkes's study (1982), where emotions in dreams were scarcely found, the most frequent type was still "happiness". Honig and Nealis (2012) found that joy is the most frequent emotion in children's dreams, and the emotional impact of dreams in the waking period following the dream is classified as "positive" (41.8%) twice as often than "negative" (21.4%).

Recent studies conducted on the dreams of 3- to 5-year-old children found a higher frequency of positive emotions (27%–33%) than negative emotions (18%–12%) (Alikhani, 2002; Lympinaki, 2001, as quoted in Gartner, 2014), and Gartner (2014) confirms these data by reporting a percentage of 52% of dreams containing at least one positive emotion. Another study involving preschool children indicates a predominance of positive emotions in their dreams (Sándor et al., 2015 p. 13).

Finally, completely compatible with the AR hypothesis is the fact that children, while reporting their dreams, often appear "serene" or "calm" rather than "troubled" or in other emotional states (Colace, 2006, 2013).

The AR hypothesis and the issue of nightmares and bad dreams

The AR hypothesis is based primarily on infantile direct wish-fulfilment dreams. However, in Marco's dreams, it was also confirmed by dreams of multiple wish-fulfilment, serial wish-fulfilment dreams and in later forms of wish-fulfilment dreams—that is, in dreams that satisfy suppressed wishes. Furthermore, we noted that the AR hypothesis is also consistent with certain infantile forms of dreaming in adults (see Chapter 16).

However, some bad dreams and nightmares *apparently* do not fit in the AR hypothesis and *seem* to contradict the wish-fulfilment theory.

Several authors have agreed that nightmares are related to a dysfunction involving the emotional regulation and coping mechanism proper of normal dreams (Helminen & Punamäki, 2008; Bauer, 1976; Wittman et al., 2010). In particular, several models view the *nightmare as failure, disruption or defeat in the processes of emotional regulation of normal dreaming*. These models therefore see *bad dreams as a particular case of dreams* in which the normal function of dreaming fails to achieve its goal (e.g., Nielsen & Levin, 2007; Levin & Nielsen, 2009).

For example, according to Nielsen and Levin's (2007) affective network dysfunction (AND) model, bad dreams and nightmares should be regarded as the expression of the blocking of the normal functioning of dreams, which is to act as a regulator of emotions, and in particular to serve the adaptive purpose of fear-memory extinction. From this perspective, the nightmare is seen as an exception to the normal functioning of dreaming.

Hartman's image-contextualizing theory suggests that the dream function is to establish new associations and contexts for emotional concerns, and this process is more evident in traumatic dreams (Hartman, 1996, 1998). However, this emotional integration and contextualization may fail in chronic post-traumatic dreams, which are viewed as a failure of the dream's emotional-regulation function.

The above mentioned models about nightmares and traumatic dreams refer to the concept of emotional regulation and are completely compatible with the concept of emotional load discharge in normal dreaming, which is the main component of the AR hypothesis. I am largely in agreement with the mentioned approaches when we refer to some types of Marco's bad dreams. Really, some of Marco's bad dreams close to the definition of true nightmares fit easily into the previous *explanations*. In particular, these dreams look like an attempt to deal with portions of strong *emotions such as big fear and anguish,* failing (totally or partially) in the function of their emotional regulation. So when the dream has to manage more challenging emotions, such as a trauma, it may well fail in its task, but this does not mean that its primary function isn't the one that the AR hypothesis assumes.

See the following dream:

M. 14(II), 8;6mo. *I was staying with friends at home, with you* (Dad). *But then you went out one day and you were hanging out with some friends. Then the earthquake came, and I could not see you anymore. You never returned home. Then I started crying because I thought you were dead. Instead, luckily you came back later.*

Marco adds that the dream ended well, but at first, he was afraid and very sad in the dream. The dream refers to an earthquake that had occurred in Rome recently. In this type of dream, an *extraordinary affective state* is processed until its positive final outcome. In this case, the dream seems to be able to fulfil, at least in part, the function of affective-reestablishment also in the face of an extraordinary emotion (the fear of the earthquake), or at least this is its intent. Some other times, however, it may prove unsuccessful.

These types of bad dreams show that the discharge of emotional load apparently takes place also in the presence of affective overloads *not linked to the failure to satisfy a desire (in daytime state)* but to the difficulty of managing a negative strong emotion, sometimes clearly linked to extraordinary situations occurred during the day. These dreams seem to safeguard only the aspect of the affective discharge of the AR hypothesis. We must therefore believe that the AR function of dreams, although in infantile dreams it appears normally and predominantly linked to the satisfaction of a wish and is exercised through its fulfilment, can also be considered valid for the discharge of extraordinary affective negative overloads.[5] In these cases, the affective discharge is thought to occur by other mechanisms, such as Hartmann's emotional contextualization. However, we should remember that we are faced here with *an extraordinary type of dream* that occurs as the result of an *extraordinary affective negative perturbing state.*

In conclusion, nightmares, the most frequent category of bad dreams found in Marco's dreams, are to be considered as true anomalies in normal dreaming in which the function of the dream—that is, affective elaboration and discharge—may reveal its limit to prevent an affective re-establishment and to protect sleep state (i.e., for the child to wake up). But this does not change the purpose to which the dream normally aspires.

The AR hypothesis can be considered completely compatible with bad dreams that are inspired by daring actions, which are as much desired as they are feared.

In these dreams, the wish-fulfilment attempt is overwhelmed by fear. I have called these dreams by the term *false bad dreams*, since under the first apparent impression of a fearsome dream, the aspect of playful challenge is evident. In these bad dreams, through the reckless attempt to satisfy a fearsome desire, an attempt is made to process that portion of pleasant/fearsome mixed emotion present in wakefulness, but this fails to happen, and the dream has a negative ending that causes the child to wake up. In brief, these dreams may be defined as "a pleasant dangerous game with a bad ending". These dreams are thought to safeguard both aspects of the AR hypothesis—that is, the discharge of affective load (fear) and the wish-fulfilment attempt (in this case failed).

We have observed some dreams of Marco's where there was an undis-guised fulfilment of an illegitimate desire (or inadequate disguise) that was *reported in a timorous form* or with shame (i.e., an embryonal form of anxi-ety dreams). For these dreams, the assumption that they correspond to the failed attempt in disguising a repressed and intolerable wish for the child's ego (i.e., superego instance) is valid. For these dreams, the AR hypothesis remains entirely valid.

The AR hypothesis and Freudian hypothesis about the function of dreams

Marco's wish-fulfilment dreams strongly suggest that the dream is a finalized psychic process that takes place in order to satisfy, in a hallucinatory state, a strong unfulfilled daytime wish associated with an intense perturbing affective state. In these dream reports, the diurnal origin of the dream, the reason for its activation, what it does and the purpose for which it takes place, as well as its function, are clear.

One aspect is constantly emphasized in many dream reports: the first direct consequence (on the psychic level) of the hallucinatory satisfaction of a wish is probably the easing of that affective state that arose with the daytime wish, an affective state that has become perturbing because it was incompletely processed and discharged and that has left some degree of emotional load, unprocessed psychologically. This psychological situation (i.e., emotional hyperarousal) is linked, on the one hand, to the intrinsic strength of the child's wish, whose frustration generates a deeper emotional discomfort, and on the other hand, to the child's poor ability to procrastinate the fulfilment of a wish and cope with the affective load.

The result is that the dream protects the child from awakening from the state of sleep and from its possible disturbing effects (probably also of the quality of sleep), but it also acts as a way to *discharge daily emotional loads* that remain unprocessed.[6] The AR hypothesis is entirely in line with the two dream functions described by Freud—that is, (a) the *dream is a guardian of sleep* and (b) *the dream is a "safety valve" for the psyche* (Robert-Freud).[7]

The discharge mechanism at the basis of the dream function hypothesized by Freud is based more on the analysis of adult dreams (i.e., discharge of unconscious drives); however, this same mechanism seems equally applicable to infantile dreams. In adult dreams, what needs to be discharged is the unconscious drive load. In children, what needs to be discharged is the daytime affective perturbing load linked to the unresolved urge of the wish. The origin (in the psychic apparatus) and the nature of what must be discharged changes, but the function of the dream remains the same.

The AR hypothesis encompasses the concept of the dream as wish fulfilment and extends its meaning. In Freud's view, wish fulfilment is about "what the dream is" while its functions are those described previously. My observation of Marco's childhood dreams confirms that the dream is often a fulfilment of a wish and that this aspect is directly related to the essence of the dream function—that is, "what the dream is for". In fact, the satisfaction of a wish is the means by which the discharge of a disturbing affective state takes place.

Having outlined a theory on the function of infantile dreams, we can obtain a complete picture of how, in its earliest forms, the dream appears as a psychic event. The results of the analysis of the dream reports collected from Marco, together with previous systematic studies on children's dreams, suggest that early forms of dreaming are entirely in line with the basic elements that define the dream in Freudian theory (and that are complementary to his theories about the functions of dream), as follows:

- The dream is a fully valid, meaningful and finalized psychic act.
- The motive and the trigger of the dream is a wish.
- The content of the dream is the representation of wish fulfilment.
- The dream has a comprehensible individual and general meaning.
- The function of the dream is to preserve sleep and to act as a safety valve for the psyche.

Several of Marco's dream reports are a fully valid, meaningful and finalized psychic acts, with contents that have an individual and general meaning. They can by no means be considered, in their occurrence and contents, a random psychic event. This is some evidence that confirms my previous systematic observations on children's dreams. It is, in my opinion, viable and robust on an empirical level—evidence from which we may legitimately develop a general theory on dreams. The forms of dreams that occur later in development are very likely to be *deviations* and *complications*, understandable in principle from the original simple infantile dream module, which nevertheless retains its basic aspects: motivational origin, meaning as a psychic act, functions. The research and study of the forms of dreams that occur between the simple ones of young children and those of adults can help us understand the processes that intervene in the original infantile form of dreaming, and this will constitute a good part of the understanding of the dream phenomenon.

Metapsychology

The AR hypothesis closely revitalizes some basic principles of mental functioning defined by Freud in the model of the mental apparatus developed through the study of hysterical patients and that are part of metapsychology (Freud, 1900, 1915, 1920). In particular, they are the "principle of constancy", the concept of "quota of affect" or "psychical energy", the theory of affects, the concept affective discharge, the concepts of trauma and of abreaction (Breuer-Freud, 1893–1895, 1894) as well as the Freud's conception on the primacy of affective processes in psychic life and the possible presence of affective elements of perturbation also in healthy people (Freud, 1913).[8] The infantile dream, with its action and function, represents an exemplification of the way of working of the mental apparatus which is consistent with these principles and conceptions. In Freud's conception, the mind works to keep "charge of affects" or "emotional arousal" low and constant by disposing an association of ideas (i.e., thought processes) or discharging every increase through motor action (Freud, 1893).

In the wish-fulfilment dream, we see that the discharge of the perturbing affective state is realized through the experience of the satisfaction of the wish that allows the complete elaboration (i.e., zeroing) of an affective charge that in the daytime experience has been blocked with the reset or improvement of emotional mental functioning.

Dreams seem to act as a sort of cathartic therapy that, through the reactivation of the pathogenic memories of traumatic events in hysterical patients, allows for the affective load linked to them and originally blocked to be relived and get discharged (i.e., abreaction).

In this sense, the principle of constancy (i.e., the mental apparatus works to maintain the quantity of energy low and constant) and the theory of affects (e.g., affective charge/discharge) appear to us to be anything but scientifically obsolete or inadequate. Moreover, the same "principle of constancy" and concept of "psychical energy" have found a revisitation in the recent Bayesian brain hypothesis (Friston, 2010; Carhart-Harris, & Friston, 2010), which refers explicitly to the first Freudian model of mental functioning. According to this hypothesis, the brain is a "prediction machine" that works to generate predictions about the possible future state of the world and about self-conditioning. The aim of this "prediction machine" is to reduce errors in prediction and/or generate more accurate predictions in order to diminish free energy (i.e., prediction error). (On this topic, see Michael, 2018).

The AR hypothesis compared to theories on emotional adaptive function

Several theories on emotional adaptive function are inspired by the Freudian hypothesis about dream function. In particular, in the current literature, two key concepts that closely evoke the Freudian concepts of dreams as a "safety valve for the psyche" and "affective discharge" are common to different theories on the emotional adaptive function of dreams. First, the *dream experience may facilitate the elaboration and regulation of emotions and emotional conflicts.* Some authors speak explicitly of the *emotional catharsis of dreams* (Desseilles & Duclos, 2013) or of the *action of emotional reprocessing and coping* during the dreaming experience. Second, *the emotional discharge of dreams is "functional" or improves emotional regulation during the next daytime* experiences and maintaining psychological balance.

Several theories on adaptive emotional function agree on the fact that dreams *resolve* emotionally disturbing conflicts (Breger, 1967; Breger, Lane, & Hunter, 1971; Fiss, 1980; Cartwright, 2010).

Other theories suggest that the dream may *reduce* the intensity of emotional stress and *calm* intense emotions (Hartman, 1998, 2011) or serves to regulate the mood (Kramer, 2007, 2011; Schredl, 2009). Hartman, for example, hypothesized that negative emotional memory traces are neutralized by integrating them with other material in the memory network during dreaming. Cartwright (2010), too, suggested that in dreaming, emotional memories are integrated with other memories.

Kramer suggested that during REM dreaming, the inherent affective arousal (increase in limbic system activity) is regulated and contained by the dream, decreasing the intensity of the associated emotion. In this way, dream activity regulates mood.

According to Revonsuo (2000), dreams perform a biological-adaptive function because they treat threatening stimuli and improve the dreamer's ability to manage and deal with threats during the waking period and would promote an adapted behavioural response in daily life (Valli & Revonsuo, 2009).

Jouvet (1991) suggested that dreaming has the function of reinforcing species-specific behaviours. It could also play a role in maintaining the dreamer's personality stability.

Schredl (2009) suggested that dreaming reduces next-day negative mood.

According to Perogamvros and Schwartz (2012), dreaming can play a role in learning and memory, as well as in regulating emotions.

The concept of *emotional discharge* is clearly present in the theory of Nielsen and Levin (2007) and Levin and Nielsen (2009).[9] The authors suggest that the dream serves to facilitate the *extinction* of memories of fearful stimuli through the recombination of the emotions associated with them, allowing an attenuation of the emotional load. According to Nielsen and Levin (2007), fearful memories present in dream content are determined by:

> ongoing daytime demands on the emotional memory system. . . . . These demands are a function of a hypothetical factor we term *affect load*, i.e., a situational or state factor that reflects the combined influence of stressful and emotionally negative events (e.g., interpersonal conflicts, dailyhassles) on an individual's capacity to effectively regulate emotions.
>
> (p. 301)

The role of dreaming in the process of emotional regulation was also suggested by Perogamvros and Schwartz (2012) in their Reward Activation Model (RAM). According to these authors, dreaming is thought to be the result of the amplification and activation of the mesocortical/mesolimbic dopaminergic system, due to the preferential reactivation during sleep of memories with high emotional and motivational value for the individual.

Common to several theories is the concept that memories of problematic emotional situations are replicated and reorganized in the dream (for review, see Sterpenich et al., 2019).

All the previously mentioned theories are based on the study of adult dreams. The AR hypothesis differs from previous theories on the adaptive emotional role of dreams in that it is mainly based on the direct wish-fulfilment dreams of young children. Thanks to the simplicity of children's dreams and their direct connection with waking experiences, the AR hypothesis goes into the specifics of the general concept of dreams as acts of emotional processing and regulation, at the basis of many of the previous theories on the adaptive function of dreaming.

Although the AR hypothesis shares with various emotional adaptive theories the general concept that dreaming can serve as emotional regulation, it differs in assigning the dream's affective-reestablishment action specifically to the fulfilment of a wish, where emotional discomfort is connected to its non-satisfaction during the daytime experience. While most theories do not foresee psychological causes and mechanisms underlying the triggering of the dream, the AR hypothesis assumes that what instigates dreams is predominantly a wish or sometimes an alliance of wishes of different origins in the psychic apparatus and/or of different motivational drives (i.e., a simple or repressed wish). In this case, too, the infantile dream proves its strategic validity for the investigation of dream functions, allowing an in-depth study of certain aspects highlighted by the theories on dream function elaborated for adult dreams.

Sándor et al. (2015) suggested that the study of children's dreams may be a valid and important investigation for the extension of adult dream theories which emphasize the emotional regulatory functions of dreams. On this aspect, however, Sándor et al. (2014) noticed that theoretical works on the functions of dreams based on developmental dream research are extremely scarce.

Previous observation of children's dreams (Colace, 2010, 2013), together with the observation on Marco's dream reports, in addition to being in line with the several previously mentioned concepts, allow us to add, among other things, three specific indications. First, according to the AR function, the *emotional load in children* for which the dream exercises its function *must be understood* as a *certain degree of perturbing emotional arousal due to residual unelaborated portions of a daytime affective state*. Second, this perturbing emotional arousal must be limited and *circumscribed daily*, and the exercise of the function of the dream seems daily and cyclical. Third, *the disturbing emotional load is not a prerogative of the unpleasant affective state* (i.e., all affective state may become perturbing), and it should be intended in terms of quantative variation than qualitative. Indeed, the

AR hypothesis is related to every kind of emotional perturbation (unpleasant or pleasant), since *it is believed that the disturbing character of the affective state does not reside in its polarity (negative/positive) but in its degree of (residual) excitation or arousal.* Differently, most previously mentioned theories are more focused on negative emotions.

Although the AR hypothesis is consistent in several aspects with previous emotional-adaptive theories of dreaming, it differs from these because it combines the fulfilment of desire and the affective function of the infantile dream. In the AR hypothesis, the concepts of hallucinatory wish fulfilment and the discharge of disturbing emotions coexist. Sándor et al. (2014), after reviewing the literature on children's dreams and about the function of dreaming in children, considers the affective-reestablishment hypothesis a result of recent attempts to merge together psychoanalytic concepts and data coming from modern neurosciences. These authors also suggest that both concepts of "dream as safety valve for the psyche" and "dream as guardian of sleep" can be seen as precursors of the concept of emotional reprocessing and coping, in particular of the theory on fear extinction/ emotional reprocessing (Nielsen & Levin, 2007).

We have seen that the Freudian theory about dream as wish fulfilment is not about the function of the dream. It is rather a theory about what instigates dreams and what dreams consist of (hallucinatory wish-fulfilment experience). The AR hypothesis combines Freud's wish-fulfilment theory with Robert's and Freud's "safety valve" theory about the function of dreams, in the context of undisguised simple wish-fulfilment dreams. In infantile dreams, the two aspects, wish fulfilment and affective-reestablishment, cannot be separated from each other and are complementary (except for some bad dreams).

The AR hypothesis and recent findings in sleep and the emotional processing of emotions

Apart from (but in line with) the aforementioned emotional adaptive theories on the function of dreaming, in the same way, several sleep neurophysiological studies are suggesting the role of sleep state, especially REM sleep, as an emotional regulator.[10] These sleep studies are in line with the theoretical claims that emotions experienced in dreams contribute to an affective recalibration, through several mechanisms according to different theories mentioned previously (i.e., generalization, extinction, discharge, regulation, etc.) could predispose to a better coping of the emotional loads of the following day.

For example, studies show that *sleep deprivation* degrades the prefrontal inhibitory control over limbic regions during wakefulness, hence exacerbating emotional responses to negative stimuli (Yoo et al., 2007; Motomura et al., 2013). Another study suggest that the sleep loss impairs emotional regulation by increasing emotional irritability and reactivity (Kahn-Greene et al., 2006). (For a review of the effects of sleep deprivation on emotional aspects, see Deliens, Gilson, & Peigneux, 2014; Vandekerckhove & Wang, 2017).

The AR hypothesis about dreams presenting interesting convergences with all studies on the role of dreams/sleep in the full processing of daytime emotional loads in order to restore the proper functioning of the individual's emotional network system (see Desseilles et al., 2011; Deliens, Gilson, & Peigneux, 2014; Yoo et al., 2007; Van de Helm & Walker, 2009; Van der Helm et al., 2011; Gillin et al., 2001; Motomura et al., 2013; see also Desseilles et al., 2011; Deliens, Gilson, & Peigneux, 2014). In particular, the AR hypothesis is entirely in line with recent studies that show the role of dreams/sleep in the dissipation of the emotional daytime load. Van der Helm and Walker (2009), in their *emotional dissipation theory of sleep and dream*, suggested that a night of sleep contributes to "dissipating" or disempowering the emotional charge via amygdala activity in response to recent daytime emotional experiences; hence, it "may 'reset' the correct affective brain reactivity to next-day emotional challenges by maintaining the functional integrity of this (medial prefrontal cortex) mPFC-amygdala circuit and thus govern appropriate behavioural repertoires" (Van der Helm & Walker, 2009, pp. 10–11). On the other hand, Van der Helm et al. (2011) also show that amygdala activity during the exposure to emotional pictures is reduced when participants are re-exposed to the same pictures after a night of sleep, but not after a similar interval spent awake.

The AR hypothesis attributes a "cathartic" role in the discharge of perturbing emotions to the dream experience, but Van der Helm and Walker do the same by attributing this function to the state of sleep. However, when we talk about regulation and emotional processing, we are more likely to think that the most suitable function for the task of emotional discharge is constituted by the *subjective hallucinatory experience of the dream* that takes place in sleep.

By the way, we note that Van der Helm and Walker also theorize a *circadian mechanism*, much along what the AR hypothesis suggests regarding the affective function in infantile dreams. From this point of view, the dreams of young children are completely consistent with this theory, also regarding the idea that the nocturnal dream repertoire deals mainly with affective/emotional issues from the day that just passed.

In summary, the affective-reestablishment function showed by wish-fulfilment infantile dreams are in line with data coming from *sleep research* on the key role of sleep (especially REM sleep) in regulating emotion and restoring the correct functioning of the emotional affective network, preparing the appropriate emotional reactivity during post-sleep daytime experience.

Vandekerckhove and Wang (2017), in their review on studies about the emotional processing role of sleep state, concluded:

> In summary, the above mentioned research indicates that the possible function of REM-dreaming in processing emotions is to re-process the emotional events experienced during daytime, leading to the rehearsal of the possible emotion regulatory process of the brain which diminishes or adapts the impact of their emotional load on the activities of the following day in a way that is beneficial for the functioning during the day.
>
> (Vandekerckhove & Wang, 2017, p. 5)

REM dreaming functions as a central phase of the masked or unmasked reactivation and the reprocessing of emotions and emotional occurrences during the day (Vandekerckhove & Wang, 2017, p. 7–8).

Notes

1 Freud noticed the distinction between the two aspects of the diurnal experiences that are the basis of the dream. For example, he claimed, "The wishes which are fulfilled in . . . in waking life they have been accompanied by intense emotion" (1901, p. 22) and later, referring to the diurnal experience that inspired the dream in addition to the unfulfilled desire, he referred to the portion of the affective state for which the diurnal experience has not allowed complete processing: "A child's dreams is a reaction to an experience of the previous day, which has left behind it a regret, a longing, a wish that has not been dealt with" (Freud, 1916–17, p. 128).

2 Some of these examples have appeared in other parts of the book to explain other aspects of the dream. The AR function of dreams is clearly observable in several examples of wish-fulfilment dreams reported in the first part of book. Many examples of dreams to explain the AR hypothesis are reported in Colace (2012, 2013).

3 We can assume that the dream deals with the discharge of, more or less, large portions of unresolved affective states depending on the type of desire (partially satisfied or not), the abilities of the child (rationalization) and the environmental circumstances (e.g., parents who promise a future fulfilment of the desire), which may have allowed their partial elaboration during the waking state.

4 For example, Bokert (1968) observed that subjects deprived of food and liquids who reported gratifying dreams (themes of drinking and/or eating) drank less and rated themselves as less thirsty in the period of wakefulness following the dream, compared to thirsty subjects who have not had those dreams. The results of Bokert's study were also supported by Klein (1965), as quoted by Fisher (1970).

5 This interpretation is also implicit in the Freudian explanation of recurrent traumatic dreams. For these dreams, there is no a wishful impulse; however, the dream is aimed to the attempt to master the traumatic stimulus, in order to maintain psychical energy constant, by the discharging mechanism and function (Freud, 1920).

6 I believe that the description of this state of things with Freud's hydraulic theory of some psychic acts is still productive and useful.

7 The idea that sleep can be disturbed by emotional overload and stressful events we experience in daytime life is widely accepted in the literature (Vandekerckhove & Wang, 2017). From this point of view, it appears very plausible that the mental processing (dreaming) of each emotional arousal in sleep is functional to the undisturbed continuation of the same.

8 On Freud's theory of affects and other metapsychological themes, see Boag (2017) and Michael (2015).

9 Sándor et al. (2014) rightly suggested that the Freudian model and the model developed by Nielsen and Levin can overlap, especially considering that wish-fulfilment dreams could very well be a category in line with the theory about the discharge of emotional load.

10 One premise of adaptive-emotional function theories about dreams is that the brain circuits involved during emotional processing occurring during sleep and dreaming activity are the same that are involved in emotional processing during wakefulness. Some studies with different approaches and methodologies offer converging evidence that sustained this theoretical premise (e.g., Sterpenich et al., 2019; Blake et al., 2019; De Gennaro et al., 2011; Scarpelli et al., 2019). For example, studies have shown that

the fronto-limbic emotional circuits (i.e., amygdala, orbito-frontal cortex and ventro-medial prefrontal areas), which are involved (in waking state) in emotional response and regulation, show intense activity during REM sleep (Solms, 1997; Levin & Nielsen, 2009). Recently, Scarpelli et al. (2019) suggest that "the processes that regulate dreaming and emotional salience in dream experience share similar neural substrates of those controlling emotions during wakefulness" (Scarpelli et al., 2019, p. 4). Healthy sleep maintains the correct functioning of media-prefrontal cortex-amygdala connections crucial in the regulation of emotions (Vandekerckhove & Wang, 2017).

References

Alikhani, T. (2002). *Aspects of Dreaming in Pre-School Children*. Unpublished thesis, The Anna Freud Centre & University College London.

Bauer, D. H. (1976). An exploratory study of developmental changes in children's fears. *Journal of Child Psychology and Psychiatry, 17*, 69–74. https://doi.org/10.1111/j.1469-7610.1976.tb00375.x.

Blake, Y., Terburg, D., Balchin, R., Morgan, B., van Honk, J., & Solms, M. (2019). The role of the basolateral amygdala in dreaming. *Cortex, 113*, 169–183.

Boag, S. (2017). *Metapsychology and the Foundations of Psychoanalysis*. New York: Routledge.

Bokert, E. G. (1968). The effects of thirst and related verbal stimulus on dream reports. *Dissertation Abstracts, 28*, 4753b.

Breger, L. (1967). Function of dreams. *Journal of Abnormal Psychology. Monograph, 641*.

Breger, L., Lane, I., & Hunter, R.W. (1971). The effect of stress on dreams. *Psichol Issues, 7*, 3.

Breuer, J., & Freud, S. (1895). *Studies on Hysteria (1893–1895)*. S.E., II. London: Hogarth Press.

Carhart-Harris, R. L., & Friston, K. J. (2010). The default-mode, ego-functions and free-energy: A neurobiological account of Freudian ideas. *Brain, 133* (Pt 4) (April), 1265–1283. DOI: 10.1093/brain/awq010. Epub 2010 28 February. PMID: 20194141; PMCID: PMC2850580.

Cartwright, R. (2010). *The Twenty-Four Hour Mind: The Role of Sleep and Dreaming in Our Emotional Lives*. New York: Oxford University Press.

Colace, C. (2006). Children's dreaming: A study based on questionnaire completed by parents. *Sleep and Hypnosis, 8* (1), 19–32.

Colace, C. (2009). Gli studi sull'effetto della frustrazione dei bisogni primari sul sognare e la recente ricerca e teoria sui processi onirici. *Psycofenia, XII* (20), 49–72.

Colace, C. (2010). *Children's Dreams: From Freud's Observations to Modern Dream Research*. New York: Routledge.

Colace, C. (2012). Dream bizarreness and the controversy between the neurobiological approach and the disguise censorship model: The contribution of children's dreams. *Neuropsychoanalysis, 14* (2), 165–174.

Colace, C. (2013). Are wish-fulfilment dreams of children the royal road for looking at the functions of dreams? *Neuropsychoanalysis, 15* (2), 161–175.

Colace, C. (2014). *Drug Dreams. Clinical and Research Implications of Dreams about Drugs in Drug-Addicted Patients*. New York: Routledge.

Colace, C. (2017). The early forms of dreaming: A longitudinal single-case study on the dream reports of a child from the age of 4 to the age of 7, poster presentation The 18th Annual Congress of the International Neuropsychoanalysis Society, London, England 13 July 2017–15 July 2017.

Colace, C. (2020a). Dreams help us to resolve affective states. How young children's dreams could reveal the function of the dream. *Psychoanalysis Today.* https://psyc hoanalysis.today/enGB/PT-Psychoanalytic-Reflections/Dreams-Help-Us-to-Resolve-Affective-States.aspx.

Colace, C. (2020b). Dreams. In: V. Zeigler-Hill & T. K. Shackelford (Eds.), *Encyclopedia of Personality and Individual Differences.* Springer International Publishing. https://doi. org/10.1007/978-3-319-24612-3.

Colace, C. (2020c). Gambling dreams in pathological gambler outpatients: A pilot study. *Addicta: The Turkish Journal on Addictions, 7* (3). DOI: 10.5152/ADDICTA.2020.20053.

Colace, C. (2021). The affective function in infantile dream. In: T. Giacolini & C. Pirrongelli (Eds.), *Neuropsychoanalysis of the Inner Mind. A Biological Understanding of Human Mental Function.* New York: Routledge.

Colace, C., Salotti, P., & Ferreira, M. (2015). Reduction of dream bizarreness in impaired frontal cortex activity: A case report. *Sleep and Hypnosis: A Journal of Clinical Neuro-science and Psychopathology, 17* (1–2), 14–18.

Colace, C., Salotti, P., & Ferreira, M. (2019). Infantile dream reports in patients with fron-tal deficits. *Sleep Hypnosis: A Journal of Clinical Neuroscience and Psychopathology, 21* (4), 321–327. https://doi.org/10.37133/Sleep.Hypn.2019.21.0201.

De Gennaro, L., Cipolli, C., Cherubini, A., Assogna, F., Cacciari, C., Marzano, C., et al. (2011). Amygdala and hippocampus volumetry and diffusivity in relation to dreaming. *Human Brain Mapping, 32*, 1458–1470. DOI: 10.1002/hbm.21120.

Deliens, G., Gilson, M., & Peigneux, P. (2014). Sleep and the processing of emotions. *Experimental Brain Research, 232* (5), 1403–1414.

Desseilles, M., Dang-Vu, T. T., Sterpenich, V., & Schwartz, S. (2011). Cognitive and emo-tional processes during dreaming: A neuroimaging view. *Consciousness Cognition, 20* (4, December), 998–1008. DOI: 10.1016/j.concog.2010.10.005. Epub 2010 Nov 12. PMID: 21075010.

Desseilles, M., & Duclos, C. (2013). Dream and emotion regulation: Insight from the ancient art of memory. *Behavioral and Brain Sciences, 36* (6), 614; discussion 634–659. DOI: 10.1017/S0140525X13001271. PMID: 24304754.

Fisher, C. (1970). Some psychoanalytic implications of recent research on sleep and dreaming. In: L. Madow & L. H. Snow (Eds.), *The Psychodynamic Implications of the Physiological Studies on Dreams* (pp. 152–167). Springfield, IL: Thomas.

Fiss, H. (1980). Dream content and response to withdrawal from alcohol. *Sleep Research, 9*, 152.

Foulkes, D. (1982). *Children's Dreams, Longitudinal Studies.* New York: Wiley-Interscience Publication.

Freud, S. (1893). *On the Psychical Mechanisms of Hysterical Phenomena.* SE 3: 25–39. London: Hogarth Press.

Freud, S. (1894). *The Neuro-Psychoses of Defence.* S. E., 3: 41–61. London: Hogarth Press.

Freud, S. (1900). *The Interpretation of Dreams.* S.E., 4–5. London: Hogarth Press.

Freud, S. (1901). *On Dreams.* S.E., 5. London and New York: Norton & Company, Inc.

Freud, S. (1913). *The Claims of Psycho-Analysis to Scientific Interest.* S.E., 13: 163–190. London: Hogarth Press.

Freud, S. (1915). *Repression.* S.E., 141–158. London: Hogarth Press.

Freud, S. (1916–1917). *Introductory Lectures on Psycho-Analysis.* S.E., 15/16. London: Hogarth Press.

Freud, S. (1920). *Beyond the Pleasure Principle*. S.E, XVIII. London: Hogarth Press.
Freud, S. (1985). *The Complete Letters of Sigmund Freud to Wilhelm Fliess: 1887–1904*, J. M. Masson (Ed. & Trans.). Cambridge, MA: Belknap Press of Harvard University Press.
Friston, K. J. (2010). The free-energy principle: A unified brain theory? *Nature Reviews Neuroscience, 11* (2), 127–138.
Gartner, Y. (2014). *Immature Recall Ability in Dream Reporting with Children Aged 3–5*. MA Dissertation, University of Cape Town.
Gillin, J. C., Buchsbaum, M. S., Wu, J., Clark, C., Bunney, W. (2001). Sleep deprivation as a model experimental antidepressant treatment: Findings from functional brain imaging. *Depress Anxiety 14* (1), 37–49.
Hartmann, E. (1996). Outline for theory on the nature and function of dreaming. *Dreaming, 6,* 147–170.
Hartmann, E. (1998). *Dreams and Nightmares: The New Theory on the Origin and Meaning of Dreams*. London: Plenum Trade.
Hartmann, E. (2011). *The Nature and the Functions of Dreaming*. New York: Oxford University Press.
Helminen, E., & Punamäki, R.-L. (2008). Contextualized emotional images in children's dreams: Psychological adjustment in conditions of military trauma. *International Journal of Behavioral Development, 32* (3), 177–187. DOI: 10.1177/0165025408089267.
Honig, A. S., & Nealis, A. L. (2012). What do young children dream about? *Early Child Development and Care, 182* (6), 771–795.
Jouvet, M. (1991). Le sommeil paradoxal: est-il le gardien de l'individuation psychologique? *Canadian Journal of Psychology, 45,* 148–168.
Kahn-Greene, E. T., Lipizzi, E. L., Conrad, A. K., Kamimori, G. H., Killgore, W. D. (2006). Sleep deprivation adversely affects interpersonal responses to frustration. *Personality and Individual Differences, 41* (8), 1433–1443.
Kahn, M., Sheppes, G., & Sadeh, A. (2013). Sleep and emotions: Bidirectional links and underlying mechanisms. *International Journal of Psychophysiology, 89* (2) (August), 218–228. DOI: 10.1016/j.ijpsycho.2013.05.010.
Klein, G. S. (1965). Peremptory ideation. Structure and force in motivated ideas. Presented to the Conference on Cognition and Clinical Psychology, University of Colorado, Boulder, CO, 20 April.
Kramer, M. (2007). *The Dream Experience: A Systematic Exploration*. New York: Routledge, Taylor and Francis Group.
Kramer, M. (2011). The selective mood-regulatory theory of dreaming: An adaptive, assimilative, and experimentally based theory of dreaming. In: B. Mallick, S. Pandi-Perumal, R. McCarley, & A. Morrison (Eds.), *Rapid Eye Movement Sleep: Regulation and Function* (pp. 450–459). Cambridge: Cambridge University Press. DOI: 10.1017/CBO9780511921179.046.
Levin, R., & Nielsen, T. A. (2009). Nightmares, bad dreams, and emotion dysregulation. *Current Directions in Psychological Science, 18* (2), 84–88.
Lympinaki, E. (2001). *Children's Dreams*. Unpublished thesis, The Anna Freud Centre & University College London.
Mari, E., Beretta, M., & Colace, C. (2018). L'appagamento di desiderio e il ristabilimento affettivo nel sogno infantile: nuove osservazioni. *Psychofenia, XXI* (37–38), 17–28.
Michael, M. T. (2015). *Freud's Theory of Dreams: A Philosophico-Scientific Perspective*. Lanham: Rowman & Littlefield.

Michael, T. M. (2018). On the scientific prospects for Freud's theory of hysteria. *Neuropsy-choanalysis, 20* (2), 87–98. DOI: 10.1080/15294145.2018.1544851.

Motomura, Y., Kitamura, S., Oba, K., Terasawa, Y., Enomoto, M., Katayose, Y., Hida, A., Moriguchi, Y., Higuchi, S., & Mishima, K. (2013). Sleep debt elicits negative emotional reaction through diminished amygdala-anterior cingulate functional connectivity. *PLoS One, 8* (2), e56578. DOI: 10.1371/journal.pone.0056578. Epub 2013 Feb 13. PMID: 23418586; PMCID: PMC3572063.

Nielsen, T. A. (2005). Chronobiology of dreaming. In: M. H. Kryger, T. Roth, & W. Dement (Eds.), *Principles and Practices of Sleep Medicine* (4th ed., pp. 535–550). Philadelphia: Elsevier Saunders.

Nielsen, T. A., & Levin, R. (2007). Nightmares: A new neurocognitive model. *Sleep Medicine Reviews, 11*, 295–310.

Perogamvros, L., & Schwartz, S. (2012). The roles of the reward system in sleep and dreaming. *Neuroscience and Biobehavioral Reviews, 36*, 1934–1951.

Piaget, J. (1962). *Play, Dreams and Imitation in Childhood*. New York and London: W.W. Norton & Company.

Revonsuo, A. (2000). The interpretation of dreams: An evolutionary hypothesis of the functions of dreaming. *Behavioral and Brain Sciences, 23* (6), 877–901.

Sándor, P. (2015). *Formal and Content-Related Characteristics of Dreaming and Their Associations with Cognitive and Emotional Development Amongst 4–8 Years-Old Children*. Doctoral thesis. Semmelweis University. Mental Health Sciences Doctoral School, Budapest.

Sándor, P., Szakadát, S., & Bódizs, R. (2014). Ontogeny of dreaming: A review of empirical studies. *Sleep Medicine Reviews, 18* (5), 435–449.

Sándor, P., Szakadát, S., Kertész, K., & Bódizs, R. (2015). Content analysis of 4 to 8 year-old children's dream reports. *Frontiers in Psychology, 6*, 534. DOI: 10.3389/fpsyg.2015.00534.

Scarpelli, S., Bartolacci, C., D'Atri, A., Gorgoni, M., & De Gennaro, L. (2019). The functional role of dreaming in emotional processes. *Frontiers in Psychology, 10*, Article 459. https://doi.org/10.3389/fpsyg.2019.00459.

Schredl, M. (2009). Effect of dreams on daytime mood: The effects of gender and personality. *Sleep and Hypnosis, 11* (2), 51–57.

Solms, M. (1997). *The Neuropsychology of Dreams: A Clinico-Anatomical Study*. Mahwah: Lawrence Erlbaum Associates Publishers.

Sterpenich, V., Perogamvros, L., Tononi, G., & Schwartz, S. (2019). Fear in dreams and in wakefulness: Evidence for day/night affective homeostasis. *bioRXiv:534099*. DOI: 10.1101/534099.

Valli, K., & Revonsuo, A. (2009). Sleep: Dreaming data and theories. In: W. P. Banks (Ed.), *Encyclopedia of Consciousness* (pp. 341–355). Amsterdam: Elsevier Publisher.

van der Helm, E., & Walker, M. P. (2009). Overnight therapy? The role of sleep in emotional brain processing. *Psychology Bulletin, 135* (5), 731–748.

van der Helm, E., Yao, J., Dutt, S., Rao, V., Saletin, J. M., & Walker, M. P. (2011). REM sleep depotentiates amygdala activity to previous emotional experiences. *Current Biology, 21*, 2029–2032. DOI: 10.1016/j.cub.2011.10.052.

Vandekerckhove, M., & Wang, Y. (2017). Emotion, emotion regulation and sleep: An intimate relationship. *AIMS Neuroscience, 5* (1), 1–17.

Wittmann, L., Zehnder, D., Schredl, M., Jenni, O. G., & Landolt, M. A. (2010, April). Post-traumatic nightmares and psychopathology in children after road traffic accidents. *Journal of Traumatic Stress, 23* (2), 232–239. DOI: 10.1002/jts.20514. PMID: 20419731.

Yoo, S. S., Gujar, N., Hu, P., & Walker, M. P. (2007). The human emotional brain without sleep—a prefrontal amygdala disconnects. *Current Biology, 17* (20), R877–R878.

Chapter 16

Infantile forms of dreaming in adults

The infantile dream in the context of the Freudian theory

The term "*infantile*" dream, sometimes used by Freud synonymously for dreams of *children*, is also a term that designates the forms of adult dreams that show the same characteristics as children's dreams (Freud, 1916–1917, p. 126). These are dreams also defined as dreams "constructed on infantile lines" (ibid., P. 134) or dreams showing the "infantile type of fulfilment" (Freud, 1901, p. 646).[1]

> Numerous examples of dreams of this infantile type can be found occurring in adults as well . . . Under unusual or extreme conditions dreams of this infantile character are particularly common. Thus the leader of a polar expedition has recorded that the members of his expedition, while they were wintering in the ice-field and living on a monotonous diet and short rations, regularly dreamt like children of large meals, of mountains of tobacco, and of being back at home.
>
> (Freud, 1901, pp. 645–646)

> On the other hand, dreams of an infantile type seem to occur in adults with special frequency when they find themselves in unusual external circumstances.
>
> (Freud, 1900, p. 131 n. 1)

The power of triggering identified infantile dreams apparently lies in the extraordinary strength that a simple (unrepressed) and legitimate desire of the person acquires exclusively in certain environmental conditions,[2] in which the regular satisfaction of that need/wish is denied. Only in these conditions may one encounter dreams that are clear and direct gratification of desires, like in young children. From a theoretical point of view these dreams demonstrate, even in the adult, and with no need for dream interpretation, that dreaming is a sensible psychic act with an understandable meaning and not a by-product of the psyche.

DOI: 10.4324/9781003184874-22

Conditions for the appearance of infantile dreams in adults

From a close examination of Marco's dream reports, I saw clearly that the desire underlying the dream must have a minimum force to be able to trigger a dream. In children, the force of simple daytime wishes is enough within the context of the infantile psychic apparatus (i.e., poor ability to desist from the fulfilment of a wish).

In adults, it is only the extraordinary power of desires and vital needs, frustrated and impeded in their proper satisfaction, that can give rise to these infantile dreams of (direct) wish fulfilment. Otherwise, they seem to appear (as we will see later) in situations of changed psychic conditions of the individual, conditions that in some way re-propose intrapsychic situations similar to those present in young children (i.e., psychic infantilism).

In his description of the infantile dreams of adults, Freud mainly referred to infantile dreams resulting from frustrations of essential basic needs, such as eating and drinking (Freud, 1901, pp. 645–646). However, a recent review (Colace, 2009) has identified studies that, despite coming from different research areas, share the fact that they allow us to observe the effects of the deprivation of several vital needs directly in the dream content, without any interpretative work, that show the direct fulfilment of vital needs/wishes (see Table 16.1). We noted that in all these dreams, there is a strong motivational drive linked to an important frustrated desire, and/or to the lack of a vital need for the individual. Every time, the dream accomplishes the satisfaction of the desire in order to re-establish a situation of normality. In all cases, it is a matter of very strong desires/needs. From a review of the existing literature, we found that the categories of infantile dreams in adults are many and variegated (Colace, 2009, 2010a). (See Arkin & Antrobus, 1991; Fisher & Greenberg, 1977; Kline, 1971; Ramsey, 1953).

Two research paradigms for the study of childhood dreams in adults

I recently pointed out that childhood dreams in adults can manifest themselves not only in the presence of frustrated normal and vital needs/desires, but also in the presence of (a) a pathological (abnormal) wish and (b) an under-functioning of the normal functions of the ego and the superego due to frontal neurological deficits. In the first condition, we are in the presence of pathological wishes that press for their satisfaction at least as much as vital needs and are therefore capable of triggering dreams of direct fulfilment. In the second condition, we are in the presence of changed intrapsychic conditions that *make* certain persistent and strong waking-state wishes capable *again* of triggering infantile dreams and wish fulfilment as it happens in young children. In this case, I would speak of infantile dreams due to a *regression* and of true *secondary infantile dreams*.

In both conditions, the need/desire becomes intense, gaining a strong motivational power to trigger the dream, which is probably accompanied by a greater degree of general activation (emotional arousal) of the individual.

I will focus on two more recent research paradigms, as follows, that made it possible to study infantile dreams in adults.

Pathological desire: the case of drug dreams

One area in which clear forms of infantile wish-fulfilment dreams could be observed in adults is the study of *dreams about drugs* in drug-addicted patients.

Drug-addicted patients often report a specific form of dream about the direct or attempted use of drugs or about seeking, handling or buying drugs (Colace, 2000, 2001, 2010b, 2014; Colace et al., 2010, 2014) (Christo & Franey, 1996; Colace, 2000, 2004, 2010; Yee et al., 2004; Tanguay et al., 2015). These dream are a well-documented clinical phenomenon in all forms of drug addiction (i.e., alcohol, heroin, cocaine, tobacco, lysergic acid diethylamide [LSD], and benzodiazepine) with comparable frequency, phenomenology and clinical aspects.

Typically, these dreams denominated *drug dreams* that are short, with simple and clear contents that refer directly to daytime experiences of drug dependence, and do not require interpretation to understand their meaning. In drug dreams, drug-addicted patients fulfil in a direct and simple way their wish for drug of abuse. Indeed, these dreams are direct expressions of *drug craving*—that is, the pathological/compulsive desire for the previously experienced effects of a psychoactive substance typically present in drug-addicted patients (Araujo et al., 2004; Choi, 1973; Christo & Franey, 1996; Fiss, 1980; Persico, 1992; Tanguay et al., 2015; Colace, 2004, 2014a; Silva & Nappo, 2019; Christensen, 2009; Looney, 1972; Yee et al., 2004; Ziegler, 2005).

Here are some examples of drug dreams:

> Drug dream (cocaine addiction). "I dreamt I was in the cafeteria, teaching other patients here how to chop lines of cocaine and snort them."
>
> (Gillispie, 2010, p. 1)

> Drug dream (LSD addiction). "I was with friends at a rave party, and the guys were offering various drugs; they gave me LSD and I used it. It was a pleasant dream."
>
> (Colace, 2010b, p. 192)

> Drug dream (benzodiazepine addiction). "A woman doctor gave me Valium and thought it was okay, even though I was an addict. I was smiling. I really got over."
>
> (Johnson, 2001, p. 87)

> Drug dream (heroin addiction). "I found the money for the heroin, and then I went out to buy it, but I could not find the pusher."
>
> (Colace, 2014, p. 17)

196 Meaning and function of infantile dreams

Several studies have shown that the frequency of drug dreams is positively correlated with the increase in *drug craving* (e.g., Colace, 2000, 2004, 2006b,; Christo & Franey, 1996; Denzin, 1988; Fiss, 1980; Mooney, Eisenberg, & Eisenberg, 1992). Furthermore, it has been shown that increased drug craving obtained by means of active stimulation (in nature or experimentally induced) might favour the appearance of drug dreams. It is interesting to note how these dreams arise when the drug craving is somewhat frustrated—that is, in conditions where the patient does not use drugs. In the initial stages of abstinence, the drug craving is even stronger, and it is precisely in these stages of transition, from frequent use to non-use, that drug dreams are found. This tells us that only if the desire becomes very strong is it able to trigger such dreams. The strength of the drug craving is evidenced by its extraordinary resistance to time. Drug dreams can appear even after several years from the resolution of the addiction problem and after the patient has stayed clean for a long time (Colace, 2014).[3]

These dreams resemble infantile dreams not only in their *content*—that is, the presence of the *clear* fulfilment of a desire—and in their *form* (for example, *essentiality* and *brevity*) but also in certain dream-work operations and therefore in the process of the dream experience. In this regard, we note the presence of the same *exaggeration* and *caricature effects* observed in some of Marco's dreams. Exaggeration, as in the dreams of children, in these dreams serves the purpose of effective wish fulfilment. The caricature effect, similar to what was observed in Marco's dreams, appears at the service of dream censorship.

See the two following examples where the drug use in the dream is exaggerated compared to reality:

"In the dream I used heroin for three days."

(Colace, 2014, page 17)

"In the dream, I exclaimed: all this heroin for me, it can't be true! I'll be fine for a week."

(ibid. page 17)

In this dream, the dreamer uses a *great amount of drugs* or uses it repeatedly. Furthermore, the exaggerated use of drugs may be presented in the dream in the form of a change in the way of drug use: for example, a change from smoking to injecting into the vein—that is, a way of feeling the effect of the drug faster and more intensely (Colace, 2014). In these dreams, like in the dreams of children, exaggeration is to be understood as an expression of the peremptory nature of desire.

Caricatural epilogues, in the sense of "comical", "funny", "that make you laugh", are also observed in drug dreams. There are countless possibilities for the effects that the dream puts into place in order to avoid the satisfaction of the drug craving, when during the recovery therapy such craving becomes no longer tolerable and admissible for the subject, a desire that has to be repressed since the patient wants to stay clean and not use drugs. In those drug dreams where the use of drugs fails, the reasons are the most disparate and sometimes bewildering and may also lead to abrupt awakening (see Table 4). See the following examples:

"I was preparing myself a heroin shot, which I had not done for many years. While I was preparing it, I felt the usual fear of doing something wrong and spilling the drug, and so it happened. I pulled the plunger backwards too much and the drug started pouring out. Unlike in the past, I was not desperate: I let the drug pour on out, thinking that, after all, it was better that way."

(Colace, 2014, p. 17)

"I was running around town with friends looking for a variety of drugs, but when we finally got some, it was taken away by a vague authority of some kind."

(Looney, 1972, p. 25)

Other strange reasons why the dreamer cannot use the drug are, for example, the drug is dropped to the ground, the wind blows the drug away, the subject receives a phone call, the subject suddenly collapses.

Most drug dreams report the undisguised fulfilment of drug cravings as the patient does not want to stop taking drugs and does not believe it is wrong to take drugs. In these cases, the satisfaction of the drug craving is direct. However, when in the course of the therapy the patients get convinced that they are doing the right thing and want to stay clean, they may report dreams in which their attempt to satisfy their desire is abruptly and bizarrely interrupted, or the fulfilment is accompanied by anxiety and guilt.

The drug craving of addicted patients shares with other vital needs its urgency to be satisfied. It is undeniable that a neurochemical substrate is at the basis of drug craving; however, it is also undeniable that psychological dependence is what plays a crucial role in triggering this type of dream. Some studies suggested that drug dreams are not, strictly speaking, the result of a "withdrawal syndrome" or physical abstinence (Colace, 2004; Hajek & Belcher, 1991). Indeed, several abstinent patients who reported drug dreams were treated with agonist pharmacological medications that mimic the effects of the drug of abuse and prevented the onset of adverse withdrawal symptoms by replacing such drugs. For example, the presence of drug dreams was noticed among patients with heroin addiction under pharmacological treatment with methadone (Colace, 2000, 2004; Colace et al., 2010, 2014). Drug dreams seem more related to psychological abstinence and drug cravings rather than to a neurochemical deficit per se.

The latter observations have received confirmation from another recent line of study: that of *gambling dreams* in patients with a *pathological gambling disorder* (Colace, 2020). This dependence is not chemical but a form of behavioural addiction. The pathological gambling disorder is characterized by a failure to resist the compulsive urge to perform an act that is harmful to the person. Here, the addictive behaviour, however, is not confounded by a drug and/or by the effects caused by stopping its use. Therefore, gambling dreams seems strategic to understand the significance of physical and psychological abstinence in triggering this type of dream of dependence. As in the case of other forms of dependence, these patients reported having had *gambling dreams* after stopping their gaming activity. These dreams, too, are an infantile-like forms of dreaming, where the patients expressed a frustrated pathological wish. In particular, these patients dreamed of playing and engaging in other activities related to gambling or seeking a big win and feeling the urge to play. This suggests that these dreams have the wish to gamble as their main theme, similar to the way that drug dreams focus on the craving for drugs. What we observed is that at the basis of gambling dreams, there might be an increase in the *peculiarly psychological drive* similar to the push of an unstoppable desire. Gambling dreams appear when the patient is busy trying to stop playing, which probably involves his attempt to reject and control his pathological urge for gambling that nevertheless appears in his dream.

In conclusion, *drug dreams* and *gambling dreams* are a case of infantile dreams in adults, which is yet another demonstration of how a vital irresistible wish/need in the adult is capable of triggering a simple infantile dream. Drug dreams, like other infantile dreams of adults, offer an opportunity for a systematic research on the role of desire in triggering of dreams and the vicissitudes of this desire in the dream itself and in the waking period following the dream. At the same time, these dreams offer an opportunity to study the operations of dream works at the service of desire and/or, when the latter becomes inadmissible for the dreamer, at the service of the defensive transformations operated by dream censorship.

Infantile-like forms of dreams in patients with frontal deficits

As we have seen in Chapter 9, in the perspective of the Freudian dream theory, the presence of simple infantile dreams is attributed to the incomplete development of the ego, or less domination of thought on motivational drives, and of superego functions, or the lower probability of the presence of repressed psychic material at the basis of dreams and less dream bizarreness (Freud, 1900, 1901). In healthy adults, unlike in young children, due to the complete development of the ego, which, by controlling intentional motility, exerts a dominant and inhibitory influence on psychic drives, it becomes rare that a simple everyday wish finds fulfilment in their dreams since adults have learned to waive such fulfilment.

In case of changes in the psychic conditions of adults, in the sense of a regression in the ego and superego functioning (i.e., psychic infantilism), we might assume a return of *secondary* infantile dreams. This hypothesis has obtained some confirmation from the study of dream reports in patients with neuropsychological impairments/deficits. Preliminary neuropsychological observations have suggested an infantile way of dreaming in patients with frontal deficits in brain areas involved in functions at the service of the correct functioning of ego and superego activity. In particular, an early study dating back to the 1950s (Frank, 1950) and two more recent exploratory investigations (Blake, 2014; Colace, Salotti, &

Ferreira, 2015) have suggested an infantile way of dreaming—that is, the presence of direct wish-fulfilment dreams with no "bizarre" elements in their contents in patients with frontal deficits and damage to certain interconnected structures (e.g., the amygdala).

Frank (1950) observed that patients with orbital cortex ablation showed less complex dreams, with contents of clear wish fulfilment, like the dreams of young children.

Blake (2014) found infantile wish-fulfilment dreams like those of young children in patients with Urbach–Wiethe disease (UWD), which involves congenital damage to the amygdala. He concluded that the presence of infantile dreams observed in UWD patients might suggest that the basolateral amygdala is probably involved in the superego circuits that govern the pervasive unpleasant distortions and complications found in the dreams of normal adults (Blake, 2014). Furthermore, Blake suggested that "if the dreams of UWD patients are similar to those of young children, then this raises the interesting idea that the basolateral amygdala could play a role in the circuits that underlie superego functions in the human brain" (p. 66). For example, in Blake's observations (2014), a patient suffering from Urbach–Wiethe disease with damage to the amygdala reported the following dream on a simple and strong wish: "I dreamt that my deceased pet dog was alive again, and I hugged him" (Blake, 2014, p. 92). (See also Blake et al., 2019.)

Colace, Salotti and Ferreira (2015) found less "bizarreness" and reduced dream length (both typical of infantile dreams) in the dreams of a woman suffering from a chronic degenerative disease with a deficit of cerebral activity in the left dorsolateral prefrontal, operculo-insular portions of the frontal lobe and in the right superior parietal region. This patient showed problems in executive functions, with deficits in the ability to inhibit inappropriate or irrelevant response tendencies, in the executive organization and in selective or focused attention.

The infantile dreams of patients with frontal deficits may have been interpreted as the result of the dysfunction of certain executive functions involved in ego and superego activities (e.g., executive tasks of the ego, adaptation to reality, self-regulation of emotional and social behaviour, inhibition) that may have determined a lower ability of these subjects to waive or forbear from the fulfilment of their everyday unrepressed wishes and a return to the most "primordial" mode of dreaming.

These indications were replicated in a more recent study involving 10 patients who, on the basis of instrumental examinations (SPET, MRI), showed frontal deficits—such as dorsolateral, fronto-orbital, frontomesial, frontoparietal, operculoinsular, cingulate gyrus and putamen (Colace, Salotti, & Ferreira, 2019). Clinically, many of these patients showed clinical signs compatible with frontotemporal neurodegenerative disorder, such as disinhibition, apathy, loss of empathy and deficiency in social cognition. At a neuropsychological evaluation, the typical patient shows deficits in executive functions, in particular in the ability to inhibit non-relevant automatic response and attentional shifting. Among these patients, 5 reported "infantile" dreams. The infantile dreams of these patients were characterized by the presence of the direct fulfilment of a strong (conscious) wish of the patient. These dreams were rather short and lacked the complexity and bizarreness that habitually hinder the understanding of the meaning of adult dreams. They were dreams with a clear meaning with respect to the dreamer's waking experiences. Two examples are reported as follows:

> Patient A: "I dreamed of the bottom of the sea, swimming above and below the seabed, beautiful to look at. There was the joy of being at the bottom of the sea, I was happy . . . I did somersaults . . . It was a very beautiful dream."

In reality, the patient swims only on the surface of water because he is afraid of deep waters. This dream is very likely an infantile compensation dream.

> Patient B: "We were walking around casually, and there were also some friends of mine and my mother too. My sister was not there. My mother was there. We were in the garden of the house."

The patient in the dream is with the mother, who had died in reality. It is another example of a compensation dream.

The brain areas where these patients showed deficits (dorsolateral, fronto-orbital, frontomesial, fronto parietal, operculoinsular, cingulate gyrus, putamen) play an important role in executive functions (Stuss & Levine, 2002; Bechara, Damasio, & Damasio, 2000; Damasio, 1994; Myers, Swett, & Miller, 1973; Schore, 1996; Raine & Yang, 2006; Horn et al., 2003; for review, see Yu, 2003), some of which are exactly involved in ego and superego activities. In this perspective, the presence of "infantile" dreams in these patients might be interpreted as the negative result that their executive function deficits have on some aspects related to the area of impulse and inhibition, regulation of emotional behaviour and cognitive flexibility, which could serve the more general ego and superego psychic function. The altered functioning of the ego and superego in these patients might have changed their ability to waive or forbear from the fulfilment of unrepressed wishes of everyday life, now capable of acting (unlike what happens in healthy adults) as a strong wishful impulse that triggers the dreams, as it occurs in young children (i.e., a sort of "infantilizing" of psychic functioning). Thus, the presence of these dreams in these patients represents a return to an ontogenetically "earlier" mode of dreaming, which normally appears present in preschool children due to incomplete ego and superego function development.

Conclusions

The possibility to observe the presence of infantile dreams in adults under different environmental (in nature) and experimental conditions amplifies the scope of the infantile dream study paradigm by offering the possibility to study, also in adults, the role of wishes in dream triggering and how the wishes are treated in the process and content of dreams (i.e., dream work).

At present, all forms of infantile dreams, both in children and in adults, show how desires play an important role in the instigation of dreams and in the treatment of the (unresolved) affective states connected to them, something that psychoanalysts may take for granted but that nevertheless, in the conditions offered by (all) infantile dreams, can be investigated in a systematic way and with the research methodologies used in conventional sleep and dream research.

Infantile dreams, be they dreams of actual young children or "re-emerging" infantile dreams of adults, so to speak, represent strong evidence supporting that dreams are triggered by and deal with desires in a sensible and significant way. Every dream theory, even those that consider the dream phenomenon as a secondary product and/or a mere random psychic act connected to the state of sleep, must be able to provide a possible explanation for these dreams in order to be plausible.

The AR hypothesis of infantile dreams that emerged clearly in the dreams of children may also extend to the forms of infantile dreams in adults. These dreams, as well as those of children, can give useful information to understand the function of the dream. For example, Bokert (1968) observed that people deprived of food and water had dreams about drinking, but more importantly, those same subjects were less thirsty upon awakening than those who did not have such dreams. Similarly, in drug-addicted patients who satisfy their craving for drugs in their dreams (i.e., dreams about drugs or drug use), a better ability to manage the drug craving is often found upon awakening, preventing the risk of relapse (Colace, 2014).

The study of infantile dreams allows us to better understand the infantile dreams of adults. For example, mechanisms such as exaggeration and caricature effect, present in the infantile dreams of adults, appear even clearer in their meaning after having observed and understood them in Marco's dreams.

Table 16.1 Infantile dreams in adults: some representative examples from the literature

Daytime Condition	Dreams	Author
Deprivation of food and/or water	Dream with obsessive reference to food and/or eating	Baldridge (1966) and Baldridge et al. (1965); Klein (1965); Bokert (1968); Sorokin (1942)
Deprivation of personal freedom and vital necessity to join the authoritarian regime	Dreams of clear satisfaction of the desire to belong and of participation, candidly expressed in a childlike and direct form. Example: dreaming of being Hitler's adviser, or Hitler's right hand man. The author compares these dreams to those of children.	Beradt (2020)

(Continued)

Table 16.1 (Continued)

Daytime Condition	Dreams	Author
Observation of the dreams of a large sample of young people who had been in prison for 6 days	80% of the dreams concerned with their home ("home dreams").	Selling (1932)
Observation of a group of inmates	Out of the 52 dream stories collected, 42 showed to have a relationship with the inmates' common desires "to go home", "to have sexual intercourse".	Hanks (1940)
War prisoners in Vietnam	Dreams about the wish to "go home" (back-home dreams) and about the typical gestures of an ordinary daily routine	Andersen (1975)
Study on a population of 600 Zulu infertile women. In this culture, there is a great psychological need to bear children, and Zulu women base the importance of their social role precisely on their ability to bear children.	The dreams collected contained many direct references to children.	Lee (1958)
Women who had come to know that their husbands were infertile	About 60% of these reported dreams in which "they were happily pregnant".	Berger (1980)
Students entering college for the first time being away from their homes	They dreamed of their families more frequently than older students.	Eisman (1994)
People who had recently become paraplegic and quadriplegic	Their dreams contained more in-motion imagery than those of normal subjects. It is important to note that this increase in motion images occurred only in recently paralyzed subjects and not in those who had been paralyzed for a long time.	Newton (1970)

Table 16.1 (Continued)

Daytime Condition	Dreams	Author
Subjects under social isolation for a day	Undisguised wish-fulfilment REM dreams about social activities and interactions, such as, for example, "conversation groups or meetings" and, more generally, about "socializing"	Wood (1968)
An impediment to normal motility was artificially induced through the administration of meprobamate (a drug that acts as a muscle relaxant). In another similar study, imipramine (a drug similar to meprobamate) was used.	In the post-treatment period, their dreams presented a statistically significant increase in motility.	Whitman, Pierce, and Maas (1960); Kramer et al. (1968)
Study on the dreams of 72 subjects who had recently undergone a limb amputation	In the dreams of 31 of these (43%), their limbs appeared intact.	Shukla et al. (1982). See also Brugger (2008).
Amputation of a leg	In part of the dreams of people who have undergone amputation, the subjects continue to represent themselves with their limbs.	Mulder et al. (2008)

Notes

1   The presence of this type of simple and directly understandable dreams had been noticed already by dream researchers of ancient times and throughout the era's prescientific studies on dreaming (Mackenzie, 1965; Mancia, 1998; Colace, 2009; Kruger, 1992). These were often related to individual's primary needs but not solely to them. Artemidorus Daldianus, in his famous *Oneirokritikon*, described the mental activity during sleep (insomnium) that directly brought the fulfilment of desires, needs or aspirations of the moment reporting the examples of the hungry who dreamed of eating, of the thirsty who dreamed of drinking and of the lovers who dreamed of their beloved (Artemidoro di Daldi, 1976). Galen pointed out that in dreams, "the image of drinking without ever getting sated happens to the thirsty, of eating voraciously to those who are hungry" (quoted in Guidorizzi, 1988, p. 87). Dreams that refer directly to needs

(hunger, thirst) were described by Augustine (see Kruger, 1992). In the Middle Ages, Macrobius and Chalcidius defined specific categories of dreams (insomnium and/or somnium, respectively) that directly reflected hunger or thirst (see Kruger, 1992). Gregory the Great described dreams triggered by an empty stomach (Kruger, 1992).

What is interesting here is that already, in past epochs, when oracular and prophetic value was attributed to dreams and where the complex contents expressed in metaphorical and symbolic forms of dreams were highlighted and different classifications of dreams had been proposed, dreams were observed and described as differing from others in their content, being directly and simply addressed to primary needs and worldly desires (Mackenzie, 1965).

2   See for example the prisoner's dream of freedom (Freud, 1916–17). Dreams of the infantile type also include the so-called dreams of convenience, "in which a person who would like to sleep longer dreams that he is really up and is washing, or is already at school, whereas he is really still sleeping" (Freud, 1916–1917, pp. 134–135) and the dreams of impatience—that is, "if someone has made preparations for a journey, for a theatrical performance that is important to him . . . he may dream of a premature fulfilment of his expectation" (p. 134).

3   On the other hand, we have seen how certain strong desires can trigger serial dreams in Marco's dream repertoire over a long period.

References

Andersen, R. S. (1975). Operation Homecoming: Psychological observation of repatriated Vietnam Prisoners of War. *Psychiatry*, *38*, 65–74.

Araujo, R. B., Oliveira, M., Piccoloto, L. B., & Szupszynski, K. (2004). Sonhos e craving em alcoolistas na fase de desintoxicação [Dreams and craving in alcohol addicted patients in the detoxication stage]. *Revista Psiqiatria Clinica*, *31* (2), 63–69.

Arkin, A. M., & Antrobus, J. S. (1991). The effects of external stimuli applied prior to and during sleep on sleep experience. In: A. M. Arkin, J. S. Antrobus, & S. J. Ellman (Eds.), *The Mind in Sleep: Psychology and Psychophysiology* (pp. 265–307). Hillsdale: Lawrence Erlbaum Associates.

Artemidoro di Daldi. (1976). *Dell'Interpretazione de' sogni*. Milano: Biblioteca Universale Rizzoli.

Baldridge, P. B. (1966). Physical concomitants of dreaming and the effect of stimulation on dreams. *Ohio State Medical Journal*, *62* (12), 1273–1275.

Baldridge, P. B., Whitman, R. M., Kramer, M., Ornstein, P. H., & Lansky, L. (1965). The effect of external physical stimuli on dream contest. Paper presentation. Association for the Psychophysiological Study of Sleep, Washington.

Bechara, A., Damasio, H., & Damasio, A. R. (2000). Emotion, decision making and the orbitofrontal cortex. *Cerebral Cortex*, *10*, 295–307.

Beradt, C. (2020). *Il terzo reich dei sogni*. Millano: Meltemi editore.

Berger, D. M. (1980). Couple's reactions to male infertility and donor insemination. *American Journal of Psychiatry*, *137* (9), 1047–1049.

Blake, I. (2014). *The Role of the Amygdala in Dreaming*. Master Dissertation, University of Cape Town. South Africa.

Blake, Y., Terburg, D., Balchin, R., van Honk, J., & Solms, M. (2019). The role of the basolateral amygdala in dreaming. *Cortex*, *113* (April), 169–183. DOI: 10.1016/j.cortex.2018.12.016.

Bokert, E. G. (1968). The effects of thirst and related verbal stimulus on dream reports. *Dissertation Abstracts*, *28*, 4753b.

Brugger, P. (2008). The phantom limb in dreams. *Consciousness and Cognition, 17*, 1272–1278.

Choi, S. Y. (1973). Dreams as a prognostic factor in alcoholism. *American Journal of Psychiatry, 130*, 699–702.

Christensen, R. L. (2009). *A Multi-Level Analysis of Attentional Biases in Abstinent and Non-Abstinent Problem Drinkers*. Dissertation. Florida State University College of Arts and Sciences.

Christo, G., & Franey, C. (1996). Addicts' drug-related dreams: Their frequency and relationship to six month outcomes. *Substance Use Misuse, 31* (1), 1–1.

Colace, C. (2000). Dreams in abstinent opiate drug addicts: Four case reports. *Sleep and Hypnosis, 4*, 160–163.

Colace, C. (2001). Needs and dreaming processes: Observations on dreams of abstinent heroin addicts. *Sleep, 24*, A185.

Colace, C. (2004). Dreaming in addiction. A study on the motivational bases of dreaming processes. *Neuro-psychoanalysis, 6* (2), 165–179.

Colace, C. (2006). Drug dreams in cocaine addiction. *Alcohol & Drug Review, 25* (2), 177.

Colace, C. (2009). Gli studi sull'effetto della frustrazione dei bisogni primari sul sognare e la recente ricerca e teoria sui processi onirici. *Psycofenia, XII* (20), 49–72.

Colace, C. (2010a). *Children's Dreams: From Freud's Observations to Modern Dream Research*. New York: Routledge.

Colace, C. (2010b). Drug dreams in mescaline and LSD addiction. *American Journal on Addictions, 19* (2), 192.

Colace, C. (2014). *Drug Dreams. Clinical and Research Implications of Dreams about Drugs in Drug-Addicted Patients*. New York: Routledge.

Colace, C. (2020). Gambling dreams in pathological gambler outpatients: A pilot study. *Addicta: The Turkish Journal on Addictions, 7* (3). DOI: 10.5152/ADDICTA.2020.20053.

Colace, C., Belsanti, S., & Antermite, A. (2014). Limbic system irritability as neubiological substrate of drug dreaming in heroin-addicted subjects. *Heroin Addiction and Related Clinical Problems, 16* (3), 75–86.

Colace, C., Claps, M., Antognoli, A., Sperandio, R., Sardi, D., & Benedetti, A. (2010). Limbic system activity and drug dreaming in drug-addicted subjects. *Neuro-psychoanalysis, 12* (2), 201–206.

Colace, C., Salotti, P., & Ferreira, M. (2015). Reduction of dream bizarreness in impaired frontal cortex activity: A case report. *Sleep and Hypnosis: A Journal of Clinical Neuroscience and Psychopathology, 17* (1–2), 14–18.

Colace, C., Salotti, P., & Ferreira, M. (2019). Infantile dream reports in patients with frontal deficits. *Sleep Hypnosis: A Journal of Clinical Neuroscience and Psychopathology, 21* (4) (December), 321–327. https://doi.org/10.37133/Sleep.Hypn.2019.21.0201.

Damasio, A. R. (1994). *Descartes' Error: Emotion, Reason, and the Human Brain*. New York: Grosset/Put.

Denzin, N. K. (1988). Alcoholic dreams. *Alcoholism Treatment Quarterly, 5*, 133–139.

Eisman, L. M. (1994). Dreams of college students living away from home for the first time. California School of Professional Psychology at Berkeley. *Dissertation Abstracts International, 54* (June), 12.

Fisher, S., & Greenberg, R. P. (1977). *The Scientific Credibility of Freud's Theories and Therapy*. New York: Basic Books, Inc.; trad.it., La credibilità scientifica delle concezioni teoriche e della pratica terapeutica di Freud, Roma: Astrolabio, 1979.

Fiss, H. (1980). Dream content and response to withdrawal from alcohol. *Sleep Research, 9*, 152.

Frank, J. (1950). Some aspects of lobotomy (prefrontal leucotomy) under psychoanalytic scrutiny. *Psychiatry, 13*, 35–42.

Freud, S. (1900). *The Interpretation of Dreams*. S.E., 4–5.London: Hogarth Press.

Freud, S. (1901). *On Dreams*. S.E., 5. London: Hogarth Press.

Freud, S. (1916–1917). *Introductory Lectures on Psycho-Analysis*. S.E., 15/16. London: Hogarth Press.

Gillispie, C. (2010). Relapse dreams. A hidden message? *California Together, 4* (4), 1.

Guidorizzi, G. (1988). Sogno, diagnosi, guarigione: da Asclepio a Ippocrate. In: G. Guidorizzi (Ed.), *Il sogno in Grecia* (pp. 87–102). Roma-Bari: Laterza.

Hanks, L. M. (1940). An exploration of the content of dreams through an interpretation of dreams of convicts. *The Journal of General Psychology, 23*, 31–46.

Hajek, P., & Belcher, M. (1991). Dream of absent-minded transgression: An empirical study of a cognitive withdrawal symptom. *Journal of Abnormal Psychology, 100*, 487–491.

Horn, N. R., Dolan, M., Elliott, R., Deakin, J. F., & Woodruff, P. W. (2003). Response inhibition and impulsivity: An fMRI study. *Neuropsychologia, 41* (14), 1959–1966. DOI: 10.1016/s0028-3932(03)00077-0. PMID: 14572528.

Johnson, B. (2001). Drug dreams: A neuropsychoanalytic hypothesis. *Journal of the American Psychoanalytic Association, 49*, 75–96.

Klein, G. S. (1965). *Peremptory Ideation. Structure and Force in Motivated Ideas*. Conference on Cognition and Clinical Psychology, University of Colorado, Boulder, Colorado, 20 April, 1965.

Kline, P. (1971). *Facts and Fantasy in Freudian Theory*. London: Methuen.

Kramer M., Whitman, R. M., Baldridge, B., & Ornstein, P. H. (1968). Drug and dreams III: The effects of Imipramine on the dreams of depressed patients. *American Journal of Psychiatry, 124* (10), 1385–1392.

Kruger, S. F. (1992). *Dreaming in the Middle Ages*. Cambridge: Cambridge University Press.

Lee, S. G. (1958). Social influences in Zulu dreaming. *The Journal of Social Psychology, 47*, 265–283.

Looney, M. (1972). The dreams of heroin addicts. *Social Work, 17*, 23–28.

Mackenzie, N. (1965). *Dreams and dreaming*. New York: Vanguard Press.

Mancia, M. (1998). *Breve storia del sogno*. Venezia: Marsilio.

Mooney, A. J., Eisenberg, A., & Eisenberg, H. (1992). *The Recovery Book*. New York: Workman.

Mulder, T. H., Hochstenbach, J., Dijkstra, P. U., & Geertzen, J. H. (2008). Born to adapt, but not in your dreams. *Consciousness and Cognition, 17* (4), 1266–1271.

Myers, R. E., Swett, C. S., & Miller, M. (1973). Loss of social group affinity following prefrontal lesions in free-ranging macaques. *Brain Research, 64*, 257–269.

Newton, P. (1970). Recalled dream content and the maintenance of body image. *Journal of Abnormal Psychology, 76*, 134–139.

Persico, A. M. (1992). Predictors of smoking cessation in a sample of Italian smokers. *International Journal of the Addictions, 27* (6), 683–695.

Raine, A., & Yang, Y. (2006). Neural foundations to moral reasoning and antisocial behavior. *Scan, 1*, 203–213.

Ramsey, G. W. (1953). Studies in dreaming. *Psychological Bulletin, 50*, 432–455.

Schore, A. (1996). The experience-dependent maturation of regulatory system in the orbital prefrontal cortex and the origin of development psychopathology. *Development and Psychopathology, 8*, 59–87.

Selling, A. F. (1932). The effect of conscious wish upon dream content. *Journal of Abnormal and Social Psychology, 37*, 172–178.

Shukla, G. D., Sahu, S. C., Tripathi, R. P., & Gupta, D. K. (1982). Phantom limb: A phenomenological study. *The British Journal of Psychiatry, 141*, 54–58.

Silva, T. R. da, & Nappo, S. A. (2019). Crack cocaine and dreams: The view of users. *Ciênc. saúde coletiva, 24* (3), 1091–1099. DOI.org/10.1590/1413–81232018243.05072017.

Sorokin, P. A. (1942). *Man and Society in Calamity.* New York: Dutton.

Stuss, D. T., & Levine B. (2002). Adult clinical neuropsychology: Lessons from studies of the frontal lobes. *Annual Review of Psychology, 53*, 401–433.

Tanguay, H., Zadra, A., Good, D., & Leri, F. (2015). Relationship between drug dreams, affect, and craving during treatment for substance dependence. *Journal of Addiction Medicine, 9* (2), 123–9.

Yee, T., Perantie, D. C., Dhanani, N., & Brown, E. S. (2004). Drug dreams in outpatients with bipolar disorder and cocaine dependence. *Journal of Nervous and Mental Disease, 192* (3), 238–242.

Yu, C. K.-C. (2003). Neuroanatomical correlates of dreaming, III: The frontal lobe controversy (dream censorship). *Neuro-Psychoanalysis, 5*, 159–169.

Whitman, R. M., Pierce, C. M., & Maas, J. (1960). Drug and dreams. In: L. Uhr & J. G. Miller (Eds.), *Drug and Behavior* (pp. 591–595). New York: John Wiley.

Wood, P. (1968). Dreaming and social isolation. In: W. B. Webb (Ed.), *Sleep: An Experimental Approach.* London: Macmillan. Unpublished PhD thesis, University of North Carolina.

Ziegler, P. P. (2005). Addiction and the treatment of pain. *Substance Use & Misuse, 40*, 1945–1954.

Chapter 17

A new ontogenetic psychological-psychoanalytic model of dreaming

Introduction

This study focuses on the assumption that the research on early forms of dreaming in the developmental age may provide useful indications for understanding various aspects of the phenomenon of dreaming in general. The dreams reported in this study show *embryonic versions* of the same processes and mechanisms that appear in adult dreams, understood through psychoanalytic investigation.[1] Infantile dreams allow us to study how these processes and mechanisms generate and develop along the ontogenetic development of dreaming and how they come to be transformed by the typical factors of dream function, as well as by external factors related to the cognitive and psychological development of the individual.

The observations of this study on the earliest forms of dreaming, the subsequent ones during development up to the age of 10 and the previous systematic research on large samples of dreams and of children (Colace, 2010a, 2013) allow us to sketch a *new ontogenetic theoretical model of dreaming* aimed at describing dreams as they occur in the child and at providing a key to understand the phenomenon of dreaming in general.

The main assumption of this model is that, while the characteristics of dream processes change along with development, they maintain some of their basic prerogatives of functioning. In this sense, the study of early elementary forms of manifestation of the dream processes in childhood and the study of their *lines of change in dreaming in the developmental age* provides a key to understand the phenomenon of dreaming.

At the same time, this ontogenetic model of dreaming is meant as an attempt to add knowledge to, look closer at and develop Freud's first observations and hypotheses on infantile dreams, by using data obtained from broad range of systematic studies on infantile dreams (Colace, 2010a, 2013) and from this longitudinal study, which has extended the research up to 10 years of age.

In his observations, Freud used infantile dreams to substantiate, above all, his theory of dreaming as wish fulfilment, in particular the assumption that dreams are instigated by desires and that one of their functions is to act as "guardians" of sleep. Furthermore, and quite important on a theoretical level, through the dreams

DOI: 10.4324/9781003184874-23

of children, Freud could demonstrate that the dream is a finalized, fully valid and meaningful psychic act. Freud also suggested that the progressive appearance of dream bizarreness was related, at least in part, to the development of education and interiorization of parental rules and detected certain early forms of dream-work operations in the children's dreams contents, such as for example, the *omissions* (Freud, 1900).[2]

The model I am proposing includes some of the aspects of infantile dreams and of dreaming in general that were already described by Freud and proposed again here due to having received major empirical support from systematic studies. Therefore, they deserve further, more structured consideration and integration within a broader model of infantile dreams and their progress in developmental age.

I understand this model as *psychological and psychoanalytic* in its essence. Indeed, this ontogenetic model of dreaming as well as the AR hypothesis, which constitutes its most important nucleus, explicitly refer to the concepts of Freud's general theory of dreams, to Freud's general psychological theory about the human mind and to certain basic concepts of mental functioning described by Freud in his formulation of the psychic apparatus derived from the study of hysterical patients and further developed in his metapsychological writings (Breuer & Freud, 1893–1895; Freud, 1893, 1894, 1900, 1915, 1920). I am referring here in particular to the principle of constancy, the theory of affects, the theory of desire, the concepts of abreaction and affective discharge and the concept of defense.[3]

The ontogenetic model is based on the direct analysis of dreams and their contents. In this study and in previous ones, I never made use of classical psychoanalytic interpretation techniques (e.g., free association) nor of observations from clinical settings.[4] In this sense, I find Freud's assertion that observations on children's dreams—and I might add on the infantile dreams of adults—can be conducted by any research psychologist interested in the study of dreams is absolutely reasonable. Certainly, what emerged from this study is that a thorough understanding of the individual meaning of infantile dreams cannot be separated from an accurate analysis of the links between dream content and day residues: these, and the child's general daytime experiences as well as his/her desires and habits, should be known well. This is essential. Just as adults' dreams can be understood within a therapeutic context that accompanies the interpretation of dream signifiers, infantile dreams presuppose a good knowledge of the child dreamers and of their life experiences.[5]

A new ontogenetic psychological-psychoanalytic model of dreaming

The data collected shows that dreams, in their earliest forms of onset at the age of 3 and up the age of 5, are *valid and finalized psychic acts*. It is a psychic event, logically and sensibly linked to psychic experiences and events that preceded it in the daytime experience and that can be understood, in the light of these, in its individual and general meaning.

The nature of the daytime events that a dream is closely linked to is *motivational* (one or more desires drive) and *affective* (affective states).

What we observe in this *embryonic form of dreaming* is the staging of the simple and direct fulfilment of a wish of the dreamer that remained unsatisfied in his waking experience. The dream does nothing else than faithfully resume the child's waking experience and represent the hallucinatory fulfilment of his/her wish by offering an *effective experience of gratification*.

In this early form of dreaming, we clearly see that *the dream is a psychic act with the purpose of satisfying a wish* and that *the wish is itself the reason for its occurrence*, the *psychic force that activates the dream* and ultimately *makes it necessary*.

In the dream repertoire of early childhood years, this is the largely prevalent model of dreaming. Exceptions are some bad dreams and very few other frankly bizarre dreams. These latter dreams are an early form of complication of infantile dreaming, while bad dreams are true dysfunctions of the ordinary dream process. The simple, infantile kind of dream that directly satisfies a daytime wish is the crucial starting point of this ontogenetic model and, at the same time, *the prototype of dreaming*.[6] We cannot see why these dream features, so clearly present in early dreams, should disappear or be denied with the progress and evolution of dreaming. We are instead inclined to believe, as it happens with other embryonic processes, that these features are intrinsic to dreams and are bound to remain in their essence, even if dreams become increasingly complicated and eventful along the course of ontogenetic development.

On the other hand, this *infantile form of dreaming survives in adults*. It is a type of process that never extinguishes completely and is ready to return. In the adult dream repertoire, infantile dreams occur in extraordinary conditions, such as the presence of *pathological desires* and *major frustrations of vital needs*, but also in conditions of frontal neurological deficits affecting the normal functions of the ego and superego that lead to a sort of "psychic infantilization" of the individual. In other words, in these cases, the dream function *returns* to operate and manifest itself in ways that have become known from the studies on children's dreams, confirming that the infantile module of the dreaming exists in itself and can affect dreams even in more mature stages of human development.

Infantile dreams show a predominant role of wishes and motivational drives in their activation, a circumstance also indicated by neuropsychological approaches to dreaming (Solms, 1997, 2000; Solms & Turnbull, 2002). Studies based on clinical/anatomical methods on the dreams of patients suffering from various brain pathologies and/or deficits showed that the essential neuroanatomical structures involved in the primary generation of dreams (the damage to these areas produces a total cessation of dreaming) are the parieto-temporo-occipital junction and the limbic white matter of the ventromesial quadrant of the frontal lobes that accommodates the mesocortic/mesolimbic dopaminergic pathway, the most important portion of the so-called SEEKING system (Panksepp, 1998). When activated, this system triggers motivated behaviours, curiosity, interest and "appetitive" states such as hunger, thirst and craving for drugs.

According to some authors, it also closely recalls the Freudian concept of "libido" (Solms & Turnbull, 2002; Yu, 2001; Kaplan-Solms & Solms, 2000; Alcaro & Panksepp, 2011). Another similar approach also suggests the role of the dopaminergic pathway in dreaming in the activation and processing of relevant memories with high emotional and motivational value for the individual (Reward Activation Model [RAM], Perogamvros & Schwartz, 2012, 2015).

Infantile dreams show us that, in principle, dreaming is a sensible act with an understandable meaning and offers, at the same time, an opportunity to investigate the reasons why such meaning will later become harder and more obscure to decipher. The study of dreams in the developmental age shows that the evolution of certain factors related to the development of the dreaming function itself (e.g., greater dream-work operations, the type of wishful drives that the trigger the dream) and to the psychological development of the child do *clearly affect* the comprehensibility and plainness of the dream, but always in a way where a *cause-and-effect relationship* can be detected. From this point of view, the research on dreams under a developmental approach may be regarded as the study of those *lines of change* that lead to the progressive increase in dream complexity. By identifying these lines of change, we were able to see that even when dreams become complicated up to the point of resembling adult dreams, *it is never a random process*. Every aspect of infantile dreaming appears determined. Nothing changes by chance. Behind every evolutive change of dream, there is a reason.

Infantile dreams prove to be valid and finalized psychic acts with a meaning of their own and a logical connection with the dreamer's experiences. This is a clear phenomenon that can be verified empirically, in sharp contrast with those theories that concede little or no meaning to dreams—for example, certain neurobiological theories according to which dreams are mere by-products of neurobiological events occurring during REM sleep state and their contents are constructs starting from randomly activated memories and therefore inherently meaningless (e.g., activation-synthesis hypothesis [Hobson & McCarley, 1977; Hobson, 1988]; Activation-Input Source-Neuromodulation model [Hobson, Pace-Schott, & Stickgold, 2000]; reverse learning theory [Crick & Mitchison, 1983]) as well as like certain cognitive approach suggesting that dreaming is a an attempt to give a plausible sense to a persistent, widespread and dissociated mental activation of memory units without intrinsic direction (Foulkes, 1985, 1999, 2017).[7]

Dreams soon start to show operations, mechanisms and ways of acting that immediately appear peculiar to their function. Their presence, albeit sporadic, operates on elementary psychic material and within the context of an infantile psychic apparatus that is not as complex as that of adults, and yet in certain cases, we can clearly see them at work in the exercise of dream functions. These mechanisms are an integral part of dream function and perform an action "similar" to that of enzymes in the biological processes of vital human systems.

In the first place, the dream immediately makes use of its own operations to facilitate the staging of the satisfaction of desire (e.g., transformation of the optative, consideration of representability) and, ultimately, to allow its full gratification (e.g., exaggeration, caricature expression).

When exercising its function, the dream can operate, to begin with, by creating alliances between wishes. We see that this is a steady process in Marco's dreams throughout his development, from 4 to 10 years. Indeed, in the course of development, the decrease in clear wish-fulfilment dreams is accompanied by the presence of dreams that satisfy several plain wishes together and then several wishes of which one or more are plain and one is a denied (repressed) wish. The alliance between wishes is initially only functional to finding an adequate and sufficient motivational drive for triggering the dream, which is also a necessary condition for staging the fulfilment that those wishes alone would not have been able to find space for in the dream. Subsequently, it is also functional to escape dream censorship. In other words, it allows the repressed wish to rely on a simple wish to find disguised or indirect fulfilment. A side effect is that simple wishes, those that are no longer able to trigger a dream themselves, find gratification too. This mechanism can be observed directly in some of Marco's dreams. The latter is an expression of the opportunism of dreams (i.e., to seek the fulfilment of desire in every way) that appears to be a general characteristic of the dreams studied.

Many dream-work operations exist before the development of dream censorship. The alliance between wishes, considerations of representability, condensation, primary forms of displacement, caricature-like representation, and symbolism—operations that initially serve the purposes of wishes in terms of ability to activate dreams and favour their fulfilment—might later serve the purpose of dream distortion of a defensive origin (i.e., dream censorship). Our observations of dreams also showed that the repertoire of these operations increases along with development, and dream-work operations themselves act in a more structured way.

The earliest form of complication of infantile dreams is represented by those dreams that satisfy multiple simple wishes together (i.e., overdetermined dreams). This marks the start of a *line of change* that will end in the complex alliance between simple wishes and disapproved (or denied) wishes. At the same time, it is a tangible sign of the influence of the child's developing ego on dreaming. When the child begins to be able to better manage his/her wishful drives, procrastinate them and even give them up, along with his/her thought development process and through more effective rationalization and mediation processes, a single wish is no longer able to activate a dream on its own, and this is where it needs to find an alliance with other wishes. The typical infantile desire that finds its specific strength in the infantile psychic context and is able to trigger dreams alone is no longer there or is disappearing. As dreams have to deal with multiple wishes now, they become complicated and make use of dream-work operations with greater force (condensation, displacement, synthesis, consideration of representability), aiming at the simultaneous gratification of multiple wishes within the same dream experience. Sometimes they succeed, giving life to sensible dream plots and sceneries; sometimes they don't and start showing bizarreness (e.g., sudden space-time discontinuities, overlapping, etc.). This is the beginning of the end of an *era* of the ontogenetic dream development: the gradual disappearance of plain wish-fulfilment dreams. Therefore, this line of change brings into play the development of the subject's ego, which exercises a direct influence on dream function.

In these *overdetermined dreams*, dreams may be present as a primary form of bizarreness due to the intervention of dream-work operations dealing with multiple wishful drives and the difficulty of a cognitive-representative synthesis—nothing to do with defensive dream distortion. The dream simply becomes more complicated because its task becomes more serious. The motivational overdetermination of dreams should be seen as an increase and an "overload" of dream-function tasks. These dreams offer an opportunity to understand that *dream bizarreness, even in these early (non-motivational) forms, is never the expression of a random process.*

Even in these forms that start deviating from infantile forms, dreams are still understandable in their wish-fulfilment intent *thanks to the knowledge of the child and his waking experiences.*

Together with primary bizarreness, some *bizarreness that is defensive in origin also makes its appearance rather early, although sporadically up to 5 years of age.* Defensive distortions with bizarre effects in dream contents are observed when the dream, for the first time in the course of development, finds itself having to satisfy a wish that in some way goes against the child's moral and/or ethical principles (i.e., is inadmissible to the moral conscience). In Marco, the earliest examples of this concern wishes that in some way "betray" a child's exclusive love for his/her parents (preferring other affections, such as that of friends, to the mother or preferring another more permissive father). Further on in the course of development, starting as early as at the age of 6, we may observe defensive distortion applied to disapproved (or denied) wishes—that is, in conflict with parental rules or dispositions that the child is supposed to have learned to suppress or is trying to suppress. At this stage, we see that the original and routine task of dreams—that is, direct wish fulfilment—becomes complicated because the *dream is required to deal with (and is triggered by) a wish that clashes with the dreamer's ego, even in its embryonic superego aspects.* Conflict and defence therefore arise as a new possible source of dream bizarreness.

In some dreams (at ages 5–6) we already observe a phenomenon that is known in the dream reports of adults. We notice for the first time some *resistance in the child's verbal dream reports* that reflects into unwilling, selective reporting (i.e., to only one of the parents) and timorous or embarrassed/shameful reporting because the forbidden content of his/her dream is expressed too explicitly.

In other words, these early dreams that stage repressed desires, which occur more frequently from the age of 6 and even more from the age of 8, offer the possibility to understand the reasons of the distortion or of the timorous reporting: these reasons have to do with the type of wish that required fulfilment and with the psychic instances that oppose it. This is another *line of change*. This time we may say that *the dream becomes complicated because the nature of the wish that instigated it has changed.* In the previous case, instead, we had affirmed that the dream was complicated by a difficulty in the simultaneous processing of multiple wishful drives that were however simple and legitimate and not in conflict with one another.

The decline of infantile simple wish-fulfilment dreams essentially passes through the need to find more wishful inputs capable of triggering dreams and through a change in the nature of the underlying wishes that become conflicting or inadmissible with respect to the child's ego and superego.

When dreams move on from infantile form to the earliest, more complex forms, we can perceive the action of dream-work operations quite clearly. These immediately appear to us as simplified (embryonic) copies of those dream-work operations that psychoanalysis has discovered through the interpretation of adult dreams. And yet, in the context of infantile dreams, the acting of these operations appears clear to us exactly because we know *a priori* the psychic material on which they operate. It is as if we were looking in a microscope at what we normally (i.e., in adult dreams) cannot see with the naked eye.

The study of childhood dreams allows for an in-depth investigation of the *phenomenology of the wishes* that trigger dreams The observation of hundreds of clear wish-fulfilment dreams (previous study) and the various examples of dreams provided by Marco show that infantile dreams are activated by simple daytime wishes that have in common the fact of not having reached fulfilment and of having remained in some way unresolved psychologically.[8] These are important wishes concerning the child's daily life experiences, desired objects, relationships with peers, grandparents and family members.[9]

A *line of change* that helps us understand dreams is the study of the *types of wishes underlying the dream*. My extensive observation of Marco's dream reports and my direct knowledge of the child allowed me to identify a wide range of wish types that follow one another in the course of the development of dream function and of the child's development. This gives a more complete picture of the possible *motivational forces that activate dreams before adulthood*. The direct analysis of dream reports (without resorting to interpretation techniques) in relation my knowledge of the child showed that dreams from the age of 4 to the age of 10 deal mostly with (a) simple (unrepressed) wishes, unresolved in waking experience; (b) suppressed wishes that are denied by parents or go against their dispositions and rules; and (c) repressed wishes (more rarely observed) in contrast with moral/ethical principles (i.e., inadmissible to the moral conscience). On the other hand, in all the dreams that appeared as *frankly bizarre*, observed more frequently starting from the age of 6, in which there is no apparent trace of wish fulfilment, I assume that there is one or more underlying repressed wishes, especially those considered inadmissible by the moral conscience, where dream distortion was more and more completely effective in making their meaning obscure. I assume that in these latter dreams, the action of the same dream-work operations seen in dreams of veiled and disguised fulfilment of repressed desires was more effective.

Infantile dreams give us a fundamental indication that will find confirmation in the course of development and that is absolutely consistent with what we know from adult dreams: *in order to be activated, dreams need more and more powerful wishful inputs.*[10] Marco's dreams help us understand the ranges of wishes with different dream-triggering abilities and their chronological succession. If we consider as a whole the dream wishes in dreams between the ages of 4 and 10 in terms of their ability/possibility to trigger dreams, we observe these can be classified from a minimum to a maximum of dream-triggering capability: simple (unrepressed) known wishes partially fulfilled (but not enough for the child); simple (unrepressed) wishes not fulfilled at all; a combination of wishes (i.e., two or more wishes can ally to find together the ability to trigger a dream); recurring, very strong (known) wishes and historical wishes (i.e., wishes that retain an important motivational strength over the years); disapproved (suppressed) wishes (i.e., in contrast with parental rules or dispositions); moral/ethically inadmissible (repressed) wishes.

In infantile dreams, the study of daytime experiences which the dream refers to is the study of the conditions for dream activation. Infantile wish-fulfilment dreams, as they appear to us, are built on *episodic memories* of major motivational and affective experiences from the day that just passed (day residue) that are directly resumed in their entirety. This data appears to be somewhat consistent with the continuity hypothesis (Domhoff, 2017) that dreams are continuous with waking life. However, while this hypothesis refers to memories of all elements (i.e., thoughts, preoccupation, etc.) present in waking life, infantile dreams show the more *specific and selective nature of day residue*—that is, with very specific motivational and affective valence. The analysis of the diurnal sources of dreams reveals that such sources are wishes, and portions of affective states have arisen with them and remained partly unprocessed because the related wish could not be satisfied. The dream takes up these experiences, and these alone can explain the entire content of a dream as well as its individual and general meaning.

Just as the digestive system processes the food we eat, and it is the food itself that activates by triggering the digestive function and making its intervention necessary, the dream processes our wishes, and we should assume that our wishes themselves activate the dreaming. Infantile dreams, in their simplicity and evident connection with waking experiences, are proof of this. The task of the dream is to satisfy a wish, which is the reason why it is activated. The drive of the wish is the power that supports the process. In this sense, dreaming is substantially a function. This is the basic functioning of the dream, and we see no reason why it should change, in its essential characteristics, in adults. This functioning is equivalent to the wheel and transmission mechanism of a bicycle prototype, that survives—although with major changes—in all the subsequent developments of the bicycle.

When dreams become more complicated at a greater age (i.e., dreams that satisfy disapproved or inadmissible wishes or make alliances between these wishes and simple daytime wishes, certain bad dreams and frankly bizarre dreams), we see that waking experiences are no longer able to explain the dream or can only explain a part of it. While in simple wish-fulfilment dreams, the daytime experience is taken up in its entirety, in more complex dreams, the plot develops from parts of such experience and then takes other directions. In simple wish-fulfilment dreams, we see that the unresolved wishful experience from the day is the core of the dream; in more complex dreams, we see diurnal sources consist rather of multiple single elements (sometimes disparate) that act as indirect triggers of dream since these are activators of other latent dream material as they often occur in adult dreams. Sometimes the day residues are simple daytime desires that trigger repressed desires. It is in these dreams that the notion of latent dream content becomes necessary. This is another clear of *line of change* that helps our comphrension of dreams' increasing complexity: the change in the type of connection between dreams and daytime experiences from direct and detailed to indirect and incomplete, sometimes obscure.

From the study of the infantile wish-fulfilment dreams, we have very important elucidation on *the functions of the dream*. In its simplest form, the *first task* of the dream is to resume and complete the fulfilment of wishes that in the waking experience of the day preceding the dream were unsatisfied for contingent reasons. In the waking situation, with the experience of the wish and its missed fulfilment, affective states arise that accompany and characterize the entire experience that could not be completely processed, as this would have required the full satisfaction of the wish. From that moment on, unworked portions of these affective states subsist on the psychic level as a sort of perturbing emotional arousal. The disturbing emotional load is not a prerogative of unpleasant affective states (i.e., all affective states may become perturbing), and it should be intended in *terms of quantitative variation* rather than qualitative. Indeed, unprocessed affective states may be positive (contentment, excitement) as well as negative (displeasure, disappointment). The dream process offers a solution to this state of things: through the hallucinatory and gratifying experience of satisfying wishes, dreams allow those portions of unprocessed affective states to be discharged in full—that is, properly processed and extinguished. The second task of dreams is therefore what configures as its main function—that is, enabling the *affective-reestablishment* (AR hypothesis) of the child, finding a new emotional balance with respect to the little big trauma that occurred in the waking state. Therefore, apart from eliminating the wishful stimuli that press for satisfaction and risk interrupting sleep (i.e., "sleep as guardian of sleep" hypothesis), dreams allow for the complete processing of disturbing portions of affective states through a hallucinatory experience of wish fulfilment.

In young children, the dream takes charge of very simple wishful requests that are however important for the child's psyche and are more powerful than the child is able to manage and postpone in their fulfilment of reality, let alone give them up. These wishes activate the dream, which performs its tasks simply and effectively. The push of these "little big" wishes is imperative, and the mental (cognitive-psychological) context in which this process occurs is simpler (than in adults), so the dream function manifests itself in its simplest, embryonic form, to the great benefit of the researcher. We assume that affective-reestablishment is the main and ordinary function of dreams and that such function shows its limits when faced with extraordinary emotional loads, such as those resulting from fear or a big fright or even a trauma, that the dream fails to process.

With regard to the *specific meaning of dreaming*, what we see is that each time, *a specific dream* satisfies *a given wish*, bringing immediate satisfaction and providing emotional relief and reestablishment with respect *to a specific and known residual disturbing affective state of the child*. With regard to the *general meaning of dreaming*, the dream process, by repeating this action daily, contributes to the general psychic balance of the individual in two ways: *indirectly*, by securing adequate continuation (without interruptions) to the state of sleep that the wishful drive risks interrupting and thus preserving the restorative effect of sleep on the dreamer, and *directly*, by enabling the discharge of disturbing affective states and the restoration of an ideal setup of the dreamer's emotional system, making it ready to deal with new everyday emotional charges and stresses.

The tasks and functions of dreams are daily and routine. Infantile dreams show that they deal selectively with the wishes that have remained unsatisfied from the day just ended. In this sense, nocturnal dreams act by preparing the ground for the waking experience of the next day, trying to resolve the wishful experiences and give full discharge to the disturbing affective states from the day before. Therefore, we would be right in making a parallel between dream functions and other biological functions of the human being that perform routine activities, always meaningful and never random, always with a specific purpose. Digestion and breathing, for example, are by no means random: on the contrary, they perform targeted and fundamental actions for the individual.[11]

I consider this dream function that we have called affective-reestablishment hypothesis a *specific* and *essential version* of the Robert–Freud assumption that dreams act an "safety valve for the psyche". The principle in common to these hypotheses is that dreams act in order to enable the discharge of potentially disturbing psychic material. In the case of children, such material is represented by portions of diurnal affective states linked to unresolved simple wishes, but sometimes also more remote unresolved affective states linked to the non-fulfilment of repressed wishes. In the case of adults, it is represented by blocked emotional loads linked to repressed unconscious wishes. At the same time, we have seen that the AR hypothesis is inspired by some basic principles of mental functioning developed by Freud in his study of hysterical patients and in subsequent metapsychological writings—that is, the principle of constancy and the theory of affects.

The affective-reestablishment function fits consistently with certain adaptive emotional theories on dreaming developed on the basis of adult dreams and with the research on the role of sleep as emotional regulator. Yet it has some additional benefit, giving specificity to the function of dreaming: specificity with respect to the way of pursuing emotional regulation function and specificity with respect to the possible individual significance of dreaming since it suggests which is the function of one given dream for one given subject at a given moment. It also ascribes to the *subjective dreaming psychological experience*—the emotional regulation function—that various theories seem to ascribe mainly to the sleep state *itself*. These two aspects, however, as noted earlier, are complementary rather than self-excluding. My thought is that, in this case too, by presenting an elementary form of dreaming, infantile dreams allow us to witness at work—in a very simplified version but for this reason clear and clarifying—those emotional adaptive functions that have been broadly confirmed by the research on sleep/dream in adults. On the other hand, infantile dreams are in conflict with theories on dreaming that ascribe non-substantial and effective functions to dreaming, such as Domhoff's (2018) "neurocognitive theory", which considers dreams as a by-product of neural processes and not having any adaptive function, or Hobson's (2009) "protoconsciousness theory", according to which REM sleep dreaming, although having a role in virtual reality simulation and would be necessary for the development and maintenance of waking consciousness (Hobson & Friston, 2012), continues to be mere subjective epiphenomenon of REM sleep based upon chaotic and random subcortical activation as in Hobson's AIM model (Hobson, 1990).

Many of Marco's wish-fulfilment dreams provide evidence of the fact that dreams act in order to protect the state of sleep. Some of Marco's dreams clearly show that one of the dream functions is to prevent sleep interruption. Dreams do what they can through their mechanisms and operations in order to transform the stimuli that occur during sleep. These stimuli must receive some scenic representation in order to be managed—the transformation of abstract concepts into a plastic visual form, caricature representations, alliances with other material, transformations of negative stimuli into positive ones, anything goes as long as the sleeper does not wake up. Wishes are the great majority of these stimuli but not the only ones. From this point of view, dreams also prove to facilitate psychic processes and harness those stimuli that for various reasons might threaten sleep. And I feel we are not mistaken if we consider the dream process, from the point of view of sleep, as a true "biological" defence mechanism for sleep protection and, ultimately, a useful mechanism for the physical as well as psychic survival of individuals.

The development of ego influences the dream since with the progressive development of rational-thought abilities in child certain desires, even if unsatisfied in wakefulness, lose their urgency. Already at the end of the 5th year of age, we see that one wish alone may no longer be able to activate the dream. So dreams continue to take wishes in and perform their function when these wishes join together, increasing the power of the wishful request. With the further development of the ego and of superegoic components in particular, the child becomes able to give up the hallucinatory fulfilment of simple wishes and also develops the ability—and the need—to suppress forbidden wishes (e.g., those denied by parents) and wishes that are inadmissible on the ethical/ moral level that may return in the dream in a disguised way. An even more complete and structured development of these psychic structures may also be observed in a more substantial way in the influences on contents and forms of dreams at the ages of 8–10.

On the one hand, simple wishes lose their peremptory importance. On the other hand, dreams must face far more powerful and actively rejected wishes, ready to make their way as soon as the opportunity arises. The psychic material that dreams have now to deal with is different. The repertoire of dream-work operations increases in order to keep and improve dream functions.

From 6 to 7 years of age, simple daytime wishes and even the alliance between these starts to be no longer suitable for triggering dreams. The alliance between wishes now consists of a simple wish and a repressed one; this is the basic pattern that is implemented in a more articulated form in adult dreams, where unconscious repressed wishes ally with ordinary wishes and psychic material from the recent waking period. In children, we can clearly observe that both wishes draw a benefit from allying: the simple one, that alone would not find its room in the dream, and the suppressed one, that would not be fulfilled unless disguised in the simple wish. On the other hand, dreams triggered by simple wishes decrease dramatically at ages 6–7. Dreams are now activated to serve more powerful wishes, those that during the day were denied by the parents and sometime those that are morally and/or ethically inadmissible. These wishes retain their strong power exactly because they are repressed.

In this age period, the distribution of the various types of dreams in the child's repertoire changes abruptly: simple wish-fulfilment dreams decrease, frankly bizarre dreams increase and bad dreams appear in significant number. An unexpected circumstance noticed is that many dreams that are apparently bad dreams should rather be regarded as "anomalous" or "false" bad dreams. These are dreams that are only apparently "bad" and present unsuccessful attempts to satisfy the child's wish to challenge a fear and win it—that is, to dispel it, which is an attempt that gets out of hand, however.

Also, at this age, dreams achieve new dream-work operations which, together with those already present in the existing forms of dreaming, now carry out their task in order to disguise the fulfilment of forbidden wishes. Among other things, satisfaction appears through symbolic relationships and allusive means. In other words, *the level of dream bizarreness with a recognized defensive motivational origin increases*. I cannot find any other explanation for this dream distortion (that was not observed before) other than the fact that it is necessary for the very nature of the underlying wishes that go against parental rules and/or ethical or moral principles.

For example, we witness the appearance in dreams, for the first time in explicit form, of rudimentary conflicts between egodystonic and egosyntonic wishes that result in a compromise, with bizarreness in the dream. It is the most elementary example of conflict directly observed in the dreams. Other times, the fulfilment of the forbidden wish is only subtly disguised: in this case, the child is timorous in reporting his dream (at 5 years and 8 months) for fear of displeasing his parents. Other times, after telling his dream, the child asks permission to fulfil the forbidden wish that he just staged in his dream. These factors become interiorized at ages 8–10 and take the form of anxiety in the dream, or the appearance in the dream plot of a parent who approves the fulfilment of that desire (forbidden in reality) in a "permissive" form of dream censorship. These mechanisms are further signs of rudimentary dream-censorship activity, the same that operates more heavily in adult dreams.

Finally, starting from the age of 6, dreams become more and more complex, along with the psychic material that they have to deal with (stronger repressed wishes and the alliance of several wishes, some of which are suppressed), and are required to request from new psychic instances.

The first means by which dreams operate defensive distortion are (a) the strategic alliance of a repressed wish with a simple one and (b) allusive means and symbolism; the latter is also present in some clearly oedipal dreams from the previous period. The first disguised fulfilment of a forbidden wish, where the distortion is evident, consists of fulfilling something legitimate that alludes to the possibility of satisfying another (forbidden) wish. Here we find alliance, support, opportunism and allusive means.

We have described the alliance between suppressed wishes and simple wishes connected by thematic-symbolic association, which allows the former to use the latter as a Trojan horse to achieve undisturbed satisfaction. This mechanism also relates to the issue of *choosing which symbol* should represent the repressed aspect. Certain infantile dreams seem to suggest that a given repressed wish may not emerge in the dream until a suitable (i.e., thematically related) opportunity is provided by a simple wish to symbolize and ultimately satisfy it. What we observe is that the choice of the symbol coincides with the possibility that there is a simple wish ready to take action to this end, a wish peculiar to that specific individual and at a precise point in time. This would lead us to affirm that many symbolized/symbolizing relationships occur with totally personal symbols. It also gives us a hint of how complex the interpretation of symbolic relationships in adult dreams can be.

The development of dream complexity may also be intended as a sort of *progressive increase in the situations of conflict between wishes*—that is, an amplification of the range of *wishes that conflict* with *dominant wishes and thoughts of the ego* that exercise pressure on the former because they are deemed harmful, inadequate and inadmissible. For example, a clearly observed conflictual mechanism underlying the complication of dreams is that of wishes whose fulfilment contrasts with the child's aesthetic requirements. In this we see another *line of change* towards more complex dreams: *the multiplication of conflicts between wishes in contrast with one another probably represents the origin of the formation of dream censorship activity and is responsible, at least in part, for dream complexity and bizarreness.*

Ultimately, I observed that between the end of the fifth year of age and the beginning of the sixth, certain bizarre dreams originate directly from *defensive distortions* aimed at avoiding guilt, shame, embarrassment and feelings of aesthetic inadequacy. In some of Marco's dreams, this process is explicit and directly detectable. This seems to confirm the statistically significant positive correlation found in previous studies between dream bizarreness and the development of the ability to feel guilt as the expression of the completion of the superego development (Colace, 2010a), which is a relationship that is directly demonstrable in these dreams.

Studying infantile dreams in the course of development means accessing the mechanisms of dreams and the early dream-work operations employed to the service of censorship in their first elementary ways, including the early examples of suppressed wishes. Dream complexity increases depending on the type of link (metaphorical, symbolic, indirect, etc.) established between simple wishes and repressed wishes. Also in this case, we believe, based on the observation of the other dreams which, although bizarre, maintain a good degree of readability (i.e., dream of veiled disguise of repressed wishes), that the ultimate determination of dream content and form has nothing to do with random processes.

The study of dreams in the developmental age, in particular from the age of 5 onwards, offers an opportunity to study how dream bizarreness progressively appears in dreams. To synthesize, we recognize in children's dreams at least two types of processes that can lead to bizarre dreams. The very first type of bizarreness may derive from the attempt to synthesize different wishful requests (not in conflict with each other) within the same dream (i.e., primary bizarreness). Another type, the prevailing one in adult dreams, is of the defensive type, where dream-work operations serve the purpose of dream censorship to prevent the explicit representation of repressed wishes that clash with the dreamer's prerogatives (e.g., rules and principles, ethical and moral requirements). On the other hand, we may also notice that certain dream-work operations (e.g., considerations of representability) can sometime produce autonomously a "neutral" (i.e., non-defensive) alteration of the meaning of the dream for the purpose of staging the dream, achieving the fulfilment of the wish (e.g., considerations of representability, condensation, exaggeration, etc.).

In addition to studying dream-work operations and types of dream bizarreness—that is, origin and their underlying causes, we can also highlight the progression of purely phenomenological aspects. Dream reports collected in this study show types of formal bizarreness (already at 5, 6 and 7 years of age), which are the same as those observed in the phenomenological studies on the bizarreness of adulthood dreams—such as sudden temporal discontinuities, strange actions, incongruous characters and so on (Colace, 2003). This would lead to suppose that the mechanisms and reasons underlying bizarreness are also potentially present in the dreams of children. After all, we have said that dream-work operations appear rather early in children's dreams and are of the same type as those observed through the interpretation of adults' dreams. This suggests that the prevailing presence of simple wish-fulfilment dreams in young children is not due to their inability to produce more complex dreams but rather to the fact that these are the dreams that prevail at that stage of development of dream functions and at the child's psychological development. The plainness of infantile dreams is simply due to the fact that the dream process is triggered and engaged by simpler wishful drives that do not require defensive distortion nor cognitive sacrifice on the level of synthesis and scenic representation. These simple dreams show their "basic" structure, their essential skeleton on which various factors will later intervene to increase their complexity. The mechanisms of dream work can be observed in a more direct form in children's dreams because we know from the beginning the material on which they intervene, as opposed to what happens in adult dreams, where the material subject to distortion is only revealed through dream interpretation. This prepares the ground for the possibility to look closer at dream-work operations by studying the dreams of children where the researcher has detailed information and good knowledge of the experiences the child who reports the dreams.[12]

The study of dreams between the ages of 8 and 10 still offers an opportunity to observe different examples of dreams of veiled fulfilment of repressed desires (insufficiently disguised) and to go on studying directly the dream-work operations now acting on more complex psychic material and within the context of a fuller development of the psychic apparatus.

In this age period, I found confirmation of the trends that emerged in dreams starting from the age of 6. In some cases, the dreams continue to deal with simple wishes, although characterized by major strength. There are increasing dreams that satisfy repressed wishes in a disguised way, mostly wishes in contrast with parental rules and in some cases against moral and/or ethical principles. The latter are difficult to identify by direct observation, and we may suppose that they are more present in *frankly bizarre dreams* (which occur frequently in this period), where the distortion of the unconscious repressed material is complete. Probably, except in some cases where the disguising is incomplete, the study of repressed wishes going against ethical/moral principles and of how they are satisfied in dreams remains a prerogative of psychoanalytic dream interpretation. Furthermore, frankly bizarre dreams at this age appear to present a greater degree of bizarreness. Bad dreams at this age decrease in frequency and, at least with reference to "ordinary" bad dreams (i.e., not really traumatic dreams), appear to be peculiar to a specific stage of the development of dreaming and of the child. We can see in bad dreams the difficulties that the dream process encounters in dealing with the new fears that the child starts knowing and experiencing at around 6 years of age.

Also in this period, we see that dreams, in order to be triggered, require increasingly important wishful impulses. For example, we observe dreams in which two repressed wishes are satisfied at the same time or dreams based on strong repressed wishes deeply rooted in the child's mind (long-time wishes) that give rise to serial wish-fulfilment dreams (also present sometime at 4–5 years). My observation that dreams are now triggered by stronger wishes is also confirmed by another fact: in the wish-fulfilment dreams from this age period, there is a lesser presence of wishes that had been partially satisfied in the waking experience and therefore lost part of their drive (i.e., *continuation dreams*), as well as of unfulfilled wishes related to events that will occur in the future (i.e., *anticipation dreams*). In both cases, we are faced with wishes that have lost the strength required in order to trigger dreams, unlike it frequently happening in the previous age period (4–5 years). In both cases, these are wishes that the child now seems able to manage in his waking experience and are therefore no longer the object of dreaming. In the former case, the child appears satisfied with the measure of fulfilment that he managed to achieve in his waking experience; in the latter case, he has seemingly learned to manage the wish to wait for the moment in which he will see it fulfilled in his waking experience. Now, the simple wishes that are able to trigger dreams are only those that in waking have remained completely unfulfilled with no hope of seeing them ever fulfilled (i.e., *compensation dreams*). On the other hand, this trend had already been noticed in the second age period, starting from 6 years of age, where *continuation dreams* disappeared already at 6–7 years.

At this age, new dream-work operations appear in addition to those previously observed. Dream-work operations are now constantly engaged for the purposes of dream censorship, whose action in dreams becomes increasingly evident. We may affirm that at around 8–10 years of age, dreams show a consistent repertoire of dream-work operations, which is a prelude to the possibility of producing increasingly complex dreams—precursory to adult forms of dreaming.

At this age, it still possible to observe, in certain dreams, the fulfilment of a repressed wish in an allusive form and the alliance between repressed and simple wishes in order to circumvent dream censorship.

If, in the first age period, the *exaggeration* in the fulfilment of wishes in dreams was a sign of their peremptory nature and of the child being unable to moderate his drive, now appearance, albeit sporadically observed, of *moderation, rationalization* and *limitation* in the fulfilment of wishes in dreams is a clear sign that the child has developed the ability to manage his wishful drives thanks to a more complete development of the ego.

Even at this age, dreams of the direct fulfilment of simple wishes and dreams of veiled and disguised fulfilment of repressed wishes offer an opportunity to study the role of day residues. These dreams often remain understandable on the basis of the daytime experiences that preceded them and allow the researcher to study the wishful drives and affective states resumed by the dream.

Starting from 8 years of age, the level of bizarreness in the dream increases, probably due to the quantity and complexity of the latent psychic material that needs processing. The same bizarre elements noted earlier are now even more bizarre. New forms of bizarreness appear (increased complexity in the dream scenario and plot, settings and places out of their original context, etc.). On the phenomenological level, some frankly bizarre dreams now recall the dreams of adults even if they remain less complex and probably less long.

With the appearance of bizarre dreams, the hope of identifying experiences taken directly from the waking state fades out. Bizarre dreams no longer show any direct connection with waking experiences. Where there is a connection, it is obscure and indirect. In other words, the child's daytime experiences are no longer useful for explaining the dream.

Sometimes, when we do recognize a clear diurnal residue in the dream, it appears as an isolated element (or a set of isolated elements) used outside its original context for the construction of a dream plot that develops in a complex and imaginative way. The diurnal material has now become raw material used by the dream possibly to organize a context in which an unconscious wish can find disguised fulfilment. In some of these dreams, we might also assume the presence of simple wish fulfilment; however, this cannot be established clearly because there are several elements of bizarreness that make the meaning of the dream uncertain.

The study of infantile dreams may be a valid approach for understanding various aspects of dreaming, including those that have always been difficult to explain (e.g., the meaning and function of dreams). This research proves that up to the age of 10, a whole range of dreams can be observed to study directly the processes and mechanisms of dreaming that are at the basis of adult dreams as well.

The ontogenetic model of dreaming that I am presenting is aimed at guiding future research and studies in this sense, starting from assumptions that will, or will not, be confirmed.

The observations of dreams in the developmental age constitutes a true addition to Freud's general theory of dreams. This ontogenetic model that is based on the study of Marco's dream reports and from several systematic studies on children's dreams shows the validity of various core assumptions of the Freudian dream theory *through the direct analysis of dreams* in relation to the waking experiences of the dreamer: in particular, the theory concerns the motivational instigation of dreams, the role of dreams in the treatment of wishes, the existence and action of dream-work operations, the disguise-censorship theory of dream bizarreness, the role of day residues in the construction of dreams and the functions of dreams. Briefly, on a methodological level, the detailed study of infantile dreams provides another paradigm of systematic dream investigation that enables a more straightforward evaluation of the Freudian model of dreaming. Such method cannot certainly replace the in-depth understanding of the dream through its interpretation but can however work alongside it.

Some important variables of the Freudian model of dreaming (i.e., wishes, dream-work activity, day residue) in the infantile paradigm of study and particularly in studies like this one, where there is good direct knowledge of the dreamer, may be observed directly and *a priori* rather than detected through a process of interpretation and *a posteriori* reconstruction. Their confirmation in this sense is more objective and possibly open to increasingly precise measurements and replication attempts. For example, the daytime sources of dreams are well known even with respect to when they occurred; the dreamer's wishes and the daytime circumstances in which they arose are also known. The way in which dream-work operations affect repressed wishes can also be observed, insofar as repressed wishes are known too.

Given these premises, this study outlines a dream model whose mechanisms and functions are a sort of prologue to what is expected to happen in adulthood dreams, and to the extent that such mechanisms and functions are observed in infantile dreams, they are absolutely consistent with what Freud described with respect to adults' dreams. Furthermore, the conclusions of this study are completely in line with previous systematic investigations that I had carried out on large samples of dreams/children, and they allow an in-depth analysis of what was previously observed. Some of the previous initial findings have been also reinforced, such as the role of day residue in dreams, the relationship between ego and superego development and certain aspects of dreams. Other aspects—such as dream-work operations, primary bizarreness and the categorization of bad dreams—have been detected only in this study, and they help us in obtaining a more complete picture of children's dreams.

The study of the dreams of adults in the psychoanalytic tradition has suggested that dreams are the "royal road to the unconscious". The data from children's dreams show us that dreams, in their early stage, prefer being triggered by simple unrepressed wishes and subsequently by repressed wishes, the existence of some of which may be detected in their insufficiently disguised fulfilment in the dream or in the somewhat timorous attitude of the child while reporting his dream. I am under the impression that the dreams at this stage land exactly at that step that precedes the period in which dreams must have a predominantly unconscious wishful drive in order to be triggered (that can only be known indirectly through dream interpretation). This is explained with the observation that, as the development of the structure of a mental apparatus progresses and the child grows up, dreams require and deal with increasingly strong wishful stimuli, of which unconscious drives are the most extreme tip. Dreams certainly appear to us as a psychological phenomenon that is strongly affected by the state and developmental conditions of the individual's psychic apparatus. For this reason, the dream itself is an expression of its functioning and development and is therefore a changing phenomenon that does not respond to rigid and specific triggering conditions but is constantly evolving. From this point of view, the dream is certainly a precious knowledge tool to access the psychological and psychopathological state of the individual. I realize that these concepts are widely known in the clinical psychiatric and psychoanalytic fields, but I would like to re-affirm that these concepts have emerged in this study through the direct investigation of the dreams and without resorting to dream-interpretation techniques. All the mechanisms of the dream process, its modi operandi and its transformations of the underlying psychic material converge towards giving a clear indication that the dream is a psychic act with meaning and with a set of mechanisms that pursue their specific tasks and purposes. It is not only the content of dreams in relation to the daytime experiences of the child that makes us think that dreams are sensible, valid and significant psychic acts: we are led to believe so also after observing the sense and consistency of such characteristics of the dream process. For example, in adults' dreams, we suppose the existence of psychic conflicts between unconscious desires that press for satisfaction and the ego and superego agency of the individual that struggle to prevent such unconscious desires from being openly expressed in the dream. We are aware of this type of process, having discovered through dream interpretation the latent psychic material of the dream and the unconscious desire that urged satisfaction in it. In infantile dreams, we see the same conflict in a more basic, straightforward form than in adults' dreams, and this allows us to understand which pairs of wishes in the dream are in conflict with each other, what their nature is, how distortion operates and what the final result is in terms of bizarre effects.

The dreams of children have opened up the possibility of studying and understanding infantile forms of dreaming in adults too, with positive consequences for the research on dream processes and for clinical application. In the same way, the study of infantile dreams in adults has made it possible to have confirmation of the characteristics of the dream processes so far observed only in children's dreams.

In conclusion, what has been achieved is an enlargement of the infantile dream research paradigm that appears to have to interesting future perspectives. I hope that the model proposed here can serve as a guideline for future investigations into the early forms of dreaming and dreaming in general.

Notes

1 As we have seen, the observation of the present study provides support to several Freudian hypotheses on infantile dreams and on the dreaming process in general. On the other hand, in the last twenty years, several core hypotheses of the Freudian dream theory have received empirical support in various systematic research contexts (Johnson & Mosri, 2016). In addition to the studies on children's dreams (e.g., Colace, 2009a, 2010a, 2012, 2013), see the studies on infantile dreams in adults (Johnson, 2001; Colace, 1999, 2000, 2001, 2004, 2006a, 2010b, 2009b, 2014, 2020) and the anatomical clinical studies on dreaming in patients with brain injuries (Solms, 1997; Yu, 2003, 2007; Colace, Salotti, & Ferreira, 2015, 2019). More generally, several authors, starting from different theoretical and research perspectives, are contributing to a reconsideration of the Freudian theory of dreams. We may refer, in this sense, to the analysis of the philosophical/epistemological foundations of the Freudian theory of dreams (Michael, 2015, 2018, 2019; Colace, 2010a; Colace & Boag, 2015a, 2015b); the analysis of its meta-psychological aspects (Boag, 2017); the theoretical/experimental character of specific parts of the model, such as the dream censorship model (Colace, 2006b, 2009a, 2012; Boag, 2006); the study of the possible neuroanatomical correlations of central aspects of the theory, such as the SEEKING system (considered as the seat of the motivational activation of dreams) by affective neuroscience (Pankseep, 2005; Pankseep & Biven, 2012; Alcaro, Huber, & Panksepp, 2007; Alcaro & Panksepp, 2011; see Giacolini & Pirrongelli [2021] and Colace [2021]); and the applications of the Freudian dream theories in various clinical contexts with major theoretical and applicative implications (see the studies on the so-called *drug dreams* and *gambling dreams* (Colace, 2014, 2020). All these contribute to proving the vitality of the Freudian model and the fact that such a model can be investigated theoretically and empirically. Even more important is the fact that it has been clearly shown that Freud's hypotheses on dreams have been formulated in such a way that they may be

subject to an empirical control. Also from the standpoint of Popper's epistemological criterion (falsifiability criterion [Popper, 1959, 1963]), several of Freud's hypotheses about dreams do have clear *potential falsifiers*—that is, facts that, if found to be true, would clearly deny the theory (Colace, 2010a; Colace & Boag, 2015a; Michael, 2015, 2018). On the question of the empirical testability of the psychoanalytic theory in the modern epistemological debate, see Colace, (2010a) and Michael (2018, 2019).

2 I have devoted extensive discussion to Freud's observations and theses on children's dreams in previous works, to which I refer for all further information (Colace, 2010a, 2012; Colace & Boag, 2015a, 2015b).

3 These are concepts that go back, in Andersson's words, to the prehistory of psychoanalytical (Andersson, 1962) concepts concerning Freud's early theorizations on the general functioning of the mind (Greenberg & Mitchell, 1983).

4 An exception is the clinical study of some forms of infantile dreams in adults, such as the drug dreams of drug-addicted patients, where I also proceeded with a systematic approach (Colace, 2004, 2014; Colace, Belsanti, & Antermite, 2014; Colace, Claps, Antognoli, Sperandio, Sardi, & Benedetti, 2010), and the infantile forms of dreaming observed in patients with frontal deficits (Colace, Salotti, & Ferreira, 2015, 2019).

5 Since the general understanding of the dream phenomenon passes through the study of the subjective meanings of the dream for each individual, it goes without saying that the progress of knowledge about dreaming from a scientific point of view also passes through studies like this one that look closer at the subjective dimension of the dream experience. Therefore, we follow the recent assumption by Sandor et al. according to which the study of infantile dreams must use a multidisciplinary methodological approach because each method allows the researcher to observe their different aspects. For example, certain aspects of the dreams identified in this study, where the researcher could interview the child in detail and was aware of the child's experiences, are obviously precluded to more indirect dream-collection methods (questionnaires, etc.). This is the case of the repertoire of dream-work operations identified in Marco's dreams, of which there is no trace—except for rare and fortuitous cases—in previous studies.

6 I am inclined to think that the preponderance of this type of dreams cannot be considered as the result of methodological flaws or theoretical biases, since these data have been confirmed by studies that have adopted different collection methods and since there are at least two studies conducted by other researchers who have reached the same conclusions as myself regarding the frequency of simple wish-fulfilment dreams (Mari; Beretta, & Colace, 2018; Kráčmarová & Plháková, 2012). Contrary data came only from studies that did not consider the possibility of understanding the dreams better by referring to the dreamer's experiences (Colace, 2006c; Foulkes et al., 1967). Moreover, the data on the high frequency of wish-fulfilment dreams in this study cannot be considered a consequence of the collection method (e.g. selective recall) because the same method gave other indications in the observation period between 6 and 10 years of age (i.e., decrease in wish-fulfilment dreams). And this result cannot be ascribed to Marco's inability to produce more bizarre dreams since the child proved to possess the set of dream-work operations and the cognitive ability that are at the basis of certain bizarre dreams, which he started having, although sporadically, as early as at the age of 5.

7 In Foulkes's cognitive approach, despite dreams being a high-level cognitive process that reveal conceptual and personal knowledge about the dreamer, there is no special purpose nor deep meaning and nor adaptive functions (Foulkes, 1985, 1999, 2017). This approach is also based on Foulkes's longitudinal studies on children's dreams. However, I have already discussed elsewhere the differences that emerge between dreams collected in the sleep laboratory and those collected with other methodologies and the reasons for these differences (Colace, 2010a, 2013; see also Sándor et al. [2014]).

8   Children's dreams provide direct access to the subjective experience of dreaming and can represent a way to find convergent phenomenological feedback (wishes at the basis of dreams, ways of fulfilment, etc.) for the evidence coming from affective neuroscience research on the so-called SEEKING system (Panksepp, 1998; Panksepp & Biven, 2012) and its role in triggering dreams (Solms, 1997). The SEEKING system activity is well suited to represent the neuroanatomical and neurobiological counterpart of the young child's typical behaviours of curiosity, appetite and wishes in his waking experience as much as in his dream experience. These are wishes that have remained unfulfilled and that press for their satisfaction and in respect of which the SEEKING system provides the necessary energy to activate actions that can satisfy them (see Colace, 2021; Giacolini & Pirrongelli, 2021).

9   A range of wishes that I have found in my studies has been already identified by several authors (e.g., Freud, 1901; Doglia & Bianchieri, 1910–1911; Kimmins, 1920; Piaget, 1962; Coriat, 1916; Hill, 1926).

10   Freud classified wishes according to their "capacity for instigating dreams" (Freud, 1900, p. 552–553). In order to start a dream, a certain minimum wishful request, or motive force, is necessary (Freud, 1900, pp. 560–561).

11   If, due to its important and routine function, the dream is similar to other important vital biological functions of the individual, what differentiates it from these is that dreaming includes an aspect of mental representation with an emotional resonance that, in addition to being experienced in the dream experience itself, is sometimes remembered upon awakening. We know that dreams are not always remembered easily, and even what are considered "good dream recallers" can only remember a few dreams they had in the morning upon awakening and nothing more. There are also people who do not remember their dreams at all (Schredl, 2007). Given that we remember very few dreams compared to the number that we have during the night, we should ask ourselves if this has any meaning for the individual and for the human species. We have seen that the function of dreams is to allow the continuation of the state of sleep and process affective loads that have not been processed in wakefulness, a routine and daily task that occurs with no need for the subject to remember his/her dream experience. Remembering a dream upon awakening in the morning can engage the subject in various ways, for example by generating concern or distress for its contents or by getting him/her involved in exciting desires and emotions. All this can distract him from ordinary daily tasks. What would happen if dreams were remembered more often or more intensely? What would happen if a subject remembered most of the dreams during a night's sleep? Probably remembering all or many dreams upon waking up in the morning would have negative consequences for the life of the individual. I think the question we should ask ourselves is therefore not "Why don't we remember dreams?" but rather "Why should we even remember them?" It goes without saying that in all circumstances in which the memory of the dream is useful to the individual and/or the community in which he/she lives, for various reasons and purposes, the possibility of remembering dreams can be encouraged, and individuals themselves may be more inclined to remembering them. We might think of the use of dreams in psychotherapy, where it is no coincidence that patients, even those who usually do not remember their dreams, begin to remember them. Or, for example, the use of dreams in ancient times, when the memory of dreams was propitiated through a ritual of "dream incubation", where the dreams induced in a temple could give hints for medical treatment (iatromancy), or the use of dreams by religion scopes, or the dream interpretation practiced in order to predict wars and/or imminent famines—for example, the dream of Constantine (Colace, 2006d; Kruger, 1992; Riberio, Simões, & Nicolelis, 2018). We can so hypothesize that the memory of dreams, except when required—that is, solicited for the purposes above—is not adaptive at all for the survival of the individual and of the species.

12 An interesting implication of this is the following: if we have direct knowledge of the way in which these operations take place while we study infantile dreams, we would gain greater familiarity in recognizing the same mechanisms in adult dreams in the psychoanalysis section.

References

Alcaro, A., Huber, R., & Panksepp, J. (2007). Behavioral functions of the mesolimbic dopaminergic system: An affective neuroethological perspective. *Brain Research Reviews, 56*, 283–321. DOI: 10.1016/j.brainresrev.2007.07.014.

Alcaro, A., & Panksepp, J. (2011). The SEEKING mind: Primal neuro-affective substrates for appetitive incentive states and their pathological dynamics in addictions and depression. *Neuroscience & Biobehavioral Reviews, 35*, 1805–1820. DOI: 10.1016/j. neubiorev.2011.03.002.

Andersson, O. (1962). *Studies in the Prehistory of Psychoanalysis*. Stockholm: Esselte Studium AB.

Boag, S. (2006). Freudian dream theory, dream bizarreness, and the disguise-censor controversy. *Neuro-Psychoanalysis, 8* (1), 5–16. https://doi.org/10.1080/15294145.2006.1 0773503.

Boag, S. (2017). *Metapsychology and the Foundations of Psychoanalysis*. New York: Routledge.

Breuer, J., & Freud, S. (1895). *Studies on Hysteria (1893–1895)*. S.E., II. London: Hogarth Press.

Colace, C. (1999). Dreams in abstinent opiate drug addicts: A case report study. *Sleep, 22* (1), 175–176.

Colace, C. (2000). Dreams in abstinent heroin addicts: Four case reports. *Sleep and Hypnosis, 2*, 160–163.

Colace, C. (2001). Needs and dreaming processes: Observations on dreams of abstinent heroin addicts. *Sleep, 24*, A185.

Colace, C. (2003). Dream bizarreness reconsidered. *Sleep and Hypnosis, 5* (3), 105–128.

Colace, C. (2004). Dreaming in addiction. A study on the motivational bases of dreaming processes. *Neuro-psychoanalysis, 6* (2), 167–181.

Colace, C. (2006a). Drug dreams in cocaine addiction. *Alcohol & Drug Review, 25* (2), 177.

Colace, C. (2006b). "Commentary on "Freudian dream theory, dream bizarreness, and the disguise-censor controversy (S. Boag)". *Neuro-psychoanalysis, 8* (1), 24–27.

Colace, C. (2006c). Children's dreaming: A study based on questionnaire completed by parents. *Sleep and Hypnosis, 8* (1), 19–32.

Colace, C. (2006d). Nota sulle idee prescientifiche sul tema della bizzarria onirica. *Psychofenia, IX* (15), 15–23.

Colace, C. (2009a). The study of bizarreness in young children's dreams: A way to test the disguise-censorship model. Poster presented at X International Congress of Neuropsychoanalysis, Paris, France, 26–29, June.

Colace, C. (2009b). Gli studi sull'effetto della frustrazione dei bisogni primari sul sognare e la recente ricerca e teoria sui processi onirici. *Psycofenia, XII* (20), 49–72.

Colace, C. (2010a). *Children's Dreams: From Freud's Observations to Modern Dream Research*. New York: Routledge.

Colace, C. (2010b). Drug dreams in mescaline and LSD addiction. *American Journal on Addictions*, *19* (2), 192.

Colace, C. (2012). Dream bizarreness and the controversy between the neurobiological approach and the disguise censorship model: The contribution of children's dreams. *Neuropsychoanalysis*, *14* (2), 165–174.

Colace, C. (2013). Are wish-fulfilment dreams of children the royal road for looking at the functions of dreams? *Neuropsychoanalysis*, *15* (2), 161–175.

Colace, C. (2014). *Drug Dreams. Clinical and Research Implications of Dreams About Drugs in Drug-Addicted Patients*. New York: Routledge.

Colace, C. (2020). Gambling dreams in pathological gambler outpatients: A pilot study. *Addicta: The Turkish Journal on Addictions*, *7* (3). DOI: 10.5152/ADDICTA.2020.20053.

Colace, C. (2021). The motivational trigger and the affective function in infantile dream. In: T. Giacolini & C. Pirrongelli (Eds.), *Neuropsychoanalysis of the Inner Mind a Biological Understanding of Human Mental Function*. New York: Routledge.

Colace, C., & Boag, S. (2015a). Persisting myths surrounding Sigmund Freud's dream theory: A reply to Hobson's critique to scientific status of psychoanalysis. *Contemporary Psychoanalysis*, *51* (1), 107–125.

Colace, C., & Boag, S. (2015b). The empirical study of infantile wish-fulfillment dreams. A reply to response of Allan J. Hobson. *Contemporary Psychoanalysis*, *51* (1), 132–134.

Colace, C., Belsanti, S., & Antermite, A. (2014). Limbic system irritability as neurobiological substrate of drug dreaming in heroin-addicted subjects. *Heroin Addiction and Related Clinical Problems*, *16* (3), 75–86.

Colace, C., Claps, M., Antognoli, A., Sperandio, R., Sardi, D., & Benedetti, A. (2010). Limbic system and activity and drug dreaming in drug-addicted subjects. *Neuropsychoanalysis*, *12* (2), 201–206.

Colace, C., Salotti, P., & Ferreira, M. (2015). Reduction of dream bizarreness in impaired frontal cortex activity: A case report. *Sleep and Hypnosis*, *17* (1–2), 14–18.

Colace, C., Salotti, P., & Ferreira, M. (2019). Infantile dream reports in patients with frontal deficits. *Sleep Hypnosis*, *21* (4) (December), 321–327.

Coriat, I. H. (1916). *The Meaning of Dreams*. Boston: Dodo Press.

Crick, F., & Mitchison, G. (1983). The function of REM sleep. *Nature*, *304*, 111–114.

Doglia, S., & Bianchieri, F. (1910–1911). I sogni dei bambini di tre anni, L'inizio dell' attivita onirica. *Contributi di psicologia*, *I*, 1–9.

Domhoff, G. W. (2017). The invasion of the concept snatchers: The origins, distortions, and future of the continuity hypothesis. *Dreaming, 27* (1), 14–39.

Domhoff, G. W. (2018). *The Emergence of Dreaming: Mind-wandering, Embodied Simulation and the Default Network*. New York: Oxford University Press.

Foulkes, D. (1985). *Dreaming. A Cognitive-psychological Analysis*. New York: Routledge.

Foulkes, D. (1999). *Children's Dreaming and the Development of Consciousness*. Cambridge and London: Harvard University Press.

Foulkes, D. (2017). Dreaming, reflective consciousness, and feelings in the preschool child. *Dreaming, 27* (1), 1–13. https://doi.org/10.1037/drm0000040.

Foulkes, D., Pivik, T., Steadman, H. S., Spear, P. S., & Symonds, J. D. (1967). Dreams of the male child: An EEG study. *Journal of Abnormal Psychology*, *72*, 457–467.

Freud, S. (1893). *On the Psychical Mechanisms of Hysterical Phenomena*. SE., 3: 25–39. London: Hogarth Press.

Freud, S. (1894). *The Neuro-Psychoses of Defence*. S.E., 3: 41–61. London: Hogarth Press.

Freud, S. (1900). *The Interpretation of Dreams*. S.E., 4–5. London: Hogarth Press.

Freud, S. (1901). *On Dreams*. S.E., 5. London and New York: Norton & Company, Inc.

Freud, S. (1915). *Repression*. S.E., 141–158. London: Hogarth press.

Freud, S. (1920). *Beyond the Pleasure Principle*. S.E., XVIII. London: Hogarth Press.

Giacolini, T., & Pirrongelli, C. (2021). *Neuropsychoanalysis of the Inner Mind: A Biological Understanding of Human Mental Function*. New York: Routledge.

Greenberg, R., & Mitchell, S. A. (1983). *Object Relations in Psychoanalytic Theory*. Cambridge: Harvard University Press.

Hill, J. C. (1926). *Dreams and Education*. London: Methuen & Co.

Hobson, J. A. (1988). *The Dreaming Brain*. New York: Basic Books.

Hobson, J. A. (1990). Activation, input source, and modulation: Neurocognitive model of the state of the brain-mind. In: R. R. Bootzin, J. F. Kihlstrom, & D. L. Schacter (Eds.), *Sleep and Cognition* (pp. 25–40). University of Arizona: American Psychological Association.

Hobson, J. A. (2009). Rem sleep and dreaming: Towards a theory of protoconsciousness. *Nature Reviews Neuroscience, 10* (11), 803–813.

Hobson, J. A., & Friston, K. J. (2012). Waking and dreaming consciousness: Neurobiological and functional considerations. *Progress in Neurobiology, 98* (1), 82–98. DOI: 10.1016/j.pneurobio.2012.05.003. Epub 2012 15 May. PMID: 22609044; PMCID: PMC3389346.

Hobson, J. A., & McCarley, R. W. (1977). The brain as a dream-state generator: Activation-synthesis hypothesis of dream process. *American Journal of Psychiatry, 134*, 1335–1348.

Hobson, J. A., Pace-Schott, E. F., & Stickgold, R. (2000). Dreaming and the brain: Toward a cognitive neuroscience of conscious states. *Behavioral and Brain Sciences, 23*, 793–842.

Johnson, B. (2001). Drug dreams: A neuropsychoanalytic hypothesis. *Journal of the American Psychoanalytic Association, 49*, 75–96.

Johnson, B., & Mosri, F. D. (2016). The neuropsychoanalytic approach: Using neuroscience as the basic science of psychoanalysis. *Frontiers in Psychology, 7*, 1459. DOI: 10.3389/fpsyg.2016.01459.

Kaplan-Solms, K., & Solms, M. (2000). *Clinical Studies in Neuro-psychoanalysis: Introduction to a Depth Neuropsychology*. Milton Park: Taylor & Francis.

Kimmins, C. W. (1920). *Children's Dreams*. London: Longmans, Green and Co.

Kráčmarová, L., & Plháková, A. (2012). Obsahová analýza dětských snů. *E-psychologie* [online], *6* (4), 1–13 [cit. vložit datum citování]. Dostupný z www: http://e-psycholog. eu/pdf/kracmarovaplhakova.pdf. ISSN 1802–8853.

Kruger, S. F. (1992). *Dreaming in the Middle Ages*. Cambridge: Cambridge University Press.

Mari, E., Beretta, M., & Colace, C. (2018). L'appagamento di desiderio e il ristabilimento affettivo nel sogno infantile: nuove osservazioni. *Psychofenia, XXI* (37–38), 17–28.

Michael, M. T. (2015). *Freud's Theory of Dreams: A Philosophico-Scientific Perspective*. Lanham: Rowman & Littlefield.

Michael, T. M. (2018). Why aren't more philosophers interested in Freud? Re-evaluating philosophical arguments against psychoanalysis. *Philosophia*. DOI: 10.1007/S11406-018-0020-8.

Michael, T. M. (2019). The case for the Freud-Breuer theory of hysteria: A response to Grunbaum's foundational objection to psychoanalysis. *International Journal of Psychoanalysis, 100* (1), 32–51.

Panksepp, J. (1998). *Affective Neuroscience: The Foundations of Human and Animal Emotions*. Oxford: Oxford University Press

Panksepp, J. (2005). *Affective Neuroscience: The Foundations of Human and Animal Emotions*. Oxford: Oxford University Press.

Panksepp, J., & Biven, L. (2012). *The Archaeology of Mind: Neuroevolutionary Origins of Human Emotion*. New York: W. W. Norton & Company.

Perogamvros, L., & Schwartz, S. (2012). The roles of the reward system in sleep and dreaming. *Neuroscience and Biobehavioral Reviews, 36,* 1934–1951.

Perogamvros, L., & Schwartz, S. (2015). Sleep and emotional functions. *Current Topics in Behavioral Neurosciences, 25,* 411–431. DOI: 10.1007/7854_2013_271. PMID: 24385222.6, pp. 1934–1951.

Piaget, J. (1962). *Play, Dreams and Imitation in Childhood*. New York and London: W.W. Norton & Company.

Popper, K. (1959). *The Logic of Scientific Discovery*. London: Hutchinson.

Popper, K. (1963). *Conjectures and Refutations*. The Growth of Scientific Knowledge. London: Routledge.

Ribeiro, S., Simões, C., & Nicolelis, M. (2018). Genes, sleep and dreams. In: D. L. Ernest & L. Rossi (Eds.), *Ultradian Rhythms from Molecules to Mind*. New York: Springer.

Sándor, P., Szakadát, S., & Bódizs, R. (2014). Ontogeny of dreaming: A review of empirical studies. *Sleep Medicine Reviews, 18* (5), 435–449.

Schredl, M. (2007). Dream recall: Models and empirical data. In: D. Barret & P. McNamara (Eds.), *The New Science of Dreaming: Vol. 2 Content, Recall, and Personality Correlates* (pp. 79–114). Westport: Praeger Publishers/Greenwood Publishing Group.

Solms, M. (1997). *The Neuropsychology of Dreams: A Clinico-Anatomical Study*. Mahwah, NJ: Lawrence Erlbaum Associates Publishers.

Solms, M. (2000). Dreaming and REM sleep are controlled by different brain mechanisms. *Behavioral Brain Science, 23* (6), 843–850.

Solms, M., & Turnbull, O. (2002). *The Brain and the Inner World: An Introduction to the Neuroscience of Subjective Experience*. New York: Other Press.

Yu, C. K. C. (2001). Neuroanatomical correlates of dreaming. II: The ventromesial frontal region controversy (dream instigation). *Neuropsychoanalysis, 3,* 193–202.

Yu, C. K.-C. (2003). Neuroanatomical correlates of dreaming, III: The frontal lobe controversy (dream censorship). *Neuro-psychoanalysis, 5,* 159–169.

Yu, C. K.-C. (2007). Cessation of dreaming and ventromesial frontal region infarcts. *Neuro-Psychoanalysis, 9,* 83–90.

Conclusion

At the beginning of the twentieth century, Freud had the intuition that the study of infantile dreams would have opened a possibility to obtain useful information about the dream process.

It was an intuition, however, that he then failed to follow in the practice with extensive and in-depth studies. He investigated a few dreams and only in children aged not above 8. However, thanks to his ingenuity and to the direct knowledge of the children he was interviewing, he was able to outline various characteristics of infantile dreaming that fit in and supported his findings from the interpretation of the dreams of adult patients. Freud found in infantile dreams the confirmation of many of his general theories about dreaming, which led him to always consider children's dreams in the foreground and to present the results of his observations as preliminary and preparatory to the understanding of adults' dreams.

Over the past 30 years, I have followed Freud's intuition, proving the validity and usefulness of a developmental approach to the study of dreams. This approach turned out to be useful and fruitful not only for the purpose of looking closer at the empirical credentials of Freud's theory on dreams but also for the purpose of gaining a better understanding of adults' dreams and for the study of infantile forms of dreaming in adults.

This study, together with my previous ones, has confirmed that the Freudian theories of dreaming can be submitted to systematic investigation with several research methodologies that go beyond (without by any means excluding) the investigation of dreams in the psychoanalytic setting. The latter is a proven approach to the study of dreams in their psychological essence and in their peculiar characteristics that would not have been achieved by any other method. However, the systematic study of infantile dreams represents a valid approach, capable of finding direct and concurrent confirmation of many psychoanalytic concepts about dreams.

The potential of the ontogenetic approach to dreaming is very promising, but although several researchers have courageously tried to follow it, greater effort should be put in starting more structured and long-lasting research programmes for the investigation of the earliest forms of dreaming.

DOI: 10.4324/9781003184874-24

At present, in terms of research and study programs, infantile dreams remain a "no man's land" where I, however, have discovered—or I believe I have discovered—important information for understanding the most impenetrable aspects of the dreaming phenomenon, a "no man's land" where we will travel far, in our path towards the understanding of dreams.

Appendix A: general contents of dreams

Frequency percentage of Marco's dreams with the presence of active self-representation, main general contents categories by age group

	4–5 years of ages	6–7 years of ages	8–10 years of ages
Total dream reports	n 36	n 34	n 56
Active self-representation	75% (27)	76% (26)	93% (52)
Human characters (all)	83% (30)*	76% (26)*	89% (50)*
Animal characters	17% (6)	15% (5)	5% (3)
TV/Play characters	39% (14)	56% (19)	45% (25)
Daily life action of dreamer	67% (24)	53% (18)	55% (31)
Fantastic action of dreamer	19% (7)	18% (6)	14% (8)
Home or other house	33% (12)	29% (10)	30% (17)
Public place	47% (17)	26% (9)	43% (24)
School	17% (6)	12% (4)	9% (5)
Length of dream report (median word count)	35	25	42

*The most frequent characters are family members (father, mother, grandparents, uncles, cousins).

Self-representation. Marco frequently reports dreams in which an active self-representation appears from the age of 4 (i.e., there is an explicit statement of presence and/or action in the dream scene). This result confirms previous investigations based on children's dreams collected in home and school settings as well as studies based on questionnaires (Colace, 2006a, 2006b; Colace, Violani, & Tuci, 1995; Colace, Tuci, & Ferendeles, 2000; Beaudet, 1990; Resnick et al., 1994; Honig & Nealis, 2012; Sándor et al. (2015). On the other hand, these results disagree with the hypothesis based on children's dreams collected in the sleep laboratory setting that young children do not have the cognitive skills to represent themselves actively in their dreams (Foulkes, 1982; Foulkes et al., 1990).

General contents. These results are mainly congruent with those of previous studies based on school, home and questionnaire-collected dreams (Colace, 2006a, 2006b; Colace & Tuci, 1995; Beaudet, 1990; Sándor et al. (2015).

Dream length. For comparison with previous data, see Colace (2010) and Sándor, Szakadát and Bódizs (2014).

For a review on the general contents of children's dreams, see also Colace (2010, 2015) and Sándor, Szakadát and Bódizs (2014).

References

Beaudet, D. (1990). *Encountering the Monster: Pathways in Children's Dreams* (1st ed.). London: Continuum Intl Pub Group.

Colace, C. (2006a). A content analysis of young children's dreams collected in school setting. *Sleep, 29* (0152), A51.

Colace, C. (2006b). Children's dreaming: A study based on questionnaires completed by parents. *Sleep and Hypnosis, 8* (1), 19–32.

Colace, C. (2010). *Children's Dreams: From Freud's Observations to Modern Dream Research.* New York: Routledge.

Colace, C. (2015). *Iniziazione ai sogni dei bamini.* Roma: Edizioni Mediteranee.

Colace, C., & Tuci, B. (1995). A content analysis of children's dreams at ages 4–6: Preliminary data. *Sleep Research, 24,* 68. University of California, Los Angeles.

Colace, C., Tuci, B., & Ferendeles, R. (2000). Self-representation in young children's dream reports. *Sleep, 23* (Suppl. 2), A176–A177, 1198.D.

Colace, C., Violani, C., & Tuci, B. (1995). Self-representation in dreams reported from young children at school. *Sleep Research, 24,* 69. University of California, Los Angeles.

Foulkes, D. (1982). *Children's Dreams, Longitudinal Studies.* New York: Wiley-Interscience.

Foulkes, D., Hollifield, M., Sullivan, B., Bradley, L., & Terry, R. (1990). REM dreaming and cognitive skills at ages 5–8: A cross-sectional study. *International Journal of Behavioral Development, 13* (4), 447–465.

Honig, A. S., & Nealis, A. L. (2012). What do young children dream about? *Early Child Development and Care, 182* (6), 771–795. DOI: 10.1080/03004430.2011.579797.

Resnick, J., Stickgold, R., Rittenhouse, C. D., & Hobson, J. A. (1994). Self-representation and bizarreness in children's dream reports collected in the home setting. *Consciousness and Cognition, 3,* 30–45.

Sándor, P., Szakadát, S., & Bódizs, R. (2014). Ontogeny of dreaming: A review of empirical studies. *Sleep Medicine Reviews, 18* (5), 435–449.

Sándor, P., Szakadát, S., Kertész, K., & Bódizs, R. (2015). Content analysis of 4 to 8 year-old children's dream reports. *Frontiers in Psychology, 6,* 534. DOI: 10.3389/fpsyg.2015.00534.

Index

For Product Safety Concerns and Information please contact our EU
representative GPSR@taylorandfrancis.com
Taylor & Francis Verlag GmbH, Kaufingerstraße 24, 80331 München, Germany

www.ingramcontent.com/pod-product-compliance
Lightning Source LLC
Chambersburg PA
CBHW050640280326
41932CB00015B/2718